You're On Your Own

(BUT I'M HERE IF YOU NEED ME)

MENTORING YOUR CHILD

DURING THE

COLLEGE YEARS

Marjorie Savage

A FIRESIDE BOOK

Published by Simon & Schuster

New York   London   Toronto   Sydney

FIRESIDE
A Division of Simon & Schuster, Inc.
1230 Avenue of the Americas
New York, NY 10020

Copyright © 2003 by Marjorie Barton Savage

FIRESIDE and colophon are registered trademarks
of Simon & Schuster, Inc.

For information regarding special discounts for bulk purchases,
please contact Simon & Schuster Special Sales at 1-800-456-6798
or business@simonandschuster.com.

The Simon & Schuster Speakers Bureau can bring authors to your live event.
For more information or to book an event contact the Simon & Schuster Speakers
Bureau at 866-248-3049 or visit our website at www.simonspeakers.com.

Manufactured in the United States of America

3   5   7   9   10   8   6   4   2

Library of Congress Cataloging-in-Publication Data

ISBN-13: 978-1-4165-9607-3
ISBN-10: 1-4165-9607-0

THIS BOOK IS DEDICATED TO THE COLLEGE STUDENTS AND
THEIR PARENTS WHO HAVE TAUGHT ME WHAT IS TRULY
IMPORTANT IN LIFE.

Acknowledgments

I am grateful every day for the support, goodwill, and good humor of my colleagues at the University of Minnesota and for my friends who work in parent services around the country. These professionals share their skills and wisdom freely, to the everlasting benefit of students and the members of their families. There is not enough space on this page to list them, so I will do my best to thank them individually.

I would like to express deep appreciation for all the people at the University of Minnesota who have committed resources to parent services and encouraged research on the topic of parent–university relations. Among these are my previous supervisors, Marvalene Hughes, now president of Dillard University; Jane Canney, now at the University of St. Thomas; Steven Baker at the University of Minnesota; and my current supervisor, Gerald Rinehart.

Special acknowledgments are due to Deb Parker, Kathy Allen, Pauline Oo, Melanie Clark, Bill Magdalene, and Jodi Dworkin, without whom I could not do my job, and to my literary agent, Betsy Amster, without whom there would be no book.

Finally and most important, I want to express my gratitude and love for my own family.

Contents

Introduction

Each day as I work with parents of college students, I hear variations on a common theme:

"I hope it's all right that I'm calling. I know my son is supposed to be able to handle these things, but I have a question about his health service bill."

"My daughter is twenty-one, so she's an adult, but can I ask if there's someone who could help her with career advising?"

"I'm sorry to bother you, but I have to talk to someone about a problem my son is having in the residence hall."

Parents apologize when they call to ask for information about their child's college experience. They cannot decide if their involvement is helpful or if they're meddling. In recent years, media descriptions of college parents as "helicopters" or worse— lawn mowers, submarines, stealth bombers—have created an image of parents as overly protective and intrusively involved in their child's life. Although families have questions that genuinely need to be answered, parents fear the reaction they may receive if they call their student's college. "I don't mean to be a helicopter parent," they explain. "Is it all right if I ask a question?"

The reason behind all those phone calls is that mothers and fathers are trying to figure out how to work *appropriately* with their children and the school they attend. The college experience creates a host of new issues to work through, at the same time as families are trying to establish a whole new way of relating.

Ultimately, students, parents, and colleges all are hoping for the same outcome at the end of four years of college: a graduate who is mature, responsible, and ready for the next step in life—either a fulfilling (and hopefully well-paying) job, or admission to a graduate program that will help the student continue preparing for that desirable career a few years down the road.

The student role in the college process is well defined: select a major, attend classes, study hard, and develop the social, personal, and academic skills that will provide that successful and fulfilling life. The college role is also clear: provide the educational instruction, along with the academic and personal support that students need to gain those skills in a safe and stimulating environment. It's the parent role in the process that is confusing and ill-defined.

A generation ago, parents were simply told to "let go" when their children started college. But the educational experience today is not the same as it was twenty-five years ago, and families are very different as well. As the average cost of attendance at a public college or university approaches $15,000 a year, with typical costs at private institutions more than double that amount, a child's education has become a major family investment. Being told to "just let go" is not a message they can accept when they are making that kind of financial sacrifice to send their child to college.

Moreover, families today have a much closer relationship than was common in generations past. Parents of current college students have been told since they first dropped their children off at day care that they should be involved in their children's life.

"Know their teachers, know their friends, know what they're doing and who they're doing it with." That involvement has even been legislated. No Child Left Behind, the federal education legislation that defines outcomes for elementary and secondary schools, includes steps for schools to take in promoting parent involvement in their children's education. And for the children who go on to college, family involvement has worked. Today's college students identify their parents as their most trusted advisers and turn to a family member when they face problems, or when they simply want someone to talk to. About half of the so-called Millennial generation (those born after 1982) are in touch with their parents daily, and another 40 percent contact their parents one or more times a week. Indeed, more than half *see* their parents at least once a week.[1]

College faculty and staff, along with many parents of college students, are confused by this close relationship among parents and their college-aged children. The common refrain is, "When I went to college, my parents just dropped me off outside the dorm and said 'good luck.' They never would have called the school. I never would have talked to them every day. But I figured things out and did just fine. I learned a lot by doing things on my own—parents should just back off."

But little about college is the same as it was a generation ago. Like consumerism, communication, and technology, education has evolved significantly in the past few decades. Most college graduates from the 1970s and 1980s recall their orientation to college as a time to take personality tests and register for classes. Now comprehensive orientation programs teach first-year students how to manage their time, study effectively, and make

---

1. Pew Research Center for the People and the Press, "How Young People View Their Lives, Futures and Politics: A Portrait of 'Generation Next.' " Washington, D.C., January 2007, pp. 18–19.

smart choices. Where dorms had open-door visitation and 24/7 access a decade or so ago, colleges now have meticulous safety procedures in place in residence halls and detailed campus-wide crisis plans to respond to emergencies. Technology now touches every detail of college life, from online instruction and Web-based class discussions to podcast lectures. Online social networks—Facebook, MySpace, YouTube, Twitter, and campus portals—have changed the way students meet, establish friend-ships, and keep up with friends and family. It's simply a fact of contemporary life that every purse or backpack is equipped with a cell phone providing free long-distance minutes and texting capabilities. Parents today may not just talk or text with their student daily, they may *see* them every day via webcams and cell-phone cameras. Why would families *not* know the details of their child's life?

I have worked with parents and their students at the University of Minnesota since 1993, and during that time, I have seen these changes in parent–student relations, in family involvement with higher education, and in higher education itself. My col-leagues at colleges and universities around the country confirm the changes: A generation ago, parents rarely knew what classes their student was taking; now they know when their child is even *considering* dropping a course. Parents are included in the "think-ing through" process, and they ask their student the important questions: How will a reduced credit load affect a four-year grad-uation plan? Scholarships? Health insurance coverage? Campus job eligibility? Will the student still qualify to live in on-campus housing?

One of the critical developmental steps for eighteen- to twenty-two-year-olds is to learn to make their own deci-sions. Today's students know that thoughtful decision mak-ing includes gathering solid information and seeking reliable advice. The youth of this generation realize that their mothers and fathers have helped them get this far, and they recognize that some of their decisions can impact the family finances. They will continue to turn to their parents while they are in college. Because receiving and providing guidance from a distance is a new experience for both the student and the family, it requires new parenting and communication skills as well as shared responsibility.

While students and parents are working to redefine their relationship for the college years and beyond, staff and faculty on campus are also learning how to work with the increased parent involvement they are seeing. Increasingly, colleges and universities are finding that parents can be valuable partners in a student's personal, social, and academic development during the college years, but families need a definition of an appropriate role in the process.

The details are still being debated on how colleges, families, and students can best work together, but there is growing agreement that families contribute to student success by

- Knowing the typical issues that young adults are going through during their college years and understanding how young adults are still maturing and developing between the ages of eighteen and twenty-five; knowing the resources available on campus to help with those issues and developmental stages. Parents can help in these areas when they
  1. Promote self-advocacy by allowing their student to identify and solve problems independently;
  2. Encourage their student to set and meet personal goals and make her own decisions related to academics, career planning, social interactions, and community engagement;

3. Empower their student to examine personal values while also learning about and respecting the values and beliefs of others;

4. Allow their student to accept the consequences of his actions and responsibility for his mistakes;

5. Help him examine disappointments and unexpected experiences in order to assess what caused them, what can be done about them, and how to avoid them in the future.

• Knowing when to step in to help and when to empower the student to take responsibility. Parents assist in this effort when they

1. Are alert to signs that their student is under significant stress, is taking unhealthy risks, or is ill; if parents have concerns, they should discuss them with their student and help develop a plan to address the problem;

2. Contact appropriate campus or community authorities if their student's physical or mental health is endangered.

• Using their child's college experience as an opportunity to expand their own horizons. Parents benefit personally, and students are inspired when their parents

1. Take time to explore new interests or resume old interests for themselves;

2. Put new focus on their career and their spouse, partner, friends, other family members, or their community.

In this book, parents will learn strategies that will help them work in concert with their child's college or university to support

their student and to achieve those goals. Illustrated by anecdotes and advice from experienced parents and college staff, the book describes such real-life college and family issues as:

- How to work with your student during the college selection process
- Coping with the mood changes of the entire family during the months leading up to move-in day on campus
- Why students complain about the food but still manage to gain fifteen pounds their first year
- Why you shouldn't decorate your child's dorm room
- What to do when your child comes home with a tongue piercing
- What illnesses to watch for among college-aged students and how to make sure your child stays healthy
- When parent intervention is critical
- Ideas for teaching students to take responsibility for their finances
- How to handle the transitions students and their families face after graduation

The book is written for parents, but each chapter concludes with a list of Quick Tips for Students, for parents to pass along to their child.

The information in this book comes from my own years of working in student affairs and parent services, and from the experiences of my colleagues at the University of Minnesota and at other colleges and universities throughout the country. The examples cited throughout the book are from our daily contact with parents and students, although names and identities have been changed to protect student privacy.

During the college years, parents and their children are developing a new, adult relationship—one based on love and respect—

that will last a lifetime. As mothers and fathers move away from the precollege patterns of closely monitoring and helping direct their child's daily activities, they begin to take on the role of mentor.

Mentoring is a concept that students, parents, and educators can all embrace. With roots in mythology, the word has come to mean trusted adviser and counselor. It allows respect for a student's individuality and personal responsibility, and it defines a valid and vital role for parents as partners with colleges on behalf of their students.

SECTION 1
The Path to College

CHAPTER 1

Endless Possibilities

The College Search

For parents, the college search represents the first real action step in a lifelong dream. You have imagined your child's future, and you have nurtured budding talents in preparation for the day you would deliver your son or daughter to a sun-drenched, ivy-covered campus. You look forward to college tours as an opportunity to spend quality time with your maturing teen—a chance to talk about goals and plans. You are looking for the best value for your money and the best collegiate brand for your child's future.

To high school students, however, nothing looms larger than the college choice. Despite the fact that there are some four thousand colleges and universities in the United States, for a teenager facing the college decision, it feels as though there are only two possibilities: picking the *right* school or picking the *wrong* one. For many high school students, then, fear of making the wrong choice means they will procrastinate every step of the way.

Some families survive the college search with no scars, but for most, there will be at least a few serious battles along the way. One father complained that his daughter's college search had barely started, and already the whole family was frustrated.

"I was looking forward to this 'emerging adult' stage in my

daughter's life, but every time the subject of college comes up, she ends up emotional, teary, and angry. Her only plan is to move to New York City and study cello at Juilliard. Did she have to pick the most selective music program in the country? She's talented, but really, I'm not convinced she's going to get into Juilliard. She's in one of those 'I know more than you' stages. I have no idea how to handle this!"

At least his daughter had a school in mind. For many high school students, the idea of narrowing that list of four thousand to a handful can be a daunting task. They're supposed to look for schools that offer the major they want; then they're told they will probably change their major two or three times during college. They're advised to come up with at least five schools, including one or two that might be a stretch to get into and one or two that will be a sure bet. But which five? And if you're dreaming, why not dream big and apply at *all* the top schools? If you have to pick a safety school, shouldn't you be *really* safe and pick ten? One thorough and resourceful student developed a comprehensive list of her twenty-nine favorite, must-apply schools, including six dream schools; five that would be a reach but possible; several third-, fourth-, and fifth-choice schools; and five more that she was sure she could get in to.

Colorful viewbooks, those glossy publications from college admissions offices, arrive in the mail daily, addressed to high school juniors and seniors—and sometimes to talented ninth and tenth graders. Web sites feature slick search engines that match students to scores of programs and colleges that fit their preference of major, geographical area, and special interests. Meanwhile, friends, relatives, teachers, and high school counselors offer suggestions that are meant to be helpful, and parents have their own ideas on schools they want their child to consider.

It's hard for parents to understand the confusion their child is feeling. For them, there is a logical sequence to the college search, neatly arranged into categories:

- Scanning the options; gathering information
- Comparing and assessing the possibilities, based on choice of major, cost, and location
- Drawing up a short list for further comparisons
- Applying; waiting for decisions
- Selecting a school

Getting your student to follow that sequence is not as simple as it would seem, however. High school students are living in the moment, and while they may have plans for the future, working on those plans is not top priority. For a student who has a test to study for, a new cell phone to master, an outfit to figure out for the party on Friday night, or a chat she was in the middle of, *now* is just not the right time.

Andrea had been trying unsuccessfully for weeks to get her son to come up with a list of colleges that interested him, and each time, he would have something else right then that needed to be done. Finally she told him she was no longer going to bring up the subject on weeknights when he had homework and other priorities. She asked him to meet with her for an hour every Sunday afternoon for the next month to talk about college. For the first Sunday, Andrea asked her son to come up with a stack of brochures from colleges that interested him. By scheduling an appointment, setting a time limit, and making a reasonable assignment, she helped overcome her son's feelings of being overwhelmed by "all this college talk."

On that Sunday afternoon, Andrea asked her son to tell her what seemed most interesting about each of the schools. Then she asked him to spend time over the coming week to figure out the application dates for six or seven of those schools and to take notes on which ones require an essay, which ones require an SAT or ACT test, and any other application steps for them. She suggested that he could chart out the tasks and deadlines. The week after that, she asked her son to decide what the next steps needed to be and to look at a calendar with her to start scheduling some campus visits. With Sunday afternoons established as "college planning time," the two fell into a routine that made the college search much less confrontational.

THE CAMPUS TOUR

While viewbook and Google searches help categorize colleges and universities, it takes a college visit to clarify the differences among schools. Students usually say the campus tour was the most compelling factor in their college decision.

Schools are selling you and your student on their unique opportunities, and any campus visit will be a well-scripted promotion showcasing the newest high-tech classroom, the most stunning architectural features, the largest dorm rooms, and a few minutes with the most popular professors. Enthusiastic tour guides will talk about the vast range of student activities, study abroad programs in world capitals, the expansive laboratory and library facilities, and opportunities for internships in the dynamic business community just beyond campus—or just a short bus ride away. There may be promises of all-you-can-eat-all-day dining; personal trainers, tanning beds, and water slides in the recreation center; weekend ski trips to nearby resorts; and discounted student tickets for theaters, concerts, and professional sports events. You may walk away from a college visit thinking, *This sounds like a luxury cruise, not a college campus.*

All these amenities can make a difference in the student experience, and it's hard for students to ignore them in the final decision. They also affect the cost of a college education, though. As you and your student visit campuses, it's helpful to take notes, snap photos, and consider those features that seem most valuable to a good education, as well as those that particularly resonate with your student.

Either before or after the official tour, walk the campus on your own. Stop in the student union or a nearby café for a snack, and eavesdrop. Wander into areas you may not have seen on the official tour and watch what students are doing. Are they talking about classes? Studying? Running for the parking lot? Staffing information tables for clubs or organizations? Do they seem like they not only belong there, but are happy there?

If you see people who look like staff or faculty, what are they doing? What are they talking about and whom are they talking to? Do they smile and say hello? Are they talking to—or ignoring—students? It's not wise to rush to judgment based on one person's attitude, but look for a collective impression. One father noted, "We happened to see our tour guide an hour after the tour. She didn't see us, but she was talking to another student, and they both had this happy and confident air about them. She wasn't paid to be smiling then, so we figured she actually meant everything she said."

Also pay attention to how you and your student feel on campus. If you are in the area overnight, walk the grounds in the dark. Is it well lit? Are students out and about? Does it feel safe?

During the paring-down process, you can talk about the overall atmosphere of the campuses you visited, as well as which of those extras are really necessary and which schools provide all or most of the "must-haves":

Does she like the idea of continuing her high school band skills by playing in a pep band? Which schools offer that opportunity?

Is he intrigued by the idea of working on a research project with a professor?

If she's captivated by the university with an on-campus ski hill, but the wildlife ecology major she wants is at another college, which is more important to her?

If she's undecided, or not yet completely convinced, of her career choice, how will career counseling be provided? Are there professional career advisers on campus, or is that role assigned to academic advisers?

Although some of the perks may seem too good to pass up, it is important to consider whether they will actually fit into your child's educational plan. The study abroad options sound wonderful, but if your daughter is a student athlete, can she fit a semester abroad into her competition schedule? Does the closely regimented schedule of a nursing program leave time for the sculpture class that grabbed her attention?

THE RELUCTANT APPLICANT

While every parent imagines the college search will be the basis of interesting discussions and enjoyable family trips, for many teens, parental involvement is the last thing they want. Noah refused all offers to visit colleges and universities with his parents, protesting that the college he would go to was his choice, and he didn't need his parents' help. As he began his senior year in high school with no plans in mind, his father became insistent. "You're going to have to figure this out in the next few months. You have to start looking at some colleges."

Still, he resisted. "I've got time! I don't know for sure what I want to study in college, so I have to figure that out first. Besides, some of my friends have been visiting schools for a year already, and it hasn't done any good. They still don't know where they want to go."

By October, his parents were feeling much more panicky than

Noah was, but they knew their anxiety wasn't helping. Remembering the saying "Sometimes help is not helpful," they offered Noah the car keys and a full tank of gas and asked him to choose one school within a three-hour drive from home. "It's your choice and your day. You don't need to commit to any school yet, we'd just like you to visit one so you have an idea of what the college search is all about. And we don't need to go with you." For Noah, a road trip all by himself was what he needed in order to take that first step. Other students who are reluctant to tour a campus with Mom and Dad might be willing to take a college tour with a friend's family, an older brother or sister, or a favorite relative. Although Noah did not end up attending that first college, the visit gave him the incentive to fill out his first application and start considering additional choices.

It's not uncommon for the first college visit to be a bust. No teenager likes being out of her element, and a campus tour is an entirely new experience. Students don't know what to look for or what questions to ask. They feel pressured by the tour guides and by their parents, and the only thing they have to compare this college to is their high school. They come home from the tour with more reasons to be cynical than enthusiastic. There is actually some logic in making that first visit to a school the student doesn't really want to attend, or to arrange for a repeat visit to the first college after touring other campuses.

THE PARENT PERSPECTIVE

Students, parents, and admissions officers all hope the student will make the final decision on his or her own, but parents offer unique perspectives that can help students think about factors they might not otherwise consider. The lifelong soccer player who refuses to look at any college that doesn't offer him a position on the varsity soccer team may need to be prompted to think about intermural and intramural teams that will give him plenty of opportunities to play. The future physician who doesn't see "pre-medicine" listed among the school's list of majors may need to hear about the biology, chemistry, business, or psychology programs that prepare students for medical school.

Parents also have the right to consider and communicate their own boundaries. If there are financial limitations, or if you don't want your student farther than a half day's car ride from home, talk about those restrictions from the start. While families should not automatically rule out a high-tuition, private college—your student may qualify for a financial package that makes the school more affordable than you expect—you should let your student know that attending certain schools may be contingent on a generous scholarship offer. Nothing is harder on a student than to go through the whole college search process and make a choice, only to hear, "We can't possibly afford that much," or "I simply will not let you go that far away."

Parents need to be the gatekeepers on some of the considerations that students don't think about and colleges rarely discuss. If your son or daughter has a mental or physical condition that requires special accommodations, keep that issue in front of your student and be sure that you and your child are receiving information from the school about appropriate services.

Parents are more likely than high school seniors to think about the things that may contribute to personal discomfort. The African-American student who attended a highly diverse high school may not predict how it will feel to be the only black on his floor in the residence hall; a Hmong student might not consider that she could be the only person of color in the two-hundred-seat lecture hall during psychology class. Parents are more likely than their student to ask for information about diversity on campus or support services for students of color.

Families that live abroad and send their children to U.S. colleges also tend to foresee problems their students don't consider. Lilli had attended English-speaking schools abroad all her life while her father worked in Hong Kong, Tokyo, and Singapore, but she always expected to attend college in the United States. She considered herself a New Yorker, since she spent a month or two every summer at her grandparents' apartment in New York City, and she was sold on the idea of attending a small, private college in upstate New York. She was annoyed, though, when her parents cautioned her that there was no "international community" to be found on the campus. They urged her to think about how lonely she would be there and asked her to look at some other schools with a reputation for international students.

"What are you talking about?" she asked. "I won't be lonely. It's not like there will be any language problems. I look like everyone else there. All the freshmen are pretty much in the same boat when they start out, you know. And if I do get lonely, I can always take a train to stay with Grandma and Grandpa for a weekend. I'll be fine."

"Third-culture kids," those who were raised in and adapted to life in another country, can find it hard to adjust to a college that doesn't have a strong international flavor. They frequently don't know—or don't appreciate—the norms, music, or popular culture of their classmates. They often have more knowledge of international news and events and can be put off by the lack of interest their American classmates seem to have in global issues. When Lilli and her parents were touring her first-choice campus and went downtown for their fourth meal in two days in the small college town, she began to see they might have a point. Looking at the menu, she struggled to find anything that appealed to her. "Hamburgers, french fries, pasta, ham sandwich?" she said. "I just want a bowl of noodles. Maybe something with rice. I don't know that I want to admit you're right about me being lonely here, but I sure could get hungry."

NARROWING THE OPTIONS

The stress of choosing a college grows as the senior year progresses. Students become anxious as they see their friends making choices, receiving scholarship offers, and feeling confident about their decisions. By January, when the application deadlines for some colleges have passed and when the highest-achieving students have begun to receive scholarship letters, life feels oppressive. "What's wrong with me? No one wants me."

As acceptance letters finally arrive, thick packets from multiple colleges, the emotions become more complex. "Three schools want me? So now I have to turn some of *them* down?"

Students often will vacillate between wanting parents' input and wanting no conversation at all about college. Ted's parents struggled to offer the right amount of input while assuring their son that the choice was his. "You need to make the decision that's best for you," they said. "We trust you to make the right choice."

For Ted, their faith in his decision only added to the pressure. "There are all these things to consider. Cost, location, majors, the kind of students who go there, whether I'll be happy there for four years. I know I'm supposed to figure it out and make the decision, and I know my family will support whatever I choose, but no one ever told me how to make a decision. What's *most* important? How do I know I'm making the right choice? What if I choose wrong?"

Although families might make charts with all the pros and cons of each college under consideration, ultimately the choice comes down to which school simply feels right. Among the most important questions you can ask your student after a campus visit and during the decision process are, "How did it feel to be on that campus? Is it a place you want to be? Did the students look like people you would want to be with?"

Sometimes students choose a college because of its national ranking in the major the student has chosen, or the chance to do ocean research might be the deciding factor. But more often the final decision is based on a visceral reaction. One student sat outdoors alone for an hour watching the students on a campus he was considering, then met up with his mother and declared, "I can *rule* this place!" Another student picked a college in Atlanta because she liked the furniture in the student union, and based on the people she saw hanging out in the student lounge, she could see herself there. Students have made their final choice because they fell in love with the library's view of the mountains, the sunshine in Arizona, or the campus architecture in Seattle, and in every case they felt, "I just want to be here." One student told her mother, "I want a school that's bigger than me—a place I won't outgrow in four years, and I just know this is it."

When students are finally sure of their decision, it's important for parents to honor that choice if they can. Students who are excited about college, who arrive on campus with a positive attitude, are more likely to adjust well and be successful in their first few weeks, which lays the groundwork for the entire college experience.

REJECTED? HOW CAN THAT BE?

Even as students prioritize their dream schools, the most likely schools, and the safety schools during the admissions process, they are still highly disappointed—even shocked—when they receive the letter that says, "Thank you for applying. We had many excellent applicants, and we regret to inform you . . ."

It's at least as disappointing—maybe even more frustrating—

to be placed on a wait list and told, "We will let you know." For many students, this is the first time in their lives they have ever been turned down. They have been brought up in a world where they're told they can do or be anything they want, and even when they have not excelled, they've been praised and rewarded. They have trophies and certificates declaring them an all-American scholar, a star athlete, or a clean-cabin camper. When they applied for colleges, they imagined they would get into their top choice, and they simply have no practice in dealing with rejection.

Parents are equally surprised and dismayed when their student is turned down. They have gathered eighteen years' worth of proof that their child is outstanding, and it's jarring to hear some outsider say he's "not good enough." Most college admissions officers have been told, "You are ruining my child's life." They have also heard the plea, "It's just one more student. You have ten thousand students, and it can't hurt to take one more. It's not like every seat in every class is going to be full every day. Let her in! It's all she has ever wanted!"

Students can appeal acceptance decisions, but unless there is some compelling new factor—maybe she earned all A's during her senior year after a B-plus high school career, he wrote a personal essay that was published in a national magazine, or she won first place in the state science fair—it is unlikely that the decision will be overturned. This is a time for parents to work with their student on dealing with disappointment. It may be the first rejection in a child's life, but it won't be the last.

Rejection from a college does not mean a student is not college material. It also does not mean that he is not as good as the high school classmate who was accepted at this college. It just means he doesn't quite fit into *this* college's freshman class right now.

Dealing with rejection is something like dealing with grief. There are stages to go through, and time is an ingredient in the process. Students (and their parents) are likely to react first with denial, concluding that this must all be a mistake; they will be angry; they will want to bargain with the admissions office and persuade the school that the student is, indeed, a good candidate; they will feel terrible for a while; and eventually, they will be in a place emotionally where they can consider other options.

As much as you hate to see your child in pain, students are justified in feeling bad about the rejection. Parents, too, get to feel the disappointment, but too often, students suffer when they believe they've let their parents down. It doesn't really help your child if you make that angry phone call to the admissions counselor.

You can be more helpful by acknowledging your child's feelings, giving her some time to take it in, then reminding her that she can learn from this disappointment and move on. When she's ready, she should keep in mind the things she did right in the application process, but also consider if she could have done anything differently. Since Plan A is not going to work, what is the alternative? As James Yorke, University of Maryland professor and expert on chaos theory, says, "The most successful people are those who are good at plan B." Millions of other college applicants have been rejected from their first choice schools, and the smart ones have gone on to other colleges, found them to be a great fit, and proceeded to make friends and become successful students.

BUT CAN WE PAY FOR IT?

Financing a college education has become a major family investment. It's likely to be the second biggest financial commitment a family makes, next to purchasing a home. At a high-tuition private college or with several children in the family, college costs may exceed the price tag of a house. Not so long ago, students could work during summers and a few hours a week during the school year to pay for their own education. That is no longer an option. Students who go to school full-time cannot earn enough to pay room, board, tuition, fees, books, and other expenses. A family contribution is expected.

For high-achieving students, scholarships and grants may be available, and families will be comparing offers from multiple schools. Low-income families will qualify for at least some student aid, and upper-income families may not suffer as much financial strain. Middle-income families feel particularly stressed about the cost of college since they qualify for less aid and don't have the savings or disposable income to pay the bills.

Every family's financial situation is different, every college and university has different financial packages, and different states have their own savings plans and tax credit programs, so it is beyond the scope of this book to provide specific college funding advice. The one consistent recommendation, however, is that every family should fill out the Free Application for Federal Student Aid (FAFSA) form each spring (www.fafsa.ed.gov/), even those who believe they will not qualify. About two-thirds of families are eligible for at least some financial aid; moreover, if your family's finances change during the year due to loss of job, a death in the family, or other circumstances, you will have the baseline information already on file.

After a student is accepted at a college or university, the school will send a financial estimate, outlining any scholarships or grants, defining the student's and the parents' expected contributions, and explaining any additional options such as work-study opportunities for the student. When the financial estimate arrives, parents may suffer sticker shock. "We've been saving for years, and we thought we could afford college!" Denny's parents protested. "When we went to the college fair, every private college said they offered scholarships and grants, and their school would end up costing no more than a public university. Now it looks like we'll have to borrow money, and Denny is going to graduate with debt."

Students can appeal their offer and ask if more grants or scholarships might be available. Schools that are competing for top students may consider the offers your student has received from other colleges or universities, but don't be surprised if the increase is small or the answer is no. It's certainly worth a try, but packages are carefully formulated from the start to provide an equitable and enticing offer, based on the profile of the entire incoming class.

When comparing financial packages from different institutions, you may need to create your own comparison charts. The school with the highest scholarship amount is not always the best deal. Make sure you're considering all expenses from different schools. Terminology differs, but the bottom line will be determining how much your student is expected to pay, and what the family contribution will be.

A generous scholarship offer is tempting, but keep in mind any stipulations on free money. Is it a onetime, one-year offer that will not be available in the future? If the student is expected to maintain a minimum grade-point average, is that realistic? Does your student understand the commitment? Ask if there is any leeway with grade-point requirements—the first semester of the freshman year is stressful, and it is not unusual for students to earn a full grade point below their high school average. Find out if additional scholarships might be available in future years and how students qualify for those. If there is no work-study award, is there a chance to work at an on-campus job without work-study?

When your student accepts an offer, clearly, he or she will want to accept any "free money" provided through grants and scholarships, but know that you and your student may not need to take out all the loan money that is suggested. Too often, students borrow as much as they qualify for, but their living expenses or book costs are less than anticipated. The extra money feels like a gift for a spring break trip or a new laptop. Borrowed money will have to be paid back eventually, so it's better to borrow the minimum now and owe less later.

MAKING DECISIONS: WHOSE CHOICE IS IT?

Any eighteen-year-old will react fiercely to parents who ask to see his mail or who want to read the e-mail message that just arrived. Any parent, however, who is facing the prospect of paying for college needs to know that all the paperwork is filled out correctly and on time. So whose job is it to make sure the college mail is opened, the forms are completed, and each of the tasks on the "to-do list" is checked off? With all the information that arrives each week from various campus offices, who is sorting through it and keeping track of deadlines and details? And ultimately, who has the final say in the decisions these mailings require?

From your student's standpoint, these forms will affect the most basic aspects of college life: Will she live in a single room, a double, or a suite? How many meals each week will he eat in the dining center? Should he move into an all-freshmen hall, live on the Spanish language floor, or request apartment-style housing with upperclassmen? Students think their parents are encroaching on their personal space when they check the mailings and tell their children how to fill out the forms.

From the parents' perspective, these decisions will affect the student's well-being and the family finances, in some cases for years to come. As the parent, maybe you see some pitfalls in selecting an all-freshmen dorm or in choosing a hall with no quiet hours, and you want to help your child avoid the potential problems. Parents feel more urgency about meeting deadlines and more caution about answering the questions completely and thoroughly. They want to make certain everything is done "right," and they want to know how these decisions will affect their child and the family.

When Jeremy opened the application from the college housing office, he didn't think twice about what kind of a room he wanted. He wanted a single. Like many college students today, he had always had his own bedroom. After reading the housing application instructions, he quickly filled out the form and gave the papers to his mother to write in the credit-card information for the deposit fee. The first thing she noticed, though, was that his single-room selection would cost several hundred dollars more than a double. A triple or a four-person suite would be even more economical.

"Jeremy, you marked down that you want a single room. You didn't even talk to us about this. You don't seem to understand how much it's going to cost for you to go to college. You can't just pile up expenses without consulting us. I think you should consider one of these other choices."

Jeremy had plenty of reasons why he would be better off living in a single. He would study better if he was by himself, he said. He needed quiet to concentrate on his homework. He needed his sleep. What if his roommate turned out to be one of those people who wanted to party all the time? What if his roommate wanted to watch television or have friends over until all hours of the night?

In fact, there were other factors at play for both Jeremy and his mother. In addition to the financial impact of the decision, Jeremy's mother was worried that her son might not make friends easily. He had never been particularly outgoing, and his two good friends from high school were enrolling in different colleges. She was afraid that he would be lonely, and it would be much more difficult to meet people if he lived in a single room. At the same time, Jeremy had his own unspoken concern. He had never mentioned it to his parents, but on an overnight band trip the previous year, he was teased unmercifully about his snoring. He didn't want roommates complaining all year that his snoring was keeping them awake.

When they talked through the issues, Jeremy and his mother acknowledged that there were personal and financial complications of this seemingly simple decision. They set the form aside for a few days and agreed to give it some more thought. Jeremy's mother made a call to the nurse at their clinic, who suggested that nasal strips from the drugstore might reduce the snoring. In a moment of enlightenment, Jeremy agreed to a four-person, two-bedroom suite on the grounds that he would have good odds of being matched with at least one other snorer. At any rate, in a quad, he had a one-in-three chance of finding a roommate who was a heavy sleeper. And, as it turned out, Jeremy's roommate was a sound sleeper who almost always went to bed earlier than Jeremy. There were never any complaints about snoring.

Not all paperwork decisions end quite as well, though. Many students, caught up with the closing events of high school, set the mail aside, figuring they'll get to it later. As the papers pile up, critical responses filter to the bottom of the stack, and deadlines are missed.

One afternoon, Melanie was talking with a coworker who mentioned that his daughter had received her orientation schedule and had taken a language test online to determine what Spanish course she would be taking in the fall. Melanie's son was going to the same college, but he hadn't said anything about orientation or placement tests. That evening, Melanie asked her son about his orientation schedule, and he said he was sure he had "some brochure or letter about that in my room." She went with her son to look for the schedule and discovered a small mountain of envelopes, forms, and e-mail printouts from the college.

"What is all this? I didn't even know you were *getting* these things—letters about financial aid, orientation, testing dates. Have you responded to any of these?" she asked.

College mail is addressed to the student, and when your student is accepted at a college, he or she is likely to receive a campus e-mail account and password. Parents don't always see what arrives, and the only way you will know what needs to be done is if your student tells you. Because federal law recognizes college students as adults, the information goes to the student, no matter who will be paying the bills. From a parent's viewpoint, this might seem absurd; from a developmental view, it makes sense. Students are facing a significant transition as they prepare for college, and they need to begin assuming responsibility.

Obviously, you would like to be kept up-to-date on the choices your student is making, and it's not at all unusual for parents to end up doing some of the work through those online accounts. Some parents ask their student for the passwords or PIN numbers. When students give away their password to a family member, however, they are learning that "It's okay to share passwords with the people who love you." Too often, that translates into giving PIN numbers and passwords to best friends, boyfriends or girlfriends, or roommates. There are many examples of students signing up an ex-girlfriend on pornography Web sites, an angry roommate dropping a student out of all her classes, or a former friend using another student's e-mail account to send hurtful messages. Parents make a strong impact if they tell their child that no one, not even Mom and Dad, should have their password or PIN numbers.

For Melanie's son, the situation was not as hopeless as she feared—there were still orientation sessions he could register for, and by calling the college, he was given an access code to take the language exam late—but he needed to learn some organizational skills. He had an idea of what information had arrived. He just had not yet developed a system for managing records. In a single evening, his mother helped him sort through the pile of mail, using a highlighter to mark dates and a calendar to note deadlines, and he learned a quick and simple lesson on how to keep his paperwork organized. They also talked about what information his parents needed to know, and they discussed how he would share that information with them.

With each passing week, your child's anxiety and doubts will intensify. All the e-mails and letters that are pouring in can seem daunting to a prospective freshman. Every piece of mail is asking for some kind of decision. Some of those decisions seem simple, but students might not be certain whether it makes sense to order season football tickets, sign up for fraternity rush, or buy a bus pass that's good for one semester or one for the whole year. Students want to make the choices themselves, but they believe it's critical to make only the *right* choices. Any mistakes feel like clear proof that they're inept and not yet ready for college.

This is your chance to provide guidance while empowering your student to make her own choices. Let your child know that you are willing to talk about the decisions she's making, but give her authority to make most of those decisions. Let her know if you want a voice on issues that affect finances. If you are worried about health and safety, ask your student to keep you posted on these topics. Tell her she may eventually wish that she had chosen differently on some of those decisions, but that will not mean she made a mistake. She is making her choices based on the information available now.

Checklist for Record Management

Parents and their student can be overwhelmed by all the information that comes from college in the months leading up to the freshman year. What are the deadlines? When are payments due? A few simple tools and organizational skills will make life easier now and will give your child a start in record management for the college years.

Accordion files or file box, filing cabinet, or fireproof box

Students will need separate file folders for
- Housing records
- Finances (tuition and fees information, scholarship and financial aid awards, receipts from orientation, billing for residence hall and dining plan, textbook receipts)
- Health (immunization records, insurance numbers, name and phone number of home clinic or physician, prescriptions, dental information, pharmacy prescriptions, lens prescription)
- Academic information (academic counselor's name and contact information, registration records, lists of graduation requirements, course requirements)
- Computer information (warranty information, helpline numbers, software support information, e-mail addresses)
- Auto insurance, repair records, and parking information (for commuter students or students who have a car at school)

Highlighter and Calendar or Planner

When mailings or e-mails arrive, the student should read it and then determine what action the letter or form is requesting. The student can mark deadlines on the calendar, along with any fees or costs due. By highlighting the steps of action and the date for responding, a later review of the letter will be quick and simple.

E-mail Folders

Aside from printing out and filing e-mail messages, your student should set up a filing system for college messages in his or her e-mailing program. If information is coming from different colleges, a separate folder should be identified for each school.

Talk to your child about how detailed the filing system should be; you may agree that information could be separated into more specific categories. Academic information can be further segmented into course planning, career planning, advising records, and transcripts or grade reports. For a first-year student who is unaccustomed to managing records, simpler is better. The more detailed the filing system, the more sections he will have to search when looking for records later. "Did I file that housing bill under housing, finances, or contracts?" As students gain experience, they should be able to handle increasingly complex record keeping.

LIFE SMARTS: THE REAL MEASURES OF COLLEGE SUCCESS

The college search and first steps to enrollment demand new skills from maturing teens—decision making, critical thinking, comparison and analysis—and your student's active participation in the process will contribute to his or her success as a college student. After all, it's not purely brain power that promises success in college; life smarts make all the difference.

Although high school seniors don't realize it, much of the risk of college failure is filtered out through the acceptance process. An amazing number of high school seniors neglect to complete their college applications, even after reminders are sent. An incomplete application is a common reason for rejection.

Students have the ability to either get by or excel at nearly any school that accepts them; schools don't admit students who are not academically prepared for the rigor of their coursework. When students fail, it's usually because of problems outside the classroom. The most serious issues are because students don't know how to manage their time, or they make bad choices that affect their health. They don't think through potential negative outcomes, or they believe they can talk their way out of any consequences they face. As your child goes through the final year of high school, parents can promote the chances of college success by turning over some of the responsibility for these areas now.

Time management: The most common reason for college failure is lack of time management skills. Parents—especially mothers—have been managing their student's schedule for years, for very good reasons. You need to coordinate your whole household. You know your student has a scouting banquet on Wednesday, and he has a chemistry test Thursday, so you remind him to be sure to study for the exam on Tuesday night. You want to avoid arguments about the bathroom in the mornings, so you wake your children at different times and set limits on their time at the breakfast table or in front of the mirror. Consequently, students arrive at college with little experience in managing their own schedules.

Sometime before the end of the senior year, start asking your student to take over more of those scheduling responsibilities, and tell him why learning time management will be important as a college student. If he misses his ride to school because he didn't get up on time, or he does poorly on a test because he didn't study, let him handle the consequences. It's much better to deal with the outcome of a high school gaffe while living in the protective environment of home than it will be when he's in college, on his own.

Health tips: In most cases, when a child or teenager gets sick, parents take over. It's what parents are supposed to do. But in the last year of high school, when anyone in the family gets sick—or if you hear about a friend who is sick—use the situation as a teachable moment. Talk about the fact that, as a college student, your child will come down with a cold or the flu. There's always the possibility of scrapes, bruises, or other injuries and illnesses. When that happens, what will your child do? How will he decide whether to call a doctor? Let your student start managing his doctor's appointments now, keeping in mind that you may have to approve the appointment or go along if your child is under eighteen.

When a student is ill and away from home, the last thing he needs is the added stress of figuring out how to make a medical appointment and how to deal with health insurance. There are some things you can do before your child leaves for college:

- Be sure that you and your student know what services are available on campus and when he should seek help off campus. Even schools with a campus health service, for example, might require students to seek urgent care or weekend appointments at a local hospital.
- If your student is covered on your health insurance, he must know how to make a claim. Many family health insurance plans are tied to specific clinics or a provider area; coverage is different when the student is away from home, and a doctor's appointment may need preapproval. In some cases, co-payments are higher for care outside of the coverage area. Let your student know if he is required to contact the insurance company before seeking nonemergency care.
- Give your child an insurance card with the coverage information and company phone numbers. If co-payments are required at the time of service, be sure your student has some emergency funds for only that purpose.
- Explain your family prescription coverage plan if you have one, and go over the information on how to obtain new prescriptions or refills.

- If your student uses eyeglasses or contact lenses, be sure he has a copy of the most recent eyewear prescription.
- Talk about dental coverage; for a student, a chipped tooth or broken filling is a devastating problem. If you have emergency dental care, be certain your child understands the coverage. Also, discuss whether your student would prefer to have regular checkups and cleanings with the hometown dental clinic during breaks, or if a campus-area dentist is preferable.

QUICK TIPS FOR STUDENTS

- Choosing a college may not be your top priority on any given day, but a few months after high school graduation, you will want to be starting your new life. Selecting a college takes time and work; it's easier if you do a little every week. *This week* what can you do to get the process moving?
- The college choice is yours to make, but it affects your family, too. Be willing to listen to their thoughts on which schools to tour, financial restrictions on college choices, or even geographical limitations—maybe there's a good reason for them to want you to attend a state university or start at a two-year college near home. Also be willing to explain your reasons for applying at the schools you've chosen.
- If you have a dream school, it's hard to imagine any second choice, and it's discouraging to think maybe you won't be accepted there. Go ahead and apply to your first-choice college, but after you get that application sent in, look around for more options. Someplace else might end up being even better.

- Finish high school strong! When you start college, you will need the information they were giving you during your senior year.
- Review college mailings as they arrive, figure out what kind of response is needed, and reply as soon as you can.
- Tell your parents about decisions that will have a significant financial impact. If you must ask your parents to take on any unexpected expenses, give them your reasons for needing or wanting to incur the extra cost. If they can't add any more to their budget, figure out if you can fund the expense yourself.

CHAPTER 2

A Summer of Change

Making the Most of the Months Before College

Every year, as a new group of high school graduates and their parents watch the calendar pages turn toward September, emotions begin to churn. Mothers and fathers who were filled with pride when the college acceptance letters arrived a few months ago will soon find themselves wondering, *How can this kid possibly succeed in college? He can't even get out of bed in the morning by himself.*

Students who are convinced that they belong at the college of their dreams are equally convinced a day later that they will never fit in. "I think the school made a mistake when they accepted me. I was probably the last person they picked, and I'm going to be the stupidest person on campus. Besides, I don't have the right clothes. No one will like me. It's just not going to work."

For these students and their parents, the issue is simple: Everything is changing. The excitement and anticipation that peaked in late spring turns to chaos during the "senior summer." Recent graduates are rejecting curfews and failing to show up for family meals, defending their freedom by explaining that, "In a couple of months, you won't *ever* know what I'm doing."

Meanwhile, parents are failing in their efforts to maintain

peace in the family. Bickering among brothers or sisters reaches new heights. One parent or the other is locked in conflict with the child. Parents listen to their child's unending complaints about the community and the small-mindedness of the neighbors, and they begin to long for the day when they can finally take this miserable, unhappy kid to college. A minute later, they berate themselves for such thoughts. "I know I'll miss her!"

What's a parent to do? Advice flows in from every direction, but each suggestion seems to conflict with at least one other:

"Give them space." *"No, set clear boundaries."*

"Make sure you talk about the critical issues." *"Don't try to review a lifetime of lessons in one short summer."*

"Tell them you'll miss them." *"Don't lay a guilt trip on them about leaving."*

The whole family has been planning for college for years, but now parents can't keep from wondering if it's what they really want. When changes are pending, emotional flare-ups are a natural reaction. The challenges are to identify the real issues as they occur and to recognize what each of the various members of the family is feeling.

"LAST TIME" SYNDROME

As you sit at the picnic table in the backyard in mid-July, a wave of nostalgia washes over you. *She'll be leaving soon! This could be the last picnic we will ever have together,* you think. A similar nostalgic feeling overcomes you on the way to church, at the mall, watching TV, or curling up with a book on a rainy Sunday afternoon.

Some parents try so hard to savor each moment that they end up in a constant state of depression. Others react with frustration at every complaint and miss the good times. This last summer before college is a series of emotional peaks and valleys.

Your feelings might be different for your first child, a middle child, or the youngest, but no matter what, there will be trying times.

Where I work, new-student orientation begins in June and continues into July. During the first weeks of orientation, parents are still planning the high school graduation party, and they're focused on guest lists and menus for the upcoming celebration. Midway through orientation season, parents are exhausted from cleaning up after the party and are most concerned with whether their child has written all the thank-you notes. They have no problem with the notion that their student will be moving away from home in a few months—September is still too far away to take it all seriously. After the Fourth of July, though, I start to see parents in tears when they realize that their child will soon be leaving for college. "I promised myself I wasn't going to cry. I'm just not ready for this!"

And it's not only the mothers who are affected by the transition. A father will gulp back the lump in his throat when he watches his daughter walk away with her orientation group.

Each week throughout the summer, parents' reactions become increasingly intense, sometimes going beyond sadness and tears to expressions of anger. A family arrived for orientation one morning in July. The daughter registered while her parents looked on; then they all crossed the room to the check-in table for parents. When the father couldn't find name badges for himself or his wife, he began berating the student volunteer who was staffing the information desk. "We paid for this program a month ago! How can you say our names aren't on the list? This is ridiculous! I want to talk to your supervisor. Now!"

The intensity of his reaction was a surprise to the staff as well as to his wife and daughter. His daughter finally remembered that she had rescheduled her orientation date, but she forgot to change the registration for her parents. Their names were on a list for the next day's program. After the problem was solved and the family moved into the auditorium, the man's wife returned to the registration table to explain that this was their youngest child and their only daughter. "Our boys both went to a college just a few miles from home, so it didn't feel that far away. And my husband has always been very protective of our daughter—he really wanted her closer to home. I think this is really hard for him."

It is common for parents to become critical about the college or university in the last few weeks before school begins. Patience wears thin as the rosy glow of the *image* of sending their student to college collides with the stark reality both of the costs they will be facing and of their student's approaching independence. Anything about the school that seems less than perfect is cause for alarm. A mother wonders how smart the residence hall director is if he doesn't know how much space there will be under her son's bed. "I have to get him a storage box that will fit under the bed. And you don't even know how high the beds are? Have you ever *been* in the dorm rooms?"

The mother who is accusing hall directors of neglecting their duties before her son even moves into the hall is actually worried that she will not be around to make sure her boy is safe. Fathers are asking college administrators if they have run background checks on campus security monitors, when the real fear is that their daughter will be walking alone on campus at night. They advise the college to "close down those irresponsible fraternities," when the concern actually is that their son got drunk at a friend's cottage over the weekend.

The emotions you feel as school approaches are legitimate and real. You deserve rational explanations and full answers to your questions. But try to ask yourself, when you begin to fume, if your frustration is with the school, your student, or the larger situation—your family is changing, and you are going to have to trust someone else with your very precious child.

"BUT I HAVE *PLANS!*"

As the end of summer approaches, parents wonder if they have lost all control. They try to schedule a family weekend before their son leaves for college, but he has something lined up for each date they suggest. They would like to take him shopping, but he is booked every evening for the next week and a half. They expect him home for supper, but he doesn't show up. He is always "hanging out with friends."

The last few weeks before college, students are not focusing on packing, cleaning their room, or spending time with family. They are spending all their time with their high school classmates, making every effort to cement the friendships they are leaving. At this moment in your child's life, he has much more in common with his friends than he does with you.

The senior summer holds magical moments for soon-to-be college students. During the day, prospective freshmen are working their separate jobs, being treated like adults. Every evening, and stretching long into the night on weekends, they are out with friends, picturing all the possibilities the future holds. And they believe in their dreams. She will, indeed, be an international law attorney working in Paris, and ten years from now, she will fly to New York for the opening of her best friend's Broadway play. This is, for many students, the best social period of their lives so far, and while it's easy to imagine a great future in distant and exotic lands, it is impossible to think about leaving these friends from home in just a few weeks.

Leaving friends might also mean the end of a serious romance. Any student who is in a relationship during the summer before college is at least thinking about what will happen when one or both start school in the fall. There may be a mutual understanding that they'll both date at college; there may be promises that "We'll always be together"; or there may be disagreement and long talks about what comes next. On the other hand, it's not unusual for no discussion about the relationship to take place at all until a breakup phone call a week after one of them leaves home.

The significant developmental factor is that these young men and women are now looking outward, toward—and then beyond—their high school friends and away from their family, as part of the maturing process. They have learned how to relate to people who are somewhat different from themselves (although so far, not too different), how to hold a conversation, how to manage their own behaviors. These are all skills that young adults—and college students—need in order to be comfortable in new situations. Right now, even though life is easy because the faces are familiar, it feels new and exciting because the boundaries are expanding.

Your expectations that your child will take time away from friends in order to have dinner with you, to go to the mall with the family, or to pack a few boxes seem to your child like a tremendous affront. Home and family don't have that tinge of thrill that comes with being out in the world. After all, you've always been there for your child, and she fully expects that you always will be.

During these last few weeks at home, your child isn't quite sure what to think about you. When you tell your son what to do, he is resentful that you still treat him like a child; if you leave him alone to make his own decisions, he feels as though you're abandoning him. If you remind your daughter about packing, you're nagging; if you don't offer to look for boxes, you obviously don't care about her or respect her educational plans.

Your child is midway between childhood and adulthood, and every step forward is made with the assumption that things are still solid at home and the fear that they are not. Thinking about leaving home is both exciting and frightening, but young adults don't dare express their concerns about the upcoming changes. Instead they just become angry or aloof.

The turmoil will be visited upon both parents and siblings. The biggest problems seem to crop up between the student and whichever parent he or she most closely resembles. It's hard to imagine major confrontations as a compliment, but if you and your daughter are arguing constantly, and you're wondering how you could have become such a dreadful parent, this is probably a sign that she is much like you. And that disturbs her endlessly.

Younger brothers or sisters react to the feelings of change as well. Preteens are troubled by the idea of their big brother or sister leaving home, and they become clingy and emotional. "Why do you want to go away? Won't you miss me? Who will be here when I get home from school?"

Siblings who are themselves starting to think about college see great possibilities as they watch the freshman prepare to leave home. They're imagining their own transition to college someday, which seems pretty exciting from the vantage point of a fourteen- or sixteen-year-old. At the same time, they're seeing some personal potential in their sibling's departure. "Do I get to move into her bedroom now?" "If she gets a new laptop, I should get one, too." "He's going to college, so I get his car!"

Just when your soon-to-be college student feels like all the lights should be shining brightly on him, his little sister is demanding all the attention, it feels as if Dad only wants him around to mow the lawn, and Mom is enthusiastically buying him laundry detergent, deodorant, and new underwear. To the departing child, this all adds to a slowly festering suspicion that "Everyone is a little too happy that I'm leaving."

LAST-MINUTE ADVICE

All across the country, as long July days fade into sweltering August nights, parents of college-bound freshmen lie awake perspiring with dread as much as with heat: "Did I talk to him about tracking his checking account online?" "What will she do if she gets sick?" "I don't think she understands how much trouble she can get into for underage drinking."

You have only a few short weeks to pass along all the advice your child needs to know. How will you cover it all, and what happens if you forget to mention something important? High school graduates, however, rarely listen patiently as their parents deliver warnings about campus safety or lectures on the importance of earning good grades.

There are things your student needs to know for the purely practical demands of coping with life in a new situation. There are things your student's college wants you to discuss with your child. There are even a few things your child would appreciate hearing from you. The trick is to figure out when you're offering useful information as opposed to unwanted advice or an index of admonishments.

All students should know how to:

- *Do their own laundry.* This skill includes, at minimum, sorting delicates for hand washing; removing tissues, dollar bills, and other paper from pockets; separating reds, pinks, purples, and maroons from light colors; measuring laundry detergent; knowing what not to wash (most notably sports jackets, ties, and anything that is labeled *Dry Clean Only*); and keeping wool sweaters away from hot water and dryers. If possible, continue the laundry lesson with additional suggestions for separating jeans and dark clothes from light colors; using fabric softener; loosely loading clothes into the washer and dryer, rather than stuffing a whole week's worth of laundry into a single load; and removing clothes from the dryer soon after the machine stops. (Shopping tips: Most students do very well with a wardrobe of T-shirts, sweatshirts, jeans, and easy-care pants and shorts. Moreover, students report that spray-on wrinkle reducers and Febreze are essential supplies for college clothing care.)

- *Balance a checking account and manage a debit card or credit card.* Ideally, your child should have been learning about checkbooks, debit cards, or credit cards during the last years of high school. By the time college classes begin in the fall, he or she should understand the importance of recording debit and check deposits and withdrawals and the mechanics of reconciling a bank statement. Please talk to your student about the potential hazards of credit card debt and explain about late payment penalties, interest charges, and annual fees. More information about finances can be found in chapter 7.

- *Iron a shirt, replace a button, repair a ripped seam.* Be pitiless about insisting your student take care of his or her wardrobe during the summer. You will probably never get a thank you, but at least your child will have the ability to maintain a decent appearance.

- *Prepare or obtain basic food.* A missed meal means students must occasionally find food to get through the night. Residence hall staff are dismayed that college-level students are seemingly unable to read and comprehend the instructions on a popcorn package—or to clean up the orange residue in the microwave when the bag burns. Make sure your child has, at least once in his life, called in an order for pizza and paid the driver the appropriate sum plus a reasonable tip. Some first-year students become quite indignant when they find out they are being charged sales tax and maybe a delivery fee.

- *Trust their instincts when they feel uneasy or unsafe.* Most parents remember to tell their daughter to avoid walking across campus alone at night; young men need the same message. Students of both genders also need to hear about date rape and acquaintance rape. Students enter into new friendships with trust and confidence, and they often ignore or downplay suggestive and threatening behaviors. More information on this topic is presented in chapter 8.

- *Make responsible decisions regarding alcohol, drugs, and sex.* The opportunity for partying will be far greater at college than ever before. Remind your student of your expectations and encourage him or her to be careful. Alcohol, drugs, and sex are discussed more fully in chapter 8.

- *How to change a tire, where to go for an oil change, how to operate a car wash (if they will have a car at school or if they are commuting to school).* If your student spends more time worrying about or reacting to any of these issues than on studying, he or she probably should not have a car at school. Students also should know what to do if there is an accident, and how to respond if they are stopped by the police.

Throughout that last summer at home, you will think of things you want your child to know before she leaves. Your tendency might be to call her into the kitchen as a topic pops into your mind while you're fixing dinner or reading the newspaper. Your daughter, how-ever, won't be in any mood to pull herself away from the computer to submit to what sounds to her like another lecture. Some parents have suggested they have more success when they set an appoint-ment with their student and explain why the subject is important:

"When I do the taxes next winter, I'm going to need some information from you about some of your college expenses. I'd like to spend an hour or so with you this weekend to figure out how you can tag those expenses in your checking account this year. Can we plan to work on it right after lunch on Saturday, say at around one o'clock?"

"I notice you're getting a lot of credit-card applications in the mail. I get those all the time, too. I'd like to talk to you about the fine print on some of those applications so that you can see what the actual costs are."

GOOD INTENTIONS, BAD RESULTS

If New Year's Day provides incentive to commit to new resolu-tions, the start of college seems like an even greater opportunity for change. Every year, a new batch of freshmen promise themselves and their parents that they will become serious students, they will give up bad habits, and they will no longer fall into the slothful patterns of their youthful and ignorant past. Many students—with or without their doctor's advice—regard the start of college as a chance to try life without the medication, therapy, or sup-port groups that have long been part of their normal routine. The young woman with a learning disability is tired of being labeled, so she refuses to register with the college disability office. The athlete who is sure that he now can concentrate on his studies neglects to have his prescription for ADHD medication filled before he leaves for school. The student who believes she has finally outgrown her adolescent depression stops taking her antidepressants.

When absolutely everything in a student's life is changing—where and how she lives, who she lives with, even what she eats and how much she sleeps—this can be the worst possible time to give up the medications and support systems that have helped in the past.

In high school, Amy had signed up for a support group led by the school psychologist. Her parents' divorce had been hard on her. The sessions were often emotionally draining, but the group helped her find answers to many of her questions. As she prepared for college, though, she was well beyond the crisis, and she was relieved to think that she would no longer be going to group counseling every month. It felt like freedom—no more therapy!

A few weeks after Amy moved to campus, her mother became concerned about the tone of her daughter's phone calls. Amy sounded increasingly depressed and complained that she had no close friends. Her classes were hard, and she wasn't enjoying them at all. All she wanted was to come home.

Her mother urged Amy to talk to a counselor at the university, and after a few appointments, Amy began to see how leaving home for college had resurrected some of her anxieties related to the divorce. This time she was the one who had left home. She had never understood how her father could walk away from the family and start a new life; now she was doing the same thing. With a little help, Amy found ways to make a fresh start for herself and still keep room in her life for her mother.

It is understandable that students want a chance to give up those burdensome, long-term treatments or medications. Parents, meanwhile, are happy to see their child "move on with life." They want to believe that their son or daughter has overcome past problems, and college feels like the milestone that marks the cure. If the new challenges of college cause a recurrence of old illnesses or problems, though, parents are not there to monitor the signs. Students may be the last to detect their own regression, and when they need help the most, they may be incapable of seeking it out.

College disability counselors sympathize with students who want to try getting along without extra support. They will not force students with minimal physical disabilities to live in handicapped-accessible rooms, and they won't insist that students with learning disabilities use special accommodations if they don't want to. If the student eventually finds that the extra assistance is needed, however, the disability office must have the paperwork and physician's reports documenting the disability. Similarly, the student who falls into depression but has allowed his medication to lapse will have to meet with a psychiatrist to obtain a new prescription. Students are wise to file the forms before classes begin, even if they don't think they will ever want the assistance.

As challenging as it may feel for your student to tell a new roommate or hall director about his mental or physical health condition, it may lead to more challenges if the roommate or hall staff member doesn't understand. If your son's roommate doesn't understand the compulsive or antisocial symptoms of Asperger's syndrome, for instance, he may conclude that your son is simply rude, unfriendly, or has taken offense for some unknown reason.

The Boy Scout motto, "Be Prepared," is the best advice parents can give. Your child can be assertive about demanding a fresh start, but having all the appropriate health records on hand is a simple insurance policy. If the time comes when you get a sense your child needs the support systems or medications that have helped in the past, you can encourage him to visit the disability office or take the prescription along to a clinic appointment.

PARENTS WHO DO TOO MUCH

It is exciting for you, as a parent, to imagine this new life your child is about to begin at college. Perhaps you envision your daughter living in a residence hall, and you picture her friends flocking into her room because it is so warm and inviting. You want her to have nice things, and soon you find yourself shopping for a bright comforter and small appliances in coordinated colors. The next thing you know, you're online, checking the roommate's MySpace or Facebook page to make sure her favorite color won't clash with what you've picked out. Or you're on the phone calling the housing staff to find out if the doors in her room are wooden or magnetic so that you can buy the right kind of message board.

As much fun as it can be to think about your child's life at college, this is not the time to take charge of every detail. Instead of picking out matching sheets, towels, and lampshades, encourage your student to make a call or send an e-mail to her new roommate to talk about what they each will bring. Discussions between roommates about how to decorate the room can be among the most useful steps in learning about each other.

Every year, in every residence hall, there is a student who arrives a few hours after his roommate and finds the walls already plastered with posters, a futon and inflatable chair taking up two-thirds of the floor space, a sound system set to play a thousand tunes at random, and a bicycle suspended from a hook on the ceiling. The only unadorned space in the room is a single unmade top bunk and the surface of one dresser. The latecomer gets the instant message that he is an intruder in his own room. If he doesn't like the bike hanging in front of his closet or if his bookshelf isn't going to fit, he won't even be able to talk about it until the music stops.

By planning and setting up the room together, new roommates pick up useful clues about each other's personality, values, background, and financial resources. A shopping trip is often the students' first shared outing. Your role, as a parent, is to encourage your student to use these decisions as a way to meet room-mates, share ideas, and find ways to compromise.

Although you cannot get your child ready for college, you can help by breaking down the task. Instead of telling your daughter to start packing, suggest that she find a carton and pack linens (or toiletries or school supplies). Focusing on a single category at a time makes the job more manageable. She also can make her own packing list by thinking through her daily routine. What will she need as she showers and gets ready for class in the morning? What will she want to have on her desk when she's studying? On a cold, rainy day, what extra clothes will she need?

Students do not have to bring everything they own. Hall directors advise, "If your possessions won't fit into a minivan, they probably won't fit into a residence hall room." Some parents have found that it's both affordable and efficient to box and ship their child's belongings rather than haul them across the country. "He was willing to limit himself to four cartons of clothes, books, and supplies and ship them ahead, as long as we agreed to let him bring all his electronics in the car."

Most students do not want you to help with the packing, but they will not complain if you offer to put together some specific items—a get-well kit in case they come down with a cold, a batch of cookies or study rations to get them through the first week, or a tool kit and connection cords for basic repairs and computer setup. You can also offer to take on a supporting task, such as washing and folding all your child's laundry this one last time (while emphasizing that you will not accept packages of dirty laundry every week while your student is in college).

Health Kit

When your student is packing for college, put together some first-aid basics, such as a box of tissues, a packet of bandages, and acetaminophen or ibuprofen. In addition, you can pack a health kit with instructions to open it only in case of illness. In the kit, pack more of the essentials—pain medication and tissues—along with some extra items.

Digital thermometer

Cough syrup

Throat lozenges

Favorite soup (in a format that is easily prepared in a residence hall)

Bubble bath

Tea bags

Jar of honey

Some of the comforts that worked when your child was small: kids' games, books, puzzles, comic books; coloring book and crayons; favorite videos (most college students like to revert to childhood activities from time to time)

A get-well card with a caring message, signed by family members

COMMUTER CONCERNS

The transition to college is challenging even if it doesn't include packed boxes and a trip to Wal-Mart for extra-long sheets and shower shoes. Commuter students face their own set of adjustment issues. As high school friends are talking about leaving for college, commuters begin to question their decision to stay home.

Natalie had decided to enroll in a community college as a way to save money. Unfortunately, the two-year college in her town was just three miles from home and within sight of her old high school. By the beginning of August, she was disappointed that she had passed up any other opportunities she might have had, and she was envious of all her friends who were getting ready to leave. She couldn't work up any enthusiasm about college.

As she thought about the first day of classes, only two things entered her mind: "Where am I supposed to park?" and "Who am I going to hang out with?"

She also had a nagging suspicion that college should somehow feel more important to her than it did. Her friends' parents were all taking a couple days off work to go with their children to new student orientation; her own parents merely left a note on the table the morning of Nat's orientation, "Hope your day goes well! See you tonight." Her friends were comparing their residence hall assignments and talking about first phone calls with new roommates. For Natalie, nothing about college seemed different or exciting. When she came home from orientation, she complained to her mother, "The only time they offer Spanish is in the evening, and it's taught by Mrs. Jenkins from my high school. It's going to be just like last year."

For commuter students who will be attending a primarily residential school—a university where most of the freshmen live in dorms—the feelings of resentment are even stronger. They attend orientation, and everyone is asking, "So, where are you from? What hall will you be living in?" The commuter is convinced that it's far more interesting to be the girl from Florida or the guy from Chicago than the kid from a few miles away. Admitting that he's living at home—with his parents—is essentially saying, "I'm boring to the bone."

All these emotions are expressed to parents not as frustrations, but as disinterest. Commuter students often act like college is not particularly important, and it can be hard for parents to work up enthusiasm about the college experience when they see so little excitement from their child.

The little things you do before school starts can make a great difference, though. If the school has a parent orientation, your attendance will show your child that you value his college experience and his choice of schools. By scheduling a checkup on the child will see that you think his commute is important. By talking about changes in family chores and granting more flexibility for household responsibilities, you will let your student know that you understand and respect the fact that college is more demanding than high school, and that you are proud of your child's academic efforts.

Encourage your student to make the trip to school and find parking *before* the first day. Your student will not admit he's not sure about the best route to campus or where to park when he gets there; even if he's made the trip to campus before, has he driven the route during rush hour? An upperclassman tells incoming freshmen to drive the route to school at least twice— including once at the time of day they will be going to campus— before schools starts. "My first day, it took me two hours to get there, and it's only a half-hour drive. Somehow I missed the exit, and I ended up in the middle of downtown rush hour. I was ready to go home and drop out of school."

Also work with your student on multiple backup transportation plans in case the primary plan breaks down. A minor accident might mean no car for a week, but students still need to go to class. A transit strike requires alternate plans. A car pool only works if all drivers cooperate, and all riders are ready on time. Students will have odd hours—a group project that requires a 9 p.m. meeting, a lab experiment that takes longer than anticipated—and buses may run at different times or along different routes at night.

QUICK TIPS FOR STUDENTS

- Be certain you can do your laundry, iron a shirt, and replace a missing button. If you are a commuter student, or if you will be taking a car to campus, know how to change a tire, when to schedule an oil change, and what to do if you are in an accident or stopped by the police.

Assume these responsibilities during the summer, and you will have less to learn when you get to college.

- Don't save packing for the last minute. If you break the job into smaller categories, it won't seem so overwhelming.
- You will probably have doubts at some point during the summer. Did I pick the right major? Is this the right school? Maybe I should go to the same college as my best friends after all? You picked your college for a reason, and the admissions people admitted you because they believe you will be successful there. Don't second-guess yourself now. If it really turns out to be the wrong place, you can transfer next year.
- If you're living on campus and the school sends your roommate's name, phone number, and e-mail address, get in touch. You don't need to talk for an hour, but ask a few questions, tell him or her something about you, and see what happens from there. An e-mail is sometimes easier for the first contact.
- Commuter students should travel the route to school before school starts. Twice. During rush hour. Then spend a little time on campus. Figure out where your classes will be and, if you're driving, where you want to park. Scope out some places to hang out between classes. When you get it all figured out, come up with a backup plan or two for getting to and from school. If your schedule changes for a day, your car breaks down, or you miss the bus, what's another option?
- Prepare yourself to ask for help, and you'll get it. Every college has faculty and staff who can talk to you about what classes to take, how to get along with roommates—people to talk to if you're unhappy.

Section 2
Early Days

CHAPTER 3

Reality Bites

Establishing New Patterns

T he day your student starts college is a pivotal point in the change you are making from your role as primary care-taker and supervisor for your child to the role of proud mentor and supporter. The process is exciting, but it includes a degree of pain.

When we took our oldest son to college, I was confident that we all were ready for this step. I was certain I would be more pleased to see him begin this next stage of his life than sad about his departure.

We turned the journey into a family event and a weeklong vacation. We packed our two vehicles, both loaded to capacity, for a lesiurely three-day road trip from Minnesota to Houston, Texas. With our two sons in one car and my husband and me in the other, we headed south. We carefully planned meeting points for gas, meals, and hotel stops along the route so that we could change drivers and make sure the cars were both running well.

After arriving in Houston and finding the residence hall, we stood by as our son checked in at the front desk. The student worker on duty welcomed him and gave him his room key, a map of the building, and a two-page handout on bright yellow paper, covered with bullet points and bold type. "These are your hurricane instructions," I heard him say to my son. "You probably heard there's a hurricane just off the coast, and it's supposed to come ashore sometime during the night. If it does, we'll be knocking on doors to get everyone up and moved into the hallways."

I had been so confident that we had prepared our son for everything he would need to know for college, but hurricane survival tips had never entered my mind. I stepped up to the desk and said, "We've been reading all the information the university was sending us, and there was never any mention of hurricanes. How were we supposed to know about hurricanes? We're from Minnesota."

"That's okay, ma'am," the student said. "We know what to do. We'll take care of him."

This tall, lanky, straggly-haired kid—who obviously would be blown around like a soda straw by a strong gust of wind—was supposed to protect my son from a hurricane?

As hard as it was to accept, I had to admit that things would happen during the next four years that I had never predicted, and that I could not prepare my son for every contingency. I needed to trust his judgment, and I needed to have confidence in the staff at this university. As they reminded us at the parent welcome, fully trained, professional, and caring counselors, advisers, and student services personnel were on duty to deal with not only the typical problems that students experience, but also any crisis situations that might arise.

In recent years, campus shootings have made national headlines and raised fears of parents, students, and college staff. Parents want to know about emergency notification and crisis plans, and colleges and universities have responded by developing detailed protocols and promoting their strategies to students and families. While parents are wise to ask about the crisis plan for the school their child attends, it's important to keep safety factors in perspective. Educational institutions are ranked among the nation's safest workplaces,[2] and few businesses or institutions have security plans as multifaceted and transparent as colleges and universities. Most campuses have their own police or security force, trained counselors, health care providers, formal policies and procedures for handling all kinds of situations, and emergency procedures for evacuations, lockdowns, or quarantines. The odds of something going wrong are slim, but in an emergency, a college campus may be one of the safest places to be.

HOW WILL ALL THIS STUFF FIT INTO A DORM ROOM?

Until now, college was the future—something to look forward to and prepare for. Once students start packing the car, though, college finally becomes reality. A father describes his son, loading boxes into the van, suddenly turning to his parents and saying, "I'm not ready. Sure, I've got everything packed, but it's me—*I'm* not ready."

Talkative children become silent as they get closer to their college town. Quiet students chatter nervously. Arguments crop up over minor points. A student remembers the trip from his home in Virginia to college in Arizona as a cross-country argument with his younger sister, who insisted on sitting in the front seat the entire way. A mother recalls driving the width of Pennsylvania in silence following an argument with her daughter. One year, when I was helping move students into a residence hall on move-in day, I watched as a car pulled up to the curb, and the freshman in the front seat nervously scanned the scene of people hauling boxes, laundry baskets, and sports equipment across the

---

2. Bureau of Labor Statistics, www.bls.gov/iif/oshwc/cfoi/cftb0206.pdf (accessed June 8, 2008).

lawn. He opened his door, walked to the back of the car, and threw up.

Students aren't the only ones who are frightened and emotional. Parents are on edge, and anything that fails to go as planned serves as evidence that the student should return home immediately. The father who finds a line of people waiting for the elevators will be convinced that the dorm is poorly designed—an architectural nightmare. A mother who sees a box-elder bug on her daughter's windowsill will capture it in a plastic bag to prove to the hall staff that the room is not habitable. As student services professionals explain, anger, sadness, and fear stem from the same underlying feeling: "I want my child back."

Although parents can't prevent their student or themselves from being nervous, they can help make the move-in process less traumatic. The last thing your child wants on move-in day is for the family to make a scene. While you and your husband may think you're being supportive by wearing bright, new T-shirts in the yellow-and-black school colors, your student would much prefer that on this, of all days, you fade into the background in nondescript khaki. Your intentions may be good as you seek out the hall director to have her meet your son and hear about his dust allergies, but your son would rather slip anonymously into his room.

Mothers and fathers can take heart, however, that their student is already beginning to see them as more desirable parents than some of the alternatives. Although your daughter may seem shockingly embarrassed by you on move-in day, she also will be noticing that her parents are not nearly as bad as the family in the room down the hall.

So what is the recommended plan for move-in day? Do you unload your student's belongings at the curb and drive away? Do you plan to spend the weekend making certain that your child finds his classes and meets at least one new friend?

The first recommendation is to take the most direct route to campus. Many parents, especially fathers, like to think that the one thing they can do for their child on this last "family weekend" is to plan a nice, leisurely trip to college with a stop along the way for an hour-long hike at a park, a picnic lunch, and maybe a side trip to go to a ball game or to visit the former neighbors or old friends who live nearby. Your student, however, is not in the mood for a vacation. She is worried, excited, and intent upon getting to school. Your efforts to give her a memorable farewell trip will be unappreciated. Save the scenic route for the trip home or for next year.

If you must do something to keep your mind off your child's departure, put your energy into fussing over the car rather than trip planning. Clean out the car, vacuum the trunk, get the oil checked, replace the windshield wipers, put air in the tires. Any maintenance that prevents a breakdown en route to college is a good investment in family harmony. The freshman stuck on the side of the road with her family, in a stuffy car filled with every one of her most valued possessions, waiting for a tow truck, is a sure candidate for emotional meltdown.

Soon enough, your daughter, lugging a cardboard carton topped with her pillow, will walk into the room that will be the center of her life for the next eight and a half months. The focal point, the bed, will look stark and uninviting. As she drops the box on the floor and tosses her pillow onto the gray-striped, plastic-covered mattress, you will see the mix of excitement and dread on her face.

"I thought it would be bigger," she might say as she looks around. "Two of us are supposed to fit in here? Is that really the only closet?"

By my count, the average college student today brings at least seventeen electrical appliances and chargers to school. Multiply that by the number of roommates, and the challenge becomes clear: Living in a residence hall is a constant exercise in adaptation, and unpacking is the student's first step in learning to "make do." For parents, move-in day is a pop quiz in the course of relinquishing responsibility for your child. Your son or daughter will not approach the move-in and unpacking as you would. This task, however, belongs to your child, and throughout the process, you must help only if you're asked.

Your student will appreciate assistance carrying things up to the room, and most students accept their mother's offer to make the bed—as one student noted, "I think that was the only time my bed was made all year." Depending on the student's own technical ability, some are willing to let a parent or sibling help set up the computer and hook up all the peripherals. Beyond that, though, students usually prefer to do their own unpacking in their own time. Tempers become short when a parent suggests which drawer the socks belong in or where the family photo should be placed.

And this is not the time to remind your daughter that you told her she would never be able to fit everything she brought into her dorm room.

Younger brothers and sisters are intrigued by this new place, envious of their older sibling, and often at least a little disconcerted by the prospect of leaving their big brother or sister here. A burst of jealousy is common as the younger child demands attention. Steph recalls her twelve-year-old brother insisting that the first thing she should unpack was her new microwave so that he could make popcorn. To stop his whining, she dug the microwave out of the pile of boxes and let him plug it in. As she turned to arrange her closet, her brother managed to scorch the popcorn, sending out waves of smoke and an offensive odor that lingered not only in her room, but also throughout the entire hallway, for the rest of the afternoon.

When your student shows signs of irritation, it's usually best for the rest of the family to take a break. The college may be offering a family reception for parents and siblings to gather, talk to staff members, and meet other families who share the unfamiliar experience of delivering their child to college. A visit to the college's art gallery, a campus tour, or a two-hour trip to a nearby tourist highlight will give you something to do while your child makes decisions about where things will go. In a few hours, he will have had time to do some unpacking and, with luck, meet a roommate or the neighbor across the hall. Parents are usually relieved when they come back after a break and see that their child is feeling more comfortable and confident.

You can offer to take your child out for a meal or make a run to the mall for forgotten items, but let him decide if he wants to go. Some students are not ready to say good-bye yet and will appreciate time with their parents while they think through the next steps. Others will refuse any suggestion to get back into the car. Either way, it is hard for students to consider this as a family day.

If you have traveled cross-country to bring your child to school, you may be planning to spend a few days in town before heading back. Your student, however, is not likely to have the time or the inclination to fit your plans into his schedule. If she arranges her meals and spends her free time with you, she will miss opportunities to meet other students and to start exploring campus, which is the work she needs to do during the first few days at college.

Parents ask, "How do I know when to leave? Is there some sign I should watch for that tells me he's ready for me to go?" There is no magical sign, although some students will help you out by saying, "Go. Now." But eventually you do have to leave. As one residence hall director bluntly explains, "You can't stay. We don't have room for parents."

Your child will be grateful if you avoid sentimental farewells

in front of the roommates. Most students find this step less difficult if they walk their parents to the car to say good-bye. All
you need to say can be summed up in a few words: "I'm proud of
you—I love you." If you are convinced you won't be able to drive
for all the tears, just go a few blocks until you're out of sight, and
park the car for a while.

On the way home, take some time to celebrate your own success—you have reached a family milestone. Most parents have a
favorite CD their student no longer lets them listen to in the car.
Bring it and sing along on the way home. As Rice University's
School of Music emphasizes, singing releases endorphins, which
raise the spirits.[3] Chocolate and exercise release endorphins as
well, so stop for that hour-long hike you skipped on the way to
college or make a run to an ice-cream parlor for a hot-fudge sun-
dae.

When you arrive home, keep the celebration going. Curl up
with a book you've been meaning to read or a video you've been
wanting to watch, treat yourself to a bouquet of flowers, or
just go home and take a long, hot bath. You deserve some self-
indulgence. Within forty-eight hours, though, check back with
your student.

Some parents think that the "distance" their student needs
when he begins college means they should wait for the child to
make the first phone call. They make an effort not to call or write
until their student does. Although your child probably does not
want you to call every night, and he certainly does not want to
hear daily reports about how lonely you are, he does want to
know you're thinking about him. One student, Melissa, remembers that her roommate's mother sent short text messages every
morning and mailed a package of cookies or brownies once a

---

3. http://music.rice.edu/preparatory/singing02.html (accessed July 19,
2008).

week for the first month. Melissa's own mother always sounded happy to receive a call from her daughter, but she made a point of saying that she would not be an interfering mother and call all the time. One day, though, Melissa told her, "I have to say— I'm beginning to feel a little neglected here! Randi's mom sends cookies all the time, and she says she's willing to adopt me. I'm about ready to take her up on the offer."

A quick call or brief e-mail, just to say hello, is not an intrusion. And no matter how glad they were to see their parents leave on move-in day, very few students object to receiving a letter or package from home every now and then.

THE COMPLAINT DEPARTMENT

All the viewbooks and Web sites students looked at when they were researching colleges and universities captured the idealized image we have of campus life: golden autumn days with students striding past red-brick buildings or lounging with their laptops on a grassy lawn; a group of smiling and attractive young men and women studying together around a library table; fans decked out in school T-shirts at a basketball game; a student gazing into a microscope under the attentive eye of a bearded professor.

While nearly all students will have moments that resonate with those photographs, they will also have times when absolutely nothing goes right.

The first days at college usually turn out to be a relief for new students. Things may not be as ideal as they'd hoped, but neither are they nearly as bad as their worst fears—people are pretty nice, the dorm room isn't as cramped as it seemed that first day, and when a problem arises, the student manages to cope. There is almost unreasonable happiness in logging onto the school's wireless service and discovering it actually works. A huge sense of accomplishment comes from figuring out how to use the college ID card to be admitted to the cafeteria.

Before long, though, the joy fades. Fall semester for freshmen is a roller-coaster ride of ups and downs. With the transition to college, nearly every aspect of students' lives changes. Although they come to school expecting new experiences, they often don't take into account the impact of all that they will encounter.

- They will almost never be alone. In most families today, children have their own bedroom at home, and many have their own bathroom. In a residence hall, though, they may share a room with two or more people, and they will almost certainly share a bathroom—in some cases with twenty people.
- There's no accounting for what will drive them crazy. Using the shower after someone else, washing dishes in the bathroom sink, or the lack of two-ply toilet paper may prove to be far more annoying than sleeping in a single bed, waking to a roommate's alarm clock, or hearing country music from across the hall.
- There is no such thing as a quiet meal. Even if they like the food, the multiple scents, sights, and sounds of a crowded dining hall become oppressive as a three-times-a-day routine.
- Despite all the activity surrounding them, there will be times of loneliness.

THERE'S NO PLACE LIKE HOME

At some point, nearly every freshman suffers from homesickness. Even commuter students will feel times of loneliness or anxiety when they're on campus and want only to be away from this place and in the company of old friends. Feelings of homesickness often seep in during the first or second week of school, but they are more confusing when they crop up later. Some students will seem perfectly content during the first month, but then call home weeping in October after friends e-mail photos of this year's high school homecoming dance. Homesickness may not even show up until it's time to return to campus after Thanksgiving, and your son realizes he won't be able to help string the holiday lights on the roof this year.

Parents don't always know that the emotions their child is expressing stem from homesickness. It sometimes sounds more like anger or frustration: "This place is not what I expected. They never said the professors would be so picky!" They may express homesickness not through missing the family, but "I miss the dog" or "It turns out I can't sleep anywhere but my own bed." Children of single parents can turn their anxiety into a sense of responsibility: "I should never have left you home alone, Mom. You need help with the yard work, and besides, it would be cheaper if I lived at home."

The intensity of homesickness can come as a surprise, especially when these same students have happily gone off to summer camps or on choral trips abroad throughout their lives. Somehow, college feels more permanent. This is the next step that they have spent a lifetime preparing for; now that they're here, they feel they have leaped firmly into the future and there's no turning back.

Usually homesickness is temporary. It's a response to being in a new situation without the support system that got them this far. Ask your student to stay in school at least for the first semester to see if things start to feel better. As students catch on that a new support system is in place on campus, that others are feeling the same emotions, and that they can handle their new life, their anxiety will subside.

In the meantime, parents can help soothe the pain by sending a small package, a card, or an e-mail letting your student know you're thinking of him, and that things are fine at home. You can schedule a remote routine that includes the student in a traditional family activity, such as a phone call after your favorite TV show to recap the program.

Most important, though, encourage your student to get involved with campus activities. Remind him to join a campus organization, get some exercise, or invite a friend for a walk. Busy, engaged students discover they don't have time to be homesick.

STARTING OUT STRONG

The opening days of college set the patterns that can mean the difference between success and failure. The routines that students establish during the first weeks tend to last at least through the first semester, sometimes longer. The patterns they form become a part of who they are and how they interact on campus. Students who spend September weekends partying will probably look for a party every weekend in October and November. The commuters who hurry home after class every day during the first few weeks may never carve out their own niche on campus or form a study group with other students.

College students are usually in class only fifteen to eighteen hours a week. Compared to a high school schedule, college might seem like a vacation. The expectation, however, is that for every hour a student is in class, another two to three hours should be spent studying. A class schedule of fifteen credit hours, then, translates into a weekly time commitment of thirty to forty-five hours outside of class. Students who revel in their unscheduled time and postpone writing their papers until the last minute or who pull all-nighters to cram for their final exams will not be as successful as they could have been.

It's not only what students are doing, but how they are relating to the campus in the first few weeks that makes a difference. Too many students turn to the Internet for a social life, sacrificing real-life, real-time companionship. Online gambling or gaming consumes hours of free time and turns into an obsession. Students stay up long into the night, communicating with high school friends or chatting with faceless icons in cyberspace, and they fail to meet the people who live across the hall. They even use instant messaging and texting to fight with their roommates. A residence hall adviser in Wisconsin found out that two students on his hall had been feuding for months. The roommates literally did not speak to each other. They would sit at their desks on opposite sides of the room and send vitriolic messages back and forth. The hostility—and the silence—in the room was oppressive.

Listen as your child describes campus life during the first few weeks of classes. By the sixth week, students should be talking about coursework, accomplishments and challenges, instructors, and new friends. Commuter students should be spending the majority of their day on campus, doing homework, and meeting with their instructors or other students. Residential students should be dedicating blocks of time to studying, not trying to read a few pages in the ten minutes before class. All students should be making connections on campus.

If your child continues to talk exclusively about friends from high school, or if the focus of her conversations relates only to the social activities on campus, it's probably time for a serious discussion about educational goals and adjustment to college. The first semester is a transition period, and all students will waver between being thrilled to be in college and wondering if they would rather be home, but you should see some progress. At least one class should be challenging enough to talk about; at least one instructor should be engaging enough to merit attention; at least one paper or test should be worth telling you about. Even if your child is mostly just complaining, as long as she's talking about college, she is becoming involved.

COLLEGE CULTURE SHOCK

Freshmen are subjected to every possible warning and tidbit of advice about safety, security, and student success. Residence hall staff talk about fire drills, cooking regulations, nighttime security procedures, and alcohol policies. Academic advisers lecture on time management, study skills, the evils of plagiarism, and the value of setting up study groups. Student affairs staff stop by to talk about getting involved on campus, developing leadership skills, and making smart choices about finances and health.

Meanwhile, there are new words and new traditions that students are expected to somehow know—the University of Michigan freshman is confused when his classmate tells him to meet him in the "Fishbowl" between classes. At Wake Forest, he is supposed to know when to show up for "rolling the quad." And college presents first-year students with challenges far beyond the classroom. The suburban student who goes to school in a big city can't imagine life without a car. The city dweller who attends a small rural college is surprised to find there is no bus service—so how do you get to a store to buy shampoo? The farm girl from Nebraska is puzzled to see people carrying umbrellas on her California campus—*Do people really use umbrellas?* she wonders. *I thought that was something only the British do, or characters in books.* Where she comes from, if it rains you either stay indoors, drive wherever you're going, or wear a hat.

New information of all kinds is firing in from every direction, and hardly any of it is hitting its mark. First-year students are not looking for advice or wisdom, traditions or new concepts; they're looking for friends. But friend making is one of those skills no one ever thought to teach them.

Friendships, in their experience, just happen. If they grew up in a small community, their parents knew the families of all their friends. Neighborhood schools or private schools usually draw students who share similar backgrounds, and most of their friends have been much like themselves. Even those from large city schools with considerable diversity had friends from a limited social circle—people they knew from a sports team, band, their neighborhood, church, or "friends of friends." When they started dating in high school, they already knew something about the person they were going out with, or they at least knew someone who could provide some information.

In college, they don't have family references for the people they're meeting. They have to figure out not only who will be fun and interesting, but also who will be trustworthy. In their urgency to have a friend or a lover, many students make poor choices and then don't know how to break off a relationship.

Students who are not naturally outgoing can feel like outcasts and failures at making friends. The icebreaker activities that seem to be a requirement at the start of every social gathering are painful exercises in forced friendship. It seems like college is designed for the extroverts of the world, and introverts are apparently expected to somehow turn into perky and bold collegians.

Students of color might find themselves feeling particularly isolated. College was supposed to provide an intellectual environment where race didn't matter; suddenly they're expected to speak for their entire race on deep philosophical or political matters. Most colleges have culture-based student groups to give students of color a place to meet, receive support on campus, and celebrate diversity. Although most students will settle in comfortably in time, initial feelings of difference and separation can be particularly difficult in the first few weeks of college.

Everyone wants to have friends and be accepted. Lonely students seeking companionship are vulnerable to predatory religious groups as well as seemingly innocent campus-sponsored student groups that promise camaraderie, but then require proof of commitment. Initiation ceremonies and hazing by athletic teams, social organizations, or even the college band sometimes demand that students perform humiliating acts—even deadly behaviors—all in the name of fun and friendship.

Years ago, hazing was considered a harmless prank; it was a way to ritualize and build bonds between members of a group. For those doing the hazing, it was amusing, and for those being hazed, it was a way to prove their commitment. But the balance of power between old and new members of the group can lead to degradation and abuse. When college students are subjected to sleep deprivation, servitude, physical and mental abuse, or alcohol overconsumption, they are not in any condition to succeed in their classes. Colleges and universities should promote a zero tolerance on hazing, and most will have a well-publicized hazing policy. But hazing still happens. If parents have any indication that their student is being victimized, encourage him or her to contact the group's adviser, the dean of students, campus police, or the national chapter of a fraternity or sorority. For more information on hazing, see StopHazing.org.

Friendship: True or False?

Most college students develop friendships that last a lifetime. Some will meet their future partners. As students experience the revelations that come with a college education, in the classroom and out, they come to treasure the people who share those moments with them.

The friends they make can be the most positive—or the most damaging—influence of their college years. Students are vulnerable to bad relationships when they are lonely or homesick, when they have recently broken up with a boyfriend or girlfriend, when they are bored, and when they are struggling academically or financially. The following information, which compares the difference between true and false friends, can be adapted to romantic relationships as well as to social and religious organizations.[4]

True Friends

- **True friends take time for you and listen to you.** Your thoughts and opinions are important to them, even if they disagree with your ideas. They do not belittle your differences.
- **True friends encourage relationships with family and other friends.** They are not jealous or possessive. They are interested in meeting your family and friends.
- **When something goes wrong, true friends want to work through the problems with you.** They can explain why they are upset, and they can acknowledge their responsibility in the problem.
- **True friends support your goals and encourage your success.** They believe in you and want you to do well.
- **True friends are people you feel safe with.** They do not ask you to bend the rules, and they respect your values and concerns.
- **True friendships develop and grow over time.** Instant friendships can end as quickly as they begin. Friends take the time to know each other well.

---

4. Adapted from "How to Spot a Loser Lover," the Aurora Center, and "Is It an Invitation, or Is It Coercion?" Interfaith Campus Coalition, University of Minnesota.

False Friends

- **False friends demand all your attention and are jealous of your other friends.** They question your loyalty to them, and they become anxious or upset if they don't know where you are.
- **For false friends, the relationship is all about them.** They expect you to be there for them, to do what they want, and to devote yourself to them. Your thoughts and opinions are important only if they conform to their own.
- **False friends don't think anything is their fault.** When things go wrong, it's your fault or someone else's. They are never wrong, and they are never responsible for problems.
- **False friends become more controlling as time goes by.** You cannot provide enough attention, and you are asked for more and more proof of your devotion.
- **False friends live by their own rules.** They may push the limits of the law, have financial problems, or use drugs and alcohol dangerously. They convince you to do things you don't want to do, and they become angry if you challenge them.
- **False friends want too much, too soon.** When you're with them, you feel like things are out of control. If you feel that something is wrong, you're probably right.

As important as it is to be cautious about friendships, parents also should stress that "different" does not equate with "bad." Except for the smallest private schools, most colleges and universities will introduce your student to a world of new ideas, new religions, new cultures. Initially, all the differences can be fascinating. Students between the ages of eighteen and twenty-two are receptive to learning, and they are in an environment that supports them as they open their minds to new people and new experiences.

In time, some of the differences may begin to feel like challenges to their own background and beliefs. When a Muslim roommate kneels on the floor to pray multiple times a day, his new friends may feel like he is taking over the room, withdrawing from them, or making some kind of a statement. A neighbor with autism may be mistakenly identified as overly sensitive or intolerant. If a lesbian suitemate has a female visitor stop by, her roommates try to figure out what kind of "girlfriend" this is.

When students come across ideas or conditions that contrast with their past experiences or their family's values, they have to make some decisions. Should they accept or reject these new concepts? And how do they deal with the people who present them?

The black-and-white, right-or-wrong perspectives that worked for students in the past are countered by shades of gray. They almost hate to admit that what is wrong in some circumstances might be perfectly acceptable in others. Most students learn how to choose what they will accept and make allowances for what they cannot. College students as a whole not only accept diversity, but embrace it. Ideally, they will recognize that they are part of an exciting and energizing community. The fact that they are learning something new every day is proof that they're moving forward with their lives.

Mini-Calendar of the First Six Weeks

Move-in Day—A tough day for families. Students are tense, excited, scared. Parents are on edge; if anything goes wrong, they may find themselves reacting more strongly than they would expect. Advice for parents: Tell your child you love and trust her, and you have great confidence that she will be fine.

Week 1—Students establish routines as a way to adapt to change. Social acceptance is usually their first priority. Students react strongly to disappointments or problems. This may be the first time they have had to identify problems and find solutions entirely on their own. They will complain, but they usually manage to adjust. Every accomplishment feels like a significant victory. Advice for parents: Talk to your child at least once during the first week; enjoy the excitement, and acknowledge the disappointments.

Week 2—Students may go overboard with new freedoms. They figure out that attendance is not taken in classes, and they decide not to go. They realize that they have two hours between their lecture and their lab, and they spend the time with friends in a coffee shop. They see other students decorating their rooms, and they spend a small fortune on posters and pillows. Advice for parents: Listen for clues that your child might be making poor decisions. Affirm the good choices and talk about priorities.

Week 3—A mix of comfort and uneasiness confuses students. They have established a routine, and they no longer feel "new." They become extremely close to friends they have just met. They can't believe they've only known these people a couple of weeks. On the other hand, students are frustrated that there is obviously so much they don't know yet about college. They think that everyone is looking at them and thinking, *Obviously clueless. Must be a freshman.* Any mistakes feel like proof they don't belong. Advice for parents: Tell your child you believe in her.

Week 4—Students who have not yet gone home begin to want a weekend away from college. The intensity of it all has become exhausting, and they're worn out. They begin to see things from a slightly different perspective—the gregarious, outgoing friend they met the first week of school starts to seem a bit shallow; the quiet, cynical person next door might not be so bad after all; and they get tired of roommates. They long for a little quiet time. Advice for parents: Listen to complaints, but don't try to fix things. Suggest that, rather than come home for the weekend, your child can stay at school and spend some extra time sleeping and studying over the weekend. The standard recommendation is that students should stay at school until Thanksgiving break.

Weeks 5 and 6—Students begin to react to disillusionment. College turns out not to be everything they had imagined, and they have to admit that some of their initial social choices were poor. Typically, students either confront their challenges and make improvements, or they confirm their original patterns. Students will continue to cycle through frustration and action throughout the first semester, deciding to drop bad habits or bad friends or concluding that "since this is what college is, maybe I'm not cut out for it." Advice for parents: Talk with your child about the good decisions you have seen him make during the first few weeks of school. Let him know there is still time to make improvements.

QUICK TIPS FOR STUDENTS

- The first day of school, you are *not* the only one who doesn't know what's going on. All freshmen are scared and confused. Some of them simply hide it well.
- If your parents are irritable on that first day at college, it's because they're nervous, too. The fact that you're starting college is almost as big a change for them as it is for you.
- The patterns you set in the first week of school are the ones you will tend to follow for a long time. Make sure they're good ones. When you find yourself doing the same thing every day, ask yourself, *Is this a routine I want to continue?*
- Get up, get out, and get involved, even if you are

the kind of person who would rather melt into the background. Turn off the computer, meet the people across the hall and on the floor above yours. Say hello to the person sitting beside you in every class. Talk to the person next to you as you go through the cafeteria line. Someday, one of those people will say, "I am so glad you came up to me that first time!"

- The way you feel today is not how you'll feel tomorrow. You will have days when you're not at all sure you're at the right school, but you'll also have days when you know you are doing just fine. Remember the good days so you can draw on them during the rough times.

- Be willing to rethink your choices. You can drop friends who don't turn out to be what you expected; you can change majors; you can ask forgiveness for doing something stupid. The best part of being a freshman is that for a whole year, you can say, "I'm still trying to figure things out."

- For commuters, setting classes as your top priority is even harder than for students who live in a dorm. Spend your free time on campus, make a space there for yourself, and start to think of college as your "real life."

CHAPTER 4

No More Notes
on the Refrigerator

Parenting from a Distance

You and your child have been working through issues surrounding independence for years. At least once during high school, and certainly during that senior summer, your child must have declared, "You can't tell me what to do; I'm not a kid anymore." It's true. With your student in college, you really *can't* tell this "almost adult" what to do. You have much less direct control, but you do still have influence, and you will continue to care deeply about how he is and whether he is safe, comfortable, and happy. For the next four years, you will be parenting your student from a distance, which requires greater trust from you and greater responsibility from your child.

If parents have studied psychology, they will recognize that the steps they go through in transferring responsibility to their child track Maslow's Hierarchy of Needs. The psychologist Abraham Maslow said that certain basic physiological needs must be met (food, drink, and sleep) before we can move on to satisfy psychological and emotional needs. When we are confident that we have sufficient food and drink and a place to sleep, we will turn to ensuring protection against danger. With a sense of security, we're ready to seek friendship and a sense of belonging, then self-respect and self-esteem, and finally self-actualization and an outlet for creativity.

The college selection and leaving-home stages replicate Maslow's hierarchy, with parents seeking assurance that all their child's needs will be met. Parents insist on being involved as their student reviews residence hall choices to make sure that their child will have a comfortable place to live. They want to know about meal plans so they can be assured their child will eat well. On move-in day, they check to ensure the safety precautions are all in place. They flick light switches, make sure there is a smoke alarm, ask about the sprinkler system, and take a close look at the lock on the door.

When parents go home after settling their student into the dorm, they may be ready to transfer the basic responsibilities to their student, but they will require ongoing assurance that their child is safe, secure, and happy. It is not quite enough for them to know that they have provided for room, board, and safety; they want to be sure their student is making the right choices about those basic needs. They will continue to ask, "Are you eating all right? Is your room okay? Are you getting enough sleep? Are you making sure to walk with someone when you're out after dark?" Students hate the questions, but parents feel compelled to hear the answers. In reality, the question is, "Can you take care of yourself?"

With those essential needs met and confirmed, parents' worries turn to whether their student is making friends and fitting into campus life. After comfort and safety issues, parents of freshmen express the most concern about their child's social adaptation. "Are you getting along with your roommates? Have you joined any groups? Do you have any friends?"

By the sophomore or junior year, parents again track Maslow's hierarchy when they begin to wonder, has my child chosen the right field of study? It's not too late to change majors, is it? Next they will question whether this major can provide an actual career. Will she get a job? Is he doing the right things to get into graduate school? Will he be happy in this career he's chosen? And finally, during the senior year, has this whole college experience been worthwhile?

Although college parents work their way up this Pyramid of Protection, they also routinely return to that baseline of basic needs. When their third-year student moves into his first apartment, they will worry about whether he can make his own meals and how safe the neighborhood is. Indeed, it may not be enough to hear that the apartment is safe, and there is food in the cupboard; parents may need to see the evidence. Then they will move up the pyramid again and look for reassurance about the people he has selected as roommates and whether he will remember to pay the bills on time.

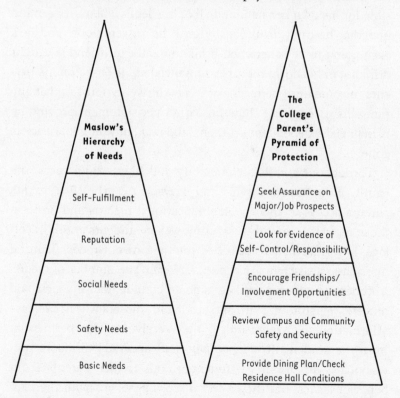

Adapted from Abraham Maslow, *The Farther Reaches of Human Nature* (New York: Viking, 1971).

I'M PAYING THE BILLS! WHAT ARE MY RIGHTS?

You're paying thousands of dollars for tuition, but you can't get a copy of your daughter's grades. You handed over all your personal financial information to the college, but you can't see your son's billing statement. Your sophomore was ordered to move out of the residence hall, but the hall director won't tell you why.

An eighteen-year-old college student is considered an adult—except, of course, for all those circumstances when he is not. If you think it's confusing for you, look at it from your child's viewpoint. The college tells him he is an adult, and he is responsible for his own behavior and all of his debts. Then they remind him that he can't drink legally until he's twenty-one, and he's even going to be sanctioned if his underage girlfriend is caught drinking in his dorm room. His financial aid is based on his parents' income until he reaches the age of twenty-four. And at any time, his parents can show up with a tax statement proving he is financially dependent on them, and suddenly all his privacy is gone.

Throughout a child's elementary and high school years, the Family Educational Rights and Privacy Act (FERPA) grants parents access to their child's educational records and protects those records from public scrutiny. When students enroll in college, however, their records become their own. Grades, financial information, disciplinary action, and even the number of credits a student is taking are all considered confidential. Financial aid officers, registration staff, and academic advisers will not release information to parents unless they receive written permission from the student. Residence hall staff and judicial affairs professionals will encourage students to talk to their parents about behavior issues, but they won't discuss problems with the family unless the student agrees. And what FERPA doesn't protect,

HIPAA (Health Insurance Portability and Accountability Act) does. Parents may have monitored their child's medical condition for eighteen years, but now medical personnel and psychologists will cite HIPAA when they explain they cannot tell you what treatment your student is receiving or even if he's had an appointment at the clinic.

A few years ago, FERPA was modified to allow, but not require, colleges to notify parents about violations of student conduct codes. Not all colleges have adopted these parent notification policies, but many schools will now tell parents if a student violates campus alcohol or drug rules. Other student records continue to be protected.

The obvious complaint—and we hear it every day—is, "I'm the parent, and I'm paying for my child's education. Why can't I get any information?" You can, but only with your child's permission or by submitting your federal income tax forms, showing that you claim your child as a dependent. No matter where their child attends college, parents can see their student's records if their child gives them access. At some schools, release processes now are routinely explained to freshmen at orientation. Because incoming freshmen tend to do what they're told, new students often don't realize they are surrendering some of their rights to privacy.

Other schools have varying approaches to granting and promoting parent access to student records. Some make the process transparent and simple, proactively telling parents how their student can give them permission to see records. Students can go online to grant access to their parents, and parents can use Internet connections to view and pay bills. Other schools may not mention privacy until the parent calls complaining, "I haven't received a statement yet for my daughter's tuition. How much do I owe?"

Although the time may come when you wish the college

would hand over your student's records, most parents agree that there are good reasons to honor student privacy. A student should have the right to prevent a noncustodial parent from receiving personal contact information; colleges and universities do not know if the person seeking information is truly the parent; stalking and harassment can and does result from access to personal information. Colleges and universities will not assume that every family is loving and caring, because, unfortunately, some are not.

INFORMATION IS POWER

As parent notification policies and release forms have become more common, parents and college administrators have expressed surprise that the voice of protest from students has been quieter than they expected. Today's students recognize the high cost of a college education, and they appreciate their parents' investment. Moreover, this generation of students is accustomed to turning to their parents for guidance, and they continue to want family support as they face the future. As first-year students, they are overwhelmed by the decisions they are required to make, as well as by the consequences for making the wrong choices, so they welcome their parents' involvement.

Although a freshman might acknowledge that there are good reasons for his parents to see his student records, parents still are likely to encounter defiance when it comes down to precisely which information they can see. Your son will be happy to have you receive and pay the tuition bill, but he wishes the bill would not reflect that he's taking only ten credits this semester. Your daughter is happy to show you her grade reports when she's earning A's and B's, but she won't want you to see the report that includes an incomplete in astronomy. She would like you to cover the co-payments for her medical appointments, but she doesn't want you to know about the 2 a.m. emergency-room visit last weekend. You feel like you are always hearing only half the story.

During Family Weekend, the college counselor offered assurance to the group of parents who were gathered for brunch. "You probably are noticing that your children will not tell you everything they're doing or show you every grade they receive, but there's a reason: They need to figure out where they, as individuals, are separate from their family, or their friends, or anyone else. An important part of that process is deciding which information they will share. It's just another step in growing up—the separation process might have begun at birth, but we're still cutting the umbilical cord eighteen years later. Over the next few months and years, you and your child will be working on establishing what we call 'appropriate boundaries.' "

To most parents, though, these boundaries seem less like clear fences than like a complicated maze. Your child will allow you to come just so far into his life, but the moment you ask a question about his new girlfriend or the state of his finances, he'll put up an impenetrable barrier: "There's really nothing to talk about! Oh—I have another phone call. Sorry, I have to go."

If you back up and wind your way down a less direct path, you might find that he's not only telling you about his girlfriend, he's asking you to stop by the dorm sometime soon to meet her. He may not tell you the balance on his credit card, but he might ask if you think it makes sense to have a debit card instead of a checking account.

From the minute your child hits campus, he is living in a world that is different from the one he grew up in. Your student controls the information you will get, partly because of data privacy laws, but mostly because he *is* growing up, and he does want some privacy. Your questions are a threat to that privacy, and he needs some time to consider which information he wants to share with you.

Since you are not part of your child's college life, most of the time you don't even know what to ask. When you do know the questions, you don't know when to ask them. And you just can't understand how your most innocent comments seem to abruptly end conversations.

Let's look at what goes on in a student's mind when you ask a simple, seemingly noninvasive question like, "What did you do this weekend?"

To begin, a weekend might include everything from Thursday evening through Sunday, and your daughter probably was busy with dozens of different activities during that time. Now that you've asked about it, she will have to sort through a long list and decide what to tell you. She figures you would be more impressed to hear that she spent five hours studying on Sunday afternoon than that she went shopping Friday evening, or that she was out with friends all day Saturday. She considers that she probably should tell you she overspent her clothing budget, but she doesn't really want to hear that same old sermon about money management. She already knows she should be more careful with her finances, so she gives herself a little reproof on your behalf, skips over all of Friday's activities, and decides she doesn't want to talk about Saturday or Sunday either.

"Nothing much" is her answer. "I'm doing laundry tonight, and actually, I better go get my clothes out of the dryer now so someone else can use it."

Nevertheless, there are things you need to know, such as when tuition is due. Or when spring break is scheduled. Or if it really makes sense for your son to be taking three physical education classes and something called "Self-Actualization."

Counselors recommend that parents ask questions that cannot be answered with a simple yes or no. At the same time, you don't want to appear to be prying for too much personal information. Once your student starts talking and is convinced that you are listening, not judging, he will share as much as feels comfortable to him. Some ideas for conversation starters:

- Ask open-ended questions that show interest in your child's experiences, such as "Are your classes what you expected?" "How does your Spanish class compare with the language classes you took in high school?" "How much variety is there in the food they serve in the cafeteria?" "What is there to do on campus on the weekends?"
- If your child doesn't seem to want to talk, don't ask about her silence; instead *you* can carry the conversation for a while. Talk about things that you know interest her. If she participated in high school sports, tell her how the team is doing and mention some of the athletes she played with. Talk about the family pet.
- Often, parents are so intrigued by their student's new life they forget that their child still needs to know at least a little about what is happening at home. Describe the repairs you're having done on the car or mention that you spent the morning doing laundry, vacuuming, and washing floors. These reports remind your child that not *everything* in his life is changing. Also tell him about anything new that he will encounter when he comes home—like the new toaster, or the new tile you're having installed in the bathroom.
- Avoid judging. Students are sensitive to any hints of disappointment or criticism. If you need to ask about

finances, student records, or other specific information, keep that part of the discussion separate from the personal conversation, and be clear about your expectations. "It sounds like you're doing well, and I'm proud of you. Before we hang up, we need to get a little business done. To keep you on my health insurance policy, my personnel office has to have a statement from the college saying you're taking at least twelve credits this semester. I need to have it by the end of the month, and they say that students usually get those forms from the registrar's office."

In the best of situations, your child will give you the information you need, even if the message is not all that you might wish. Because students don't want to disappoint their family, though, they will work hard to prevent their parents from seeing poor grade reports, finding out that they did something foolish, or hearing that they are in serious trouble. To a young adult trying to attain independence, keeping bad news from Mom or Dad is a way to avoid the reprimands and control they have been trying to escape. Almost everything you hear from your student will be filtered through the clearest possible lens. Sometimes students will be vague about what's happening in their lives, and sometimes they will flat-out lie.

When you hear something from your student that doesn't seem to ring true, consider whether there is something he or she may not want to acknowledge. If your child tells you that the college doesn't provide transcripts, or that the school doesn't post grades, you probably have a clue that there are academic difficulties. If you suddenly hear about an unexpected "hundred-dollar registration fee the college just added," it may be an indication that your child has some kind of expense she does not want you to know about.

A discussion at the start of the college experience, plus occasional follow-up conversations, can establish expectations about what kind of information you will share and which topics can be considered private or discretionary. Your student is unlikely to want to share details of every quiz or expenditure, and you will not hear about every party or date, but parents are justified in asking for general information on grades, the social scene, health issues, and bottom-line financial balances.

If you don't show an interest in your student's education, she will think you don't value how hard she is working. If you show too much interest, she will think you are infringing on her privacy. Parents struggle with the fine line they must walk, but most agree the path is smoothest when they express frequent admiration for their child's efforts. When students see that their parents use information to provide support rather than assert control, they end up offering information because they *want to* rather than because they *have to*.

"HOW DO I GET SOME ANSWERS AROUND HERE?"

It takes time to sift through the new communication processes when students start college. A parent's expectations about how and when information will be shared are rarely the same as the student's.

When Marcy's family said good-bye after moving her into the freshmen residence hall, they told her to be sure to call and let them know if she needed anything. They expected to hear from her within a day or two. The third day passed with no word, so Marcy's father placed a call to her. He was anxious to talk to his daughter, but his mood turned to irritation when Marcy's voice-mail recording brightly announced, "You know who this is, and you know what to do. Wait for the beep." Stifling his annoyance, he did his best to sound nonchalant as he left a message saying that he hoped things were going well and asking her to call when she had a chance.

She sent a short text message, "All fine here," but she still had not called home by the end of the week. On Friday her parents began phoning every couple of hours. Obviously, she was not in class every minute. They went from irritation to anger—was she even checking her voice mail? How irresponsible was she, refusing to call home like this? Then they blamed the phone—her voice mail must not be working. Maybe her phone didn't work at all. It became the university's fault: The dorm should have a backup system for getting messages to students. Next, fear set in. Was she all right? Had she left school and was afraid to tell them? Did *anyone* know where she was?

When her parents finally reached her, Marcy couldn't understand why they seemed so upset. "I got your messages, but I've been busy. I would have called if something was wrong," she said. "Am I supposed to talk to you every day? I really didn't have anything to say. Everything's fine."

Throughout high school, the only times Marcy phoned her parents were when she needed a ride or if she found that she would be later than expected. There was never a need to call home "just to talk." Marcy thought that she would call her parents from college if she had a specific question or a problem. It didn't occur to her that a quick, five-minute phone call the day after she started school would have mattered so much to her parents. She wasn't homesick for them yet, so she didn't share the urgency to give them a call.

"I'm not going to tell you everything that goes on in my life," she said. "I don't want to have to come up with a daily Marcy report."

Marcy's parents explained that while they wanted to know if their daughter had any problems, they also wanted to hear the good news. Most important, they simply needed to hear her voice and know that she was all right.

TECHNOLOGY: HIGH TECH, LOW TOUCH

Communication between students and their parents is not the same as it was a generation ago. When you first left home, you might have scheduled a collect call to Mom and Dad at a time when you knew they would be home to accept the charges. Or you waited to place the call during less expensive "evening and weekend hours." Now, however, students pull out their cell phones as they're walking between classes. Your child may be talking to you on the way to an exam, and you might get another call minutes after she turns in her test. Technology—particularly cell phones, e-mail, texting, and instant messaging—has dramatically affected the relationship between parents and students.

Some studies have shown that parents and their college-aged students are in touch more than ten times a week. Hardly any student goes a week without communicating with Mom and Dad. When something goes wrong, the first person a student talks to is a family member.

The speed of communication means that students don't spend much time processing information before they call home. Parents hear the news when it is still raw and emotional. When your student uses his cell phone to call you at work and report that he's standing outside the financial aid office, and he's missing a required form, it will seem like a major crisis to him. Your instinct will be to try to figure out a solution immediately, while he's on the line. If, on the other hand, he had waited to call until seven-thirty that evening, he would have had time to find the form himself, ask someone in the financial aid office what to do, or decide by himself how to deal with the problem. At any rate, the issue would not be complicated by such urgency.

This immediate contact is both a blessing and a curse. Parents and students are communicating more, but technology also has raised expectations. A father knows his daughter has a cell phone; if he calls and gets no answer, he may panic.

Text messages and e-mail bring similar mixed blessings. If a parent sends a text message and a response doesn't come within a couple of hours, she worries. An e-mail that doesn't elicit a reply within twenty-four hours can raise an alarm. The student, however, may have turned his phone off during class and forgotten to turn it back on. Maybe he was doing countless other things and hadn't checked that particular e-mail account in a couple of days. Or maybe he glanced at his list of messages and thought, *A message from Mom. I don't have time to write back to her now, so I'll wait and read that one later.*

Some parents insert code words into the subject line of e-mail messages when they must have a quick response. One family has agreed that urgent messages will begin "Respond Now." Another mother says she always gets a reply if she writes "Want money?" in the subject line.

"High tech" has some "high touch" benefits as well, though. Students and their parents find that e-mail allows them to say things to one another they could not say in person or over the telephone. The lack of visual cues can make for more personal communication. As they write a message, there are no interruptions and no body language or voice inflections to stop the train of thought. Consequently, e-mail users frequently disclose far more than they would in person, much as a blogger confides more online than she does out loud to a friend. Fathers, especially, are likely to communicate more openly with their child by e-mail.

"I hate talking on the phone," one father said. "I don't do

well with small talk, and once I've said whatever it is I'm calling about, I can't think of anything else to say. Then I hear my
son's roommates in the background, or the TV is on, and I feel
like he's probably got better things to do than talk to me. If I
send an e-mail message, I figure he'll read it when he has the
time. With a phone call, I feel like I have to have something
important to say, but I can send an e-mail if some little thing
pops into my mind. Yesterday, I was eating a tuna sandwich at
my desk, and I sent him a message saying, 'I'm sitting here at
work, eating your favorite kind of sandwich, and I'm thinking
about you. You're a great kid, and I love you.' I'm not the kind
of guy who could ever call and say that to him. In an e-mail, I
can."

Parents and students may reveal more through e-mail than
they ever had before. The emotion that comes out in e-mails,
however, can create unrealistic expectations the next time they
see one another in person or talk on the phone. When students
come home for a weekend or a school break, families often find
that they need a period of adjustment. Patterns of communication don't change overnight. Just because you can write to each
other about deep feelings does not mean that you can jump into
face-to-face conversations on the same topics.

Multiple technologies create more opportunities for different
kinds of communication—a brief text message just to let your
student know you're thinking of him; a short e-mail with the
latest news item from home; a lengthy phone call when you
know you both have some free time; instant messaging while
you're watching the same TV program. Ask almost any student,
though, and they'll tell you not to forget the old standby—the
U.S. Post Office. Students may not *write* letters, and they will
choose to make a phone call or dash off a text message when
they want to communicate with you, but they still check their
mailboxes, hoping something will be inside. Receiving a card, a

letter, or best of all, a package, is an increasingly rare gift in an electronic world.

Cell Phones: The Family Plan

The landline phone is hardly a factor in college residence halls anymore, and very few parents call their college student's landline phone. Some schools no longer provide a phone or voice-mail service in residence halls; even if they do, students may never record a voice-mail greeting or check for calls. Cell phones are the standard communication device on the college campus, and a quick conversation starter among students is a comparison of phone features.

Not that long ago, parents did not need to have a conversation with their college-bound child about phone services. Now you do. Your child's high school phone plan may no longer make sense. Wading through the multiple options for cell-phone plans can be confusing. Choosing the wrong carrier can be costly—if you pick a plan with poor service in your child's college community, you may be stuck with a two-year contract and penalties for changing.

Questions to consider as you assess a phone plan:

- Does your current carrier have cell-phone service and good coverage in the area where your student will be living? Either check your phone while you're visiting campus or do an online search for coverage to find out how many "bars" are available in that community.
- Does your student need a phone number from the college's area code? Local businesses, college staff, and friends may be less likely to return your student's phone calls if it means a long-distance charge for them.
- How many minutes a month will he need? What's reasonable, and what would you consider excessive?

- What features are really necessary on the calling plan? On the phone itself?
- Does your own calling plan need to be revised to accommodate having a child at college?

It's easy to get carried away with phone features and calling-plan options, but the budget may help determine limits. Maybe the free phone offered with the calling plan will be sufficient. Web capability on the phone is fun, but if you're providing a laptop—and wireless Internet service is available on campus—is it necessary for your student to pay extra for Internet phone service? If your student was given a new iPod for graduation and will be using it to listen to podcast lectures, does he need to use his phone to download music? Cameras are fun for students, and parents have noted that they will send their student a photo of the family cat every now and then, but is photo storage worth an extra fee each month?

There are reasons for college students to have text capability, beyond the friend factor. Many colleges and universities have set up text alert systems, allowing students to receive quick messages in the event of a campus emergency. Increasingly, parents and students are texting rather than making a phone call to give quick updates or check in. Ted's mother notes, "He will read a text, but he won't necessarily read an e-mail or listen to a whole voice-mail message." If text messaging has limits or incurs per-message costs, however, talk with your student about limits and who will pay for the messages.

Cell-phone safety: Many parents regard cell phones as a form of insurance. In an emergency, they want their child to be able to place a call, no matter where she is. But cell phones can also create their own emergencies. A lost or stolen phone requires quick action to cancel service. Extra costs from using minutes over the plan limits or unexpected roaming charges can break a student's budget.

Students who drive or walk while using a cell phone place themselves in danger—and I've even seen students text while Rollerblading or riding a bike. They are not paying full attention to their surroundings, and they become easy targets for theft—what's more, they are advertising that they have something a thief wants: a cell phone. Campus police advise, "Put the phone and the iPod away so you can use your ears and your mind to stay alert."

Parents recommend asking for the phone numbers of your student's roommate or good friends. If your child loses his cell phone or neglects to charge the battery, you may be unable to reach him in an emergency. It's reassuring to have someone else's number as a backup.

International calls: I asked a group of students on an international program in Argentina, "How do you communicate with your parents?" In unison, all twenty-three students replied, "Skype!" Skype is one of several international services providing Voice-over Internet Protocol (VoIP) services, allowing you to make international calls inexpensively or free. A critical question to consider when your student is preparing to study abroad is how you and your student can communicate in the country he or she will be living.

VoIP is easy and convenient, but it requires an Internet connection, which may not always be available. Before your student studies or travels abroad, contact your phone provider to ask about rates for calls placed to or from the country where your child will be. By paying an international access rate on your phone, you can usually get much less expensive rates for international calls. It may be most reasonable for your student to rent or purchase a new phone in the country where she will be studying. Currently, many phones sold in the United States do not work internationally; those that do may incur costly roaming charges. Foreign international calling rates may be less expensive than global phone service offered by a U.S. provider. Campus study abroad offices can provide suggestions on calling options for the destination your student has selected.

QUICK TIPS FOR STUDENTS

- The college or university you attend regards you as an adult. That means the school considers you the responsible party for your educational records. Unless you make other arrangements, the bills will come to you. If you expect your parents to pay the bills, make sure they receive them! And if they're paying the bills, they will probably want to see your grades.

- Talk to your parents about the kinds of information you will share with them (maybe general information on your financial standing, health issues, overall academic progress, and an overview of the social scene) and what you would prefer to keep private (maybe quiz grades, personal expenses, and details about your dating life).

- When things go wrong, you may be tempted to call home immediately and turn the problem over to your parents. Spend a little time first figuring out what the problem really is, what steps you need to take now, and—if you need help—exactly what kind of help you are asking for. Parents are impressed when their student has done the initial troubleshooting and formed a plan.

- If you do not call your parents once a week, at least send a quick e-mail or text message. They need to hear from you and know you are all right.

CHAPTER 5

Meanwhile, Back at the Ranch

College Is a Family Affair

Thea's parents expected life to be quieter after she left for college, and they knew they would miss her—she was the family storyteller and drama queen. Every night at dinner, she had at least one tale to tell, and she could stretch out a description of her day and all its woes through the entire meal.

What they didn't expect was that their younger daughter, Marissa, would become so difficult after Thea left. At fifteen, Marissa was, they thought, past that challenging adolescent stage. Instead she seemed to have a breakdown at every meal, storming out of the room before they finished eating.

Family structures and patterns develop based on all members of the household. When one person leaves, it's not just the physical presence, or the humor, or the affection that is missed. It's also the role that person plays in the family.

Thea was the lightning rod in her family. As issues arose, she could draw attention away from the problem and toward her. With Thea at college, that tension had nowhere to go. The family was going through a significant adjustment, and her sister's behavior was just one of the results.

OUT OF SIGHT, NOT OUT OF MIND

Within the lifetime of today's college students, instant communication—e-mail, cell phones, and texting—has complicated family transitions. It's no longer clear when a student actually leaves home. A daughter is no longer living at home, but she calls every day. It's hard to fully accept that a son is gone when an e-mail pops up every morning, reminding Dad that the boy needs money, advice, or a new cartridge for his printer. Parents sometimes feel like they know more about their child's daily life in college than they ever did when the student was living in the house, and they struggle to figure out how to let go when their child is still hanging on.

Allison never expected her daughter to tell her quite so much about her life at school—not just stories about her roommate and classes, but details about the boys she was meeting, the social activities in the dorm, what she was eating for every meal, even when her period started and ended. She finally told her daughter, "Honey, it's probably best that I don't know *everything* about your life. Really . . . too much information!" When the calls continued multiple times a day, Allison went so far as to set limits on when her daughter could call. "No more phone calls when I'm at work. How about if we plan on talking every other day for a while? You can text if it's an emergency, but otherwise, let's try a little less communication."

It's not just about defining communication expectations; every family develops entirely new patterns when a child leaves home. With only one or two people gathering for dinner, it might seem unnecessary to set the dining-room table and have a formal meal. If you're running late, it may be easiest to allow the only child still at home to eat in front of the TV.

Some of the changes that college brings will feel like a gift. You get your car back, or at least you don't lie awake every Friday night waiting to hear your son come in the front door. The brother or sister still living at home is receiving extra attention; morning schedules are less hectic; if your last child just left home, you and your partner can talk about sex anytime, even at the dinner table.

On the other hand, without your child as the center of your relationship, you may find yourself feeling lost and alone. For many seemingly stable families, a student's college years coincide with marriage problems. You may discover that all you have talked about together for the past five years is your kids. The dissonance in the household caused by a child's departure results in one parent rejoicing, "We can change everything!" while the other protests, "We've had change enough! Let's leave things alone."

It is common to "mourn" for a while when a child leaves home, and it's not entirely coincidental that parents' midlife crises correspond to their children's college years. Moreover, the harder one partner pushes for change, the harder the other pushes back for stability. Because transition is a process, not an event, patience will bring transformations to both partners over time more successfully than demands for immediate change.

You may even feel a touch of envy for what your child is experiencing. As you begin to see your responsibilities to your child more in terms of financial obligations, you might begin evaluating your beliefs and values, and perhaps you will decide it's time to do something for yourself. Countless parents look at the school their student is attending and say, "I wish I could go to college. Someone would fix my meals, I could take any classes I want, I would have no responsibility, and I could have intellectual conversations every day. Why do we waste all this on kids?"

You're stuck with your responsibilities, but you can still expand your mind. This is the best time in your life to do those things you've put off for years—take a class at a local college, devote time to a hobby, concentrate on your career, or pamper your partner. As your new life develops, you can look for ways to adapt and create new routines. Depending on your outlook, all the changes in your life might seem somewhat depressing, or they may feel a bit daring and exciting. As one father from Florida noted, "People talk about the 'empty nest' like it's a bad thing. I don't feel like I'm living in an empty nest, I feel like a 'Freebird.' "

Then again, you might be oblivious to any particular differences at all until the first time your student comes home for the weekend, expecting everything to be the same, and points out the new routines. "We always have pancakes for Saturday breakfast. What's with the cereal boxes on the table?"

When students come home and find life even a little different, they feel unsettled. This is partly because they did not have a voice in the changes, and partly because they don't know how these adjustments happened—"I talked to you every day. You could have *told* me you changed the cable service." They also don't know how these changes will affect them. They rarely object to new living-room furniture, as long as you save the comfortable old couch for their first apartment. There are limits to what feels like progress and what feels like an attack on their territory. They still don't want you to change their bedroom into your exercise room. Personal space is sacred, at least until your child gets his own apartment.

Students find comfort in returning to the familiar, and they rely on the stability of "family." They knew *they* were changing, but they had assumed the family would stay the same. They'll let you know they are surprised—maybe even disappointed—at any differences they see. Nevertheless, they adjust. They go back to school and tell their friends, with pride and amusement, that their mother signed up for ski lessons, their father took a first-ever trip to New York City, or Grandpa enrolled in computer classes at the community college.

THE SINGLE-PARENT FAMILY

If the college transition creates challenges for two-parent families, the dynamics for one-parent households is greater yet. Marianne knew her life would be different when her son went to college, but she wasn't worried about his adjustment. She had raised him to be independent, confident, and incredibly competent. The sense of loss they both felt when she left him at college overwhelmed her, though. His parting words haunted her all the way home and for days afterward.

"When we were saying good-bye," she recalled, "he asked if *I* was going to be all right. He said if it got to be too much, taking care of the house and the younger kids, I should call him. He said he'd come home every weekend if I wanted so that I could have a break.

"He shouldn't have to feel that kind of responsibility! And I shouldn't have been so tempted to take him up on the offer."

Children growing up in single-parent families assume household roles that create huge gaps when they leave home. The older child is the family babysitter or handles all the outdoor and home repair chores. An only child becomes more like a friend than a child every year. They are the extra hand when help is needed, and they are the other side of the conversation at the dinner table.

As a college student, the child feels ongoing responsibility for the household. They believe their parent will struggle to manage without them; and they worry about younger children still at home. They make choices at college based on concerns about the family. They turn down study abroad opportunities because that would mean being too far from Mom or Dad. They return home every summer, rather than staying on campus, in order to take back the lawn-mowing or house-cleaning duties. They even pick careers that will return them to the home community.

For a single parent seeing their last or their only child settling in at college, there are distinctly mixed feelings. There is great relief and pride in seeing that you've succeeded at this exhausting task of parenting; you've reached the goal you've been striving for all these years. At the same time, though, a major identity in your life that you have worked so hard at—being a good parent and either doing it alone or under constant negotiation with the child's other parent—is no longer paramount. Finances may need to be rearranged with ex-partners, bringing up difficult conversations and disagreements about the college choice, new expenses, and the student's academic goals. Single parents often focus more than ever on their jobs or cast about for some new identity.

Soon after her daughter started college, Amelia talked with a financial planner about quitting her secure computer programming job to go back to school herself. "He told me I could do it. It will just take two years, and I'm still young enough to have a whole new career and not have to worry so much about retirement. With me in school, my daughter will actually get a better financial package, and it turns out that as a 'returning student' myself, the local college here considers me a nontraditional student. That means I qualify for a small scholarship, a campus job, and extra advising."

LIVING WITH THE CHANGES: COMMUTER FAMILIES

When any student enters college, the sphere in which the family operates expands to include the college or university. For families of commuters, the student is bringing aspects of that new community into the house every day. College schedules are different, which means the commuter family's daily routine is directly impacted. Social expectations for young adults are different than for high school students, and those, too, filter into family relationships.

Parents may be willing—even want—to know more about the courses and the demands their college student is dealing with, but it's hard to get the information. Students are trying to become independent, and even the simplest questions can seem like intrusions. Parents can hardly avoid asking: "How was your day?" "What did you do on campus this afternoon?" "Will you be home for dinner?" "Do you need the car tonight?" The questions seem conversational or logistical to you, but your child interprets them as interference.

It is common for commuter students to feel defensive and to be silent about their education. Like everyone else their age, they've seen the films and TV shows, and they know their experience is not mirroring the media image. Commuter students believe their classmates who live on campus have more fun, more freedom, and more friends. To some extent, they're right. Although they *can* have the fun, explore the freedoms, and meet the friends, it simply takes more effort when part of their daily routine includes a mental and physical transition from home to school and back again. It also takes family support:

- Encourage your student to stay on campus between classes and to attend athletic events, concerts, and other student activities. The more time they spend on campus, the more likely they are to feel that it is "their" school.
- If commuter students work, suggest that they work on campus. Even if wages are less than they could earn off campus, the support of college-based supervisors and the time on campus is beneficial.
- Read the campus newspaper, look at online news about the school, and be alert to the campus calen-

dar. Ask your student to explain the things you don't understand. If you acknowledge the importance of what's happening at the college or university, your student will, too.

- Attend parent events on campus, such as orientation, Parents' Weekend, and especially graduation.

WHEN THE GOING GETS TOUGH, THE TOUGH CALL HOME

Parents are the sounding board for every complaint. You will hear about the tasteless food, unfair homework assignments, inconsiderate roommates, and impossible-to-understand instructors. During the first month or two of school each year, I frequently receive early morning phone calls from exhausted mothers who couldn't get back to sleep after a 1 a.m. conversation with their students.

"She called in the middle of the night, and she was so depressed. I don't know if I should bring her home or tell her to stick it out."

"He hates it there. He doesn't seem to have any friends. Maybe it was a mistake to send him so far away for college."

Parents feel terrible when their child is unhappy. In most cases, however, after your daughter purged all her frustration, she hung up the phone and went to bed feeling much better. Or after your son unloaded all his misery onto you, he saw his neighbor on the way to the vending machine and spent an hour talking about video games. In the meantime, you don't know that your child feels better. He doesn't call you back the next day to say the problem is solved. And if you call the next night but get no answer, you only worry more.

When students call home to complain, they don't necessarily expect their parents to solve the problem. If you offer advice, your child most likely will assure you that your solution is unreasonable or unworkable. You may suggest that a conversation with the professor will clarify the requirements for an upcoming project, and your student will tell you that it is impossible to talk to this professor—she only has office hours from 8 to 9 a.m., when your son has another class, which he absolutely cannot miss. This instructor would never agree to talk to him outside of her posted office hours. And what's more, not one person in the class has ever been able to talk to this instructor.

Your student is calling you because he is trying to figure out if it really is a problem, if he has to do something about it, and how to talk about it—and because he needs sympathy. Life is more challenging than ever before, and all this problem solving is hard work. He feels awful, he is recognizing that he probably caused or at least contributed to his problems, and now he must make an effort to fix things. Talking through the issue is part of the review process that allows him to understand how the situation came about. After he has vented his frustration, he will be ready for the next step: figuring out a solution.

By listening, you are providing your student with what he needs. You can't tell him what to do, and it will not help to ask why he let the problem develop, but you can ask some useful questions about moving toward a solution. "What do you think you can do now?" "Do you know of anyone who might be able to help?" "Is there any place you can think of to find some information on this problem?"

He still may argue with your suggestions, but you have done your part: you've listened, and you've given him some possibilities to think about.

IS IT A BIG PROBLEM OR A BAD DAY?

A few weeks after starting college, Leslie called home with a list of complaints. Her classes were much too difficult, she didn't have any close friends at school, the food was awful, and to top it all off, the basketball coach had rebuffed her request to try out for the varsity team.

To Leslie's mother, this sad and angry person did not sound like her daughter. In high school, Leslie had been a class officer, top athlete, and a school leader with a host of friends. Her mother began to worry that the family history of chronic depression might be affecting her buoyant, optimistic child.

Most problems are fleeting, and parent intervention not only is unnecessary, it is also unwanted. In Leslie's case, she was hurt by the basketball coach's rejection of her bid to join the team. She was embarrassed because she had not realized that all the members of the varsity team were recruited as high school players, and there were no walk-ons at her school. The confrontation was a reminder that she had a lot to learn about how the university worked, and it colored her opinion of the entire school for a couple of days. A week later, though, her physical education instructor happened to mention that there were several intramural basketball squads looking for members. Leslie found the team she needed, and she was fine.

When students call home with problems, parents often struggle to understand the true situation. Colleges are set up differently from high schools, and learning how to get information or solve problems can be complicated for new students and for their parents. Mothers and fathers who went to college themselves assume they know how higher education works because they've been there, but systems have changed in the past twenty years. For parents who attended college in another country or who didn't attend college at all, the puzzle is even more confusing. And most students, when reporting a problem, either exaggerate the severity or cast themselves in the best possible light: A bad grade on a math test is the instructor's fault; he didn't warn students what would be on the test. A parking ticket is the fault of overzealous police. Roommate problems are always caused by the other person.

AM I HELPING OR HELICOPTERING?

In recent years, newspaper stories and media reports have portrayed parents of college students as intrusive, demanding, and prepared to protect their child at the expense of all other students. In my experience, parents become involved when they are afraid for their student's educational well-being, his safety, or his life. They call because they don't have the information they need to answer critical questions. Only a small number of parents are genuinely overinvolved or inappropriate in their relationship with their student and the college. Those who are intrusive, however, make the best stories. No wonder reporters love the image of helicopter parents.

When students call, e-mail, or come home with a problem, the primary role for parents is to encourage the student to take responsibility for resolving the issue. When students take care of their own problems or seek out campus resources, they meet people who can be helpful later, they develop important problem-solving skills, and they gain confidence in themselves. You do, however, have a role in problem solving. Parents can guide their student without taking on the task of fixing their student's problems. You can help by directing your student to the right person by determining the category that best fits the concern.

But who is that right person? For new students, and for their parents, the range of offices and options can be confusing. "How are students supposed to know who to talk to?" a parent complains. "For every issue, it's a different person."

Moreover, as colleges increasingly rely on computers for everyday transactions—registration, financial aid, and official college communications are all managed online—the more concerned parents become. "Who's taking care of my kid? Where are the *people?*" Although many questions can be answered by e-mail or by directing students to the right Web site, personal contact is still the heart of student services.

Academic issue: Students can talk to their instructor if a concern is related to a specific class; otherwise students should talk to their academic adviser.

Residence hall issue: Students can first talk to the residence adviser who lives on their floor. If he or she can't help, the student should talk to the hall director; for disturbances or illegal activities in the residence hall, students can report the incident to campus security or police.

Commuter issue: Some schools provide an office for commuter students. If that's not the case at your student's college or university, the counseling office is the best resource.

Personal issue: Students can talk to a counselor or academic adviser.

Physical or mental health issue: Students should make an appointment with a medical provider at the school's health center or at a local clinic.

If your student is truly stymied about how to proceed with a problem, tell her to start by asking the closest "authority figure" she can find. It might be her residence hall assistant, her academic counselor, or an instructor. If the first person she asks does not have an answer, tell her to ask someone else. In almost every case, by the time she has talked to three people, she will have a good lead. Someone will direct her to the right office or the best expert.

Avoiding the Helicopter Label

Before parents get involved with a student's issues, consider the following:

- Can your student learn something by handling the situation on his or her own?
- Who has the full story? If your student has details about a situation, it is easiest for all involved if he or she makes the call. Otherwise, considerable time will be spent relaying information back and forth.
- Will your involvement complicate matters or make things worse?
- Would you (and your student) be comfortable with your student knowing you called about the situation?

You should be involved when:

- Your student is too ill to handle the situation.
- Your student has mental health issues that prevent him or her from making well-informed decisions.
- Your student's financial mistakes are likely to affect the family finances.
- You cannot locate your student.

SOMETIMES THE TRUTH HURTS

Parents want their students to tell them what's happening in their lives, but it's not always easy to hear what they're telling you. Some of the clues that parents pick up from their students raise red flags. Your son mentions that he went to a house party Thursday night, and you begin to worry that he is drinking. Your student says, "Everyone else in my French class seems to understand the teacher, but I don't know what she's saying." You fear that she is underprepared for college.

How do you know if your child is in real trouble? How can you support her if she is unhappy? Should you confront your child,

or stand back and wait awhile? These decisions are always difficult, but they are especially challenging if this is your first child
to attend college or if you did not attend college.

Residence hall staff and student services personnel often get
calls from parents that begin, "I don't want my son to know I'm
calling, but can you find out . . ." In most cases, university staff
can't promise to keep your concerns secret. If a residence assistant unexpectedly knocks on the door to check on your child's
well-being, your child will guess that someone has alerted the
staff person, and you will be the first suspect. Usually, we tell
parents that we can make a call or check on the student, but we
would prefer to be able to say, "Your parents asked us to look in
on you. Is everything okay? Is there anything I might be able to
help with? How about if you just give your mom a call?"

If you are looking for advice about your child's behavior, you
probably have your own circle of experts to consult. Many colleges and universities have a parent office, and you can call to
talk through your concerns. Your friends or coworkers who have
students in college can give you an opinion based on their child's
experience. A niece or nephew a few years older than your child
may be able to offer some useful perspective. A neighbor's child
or a recent college graduate who works with you is likely to
understand what your student is going through. Talk with the
people who know your child and who have some recent insights
on campus life.

At some point, it will be you, not your child, who must report
some bad news. Over the four or more years that a student is in
school, it is almost inevitable that something will happen in the
family. A grandparent may die, someone in the family could be
diagnosed with a serious illness, or the family pet may need to be
put to sleep.

During Kari's junior year, her parents decided to divorce. Traveling together from Kansas to Kari's school in Seattle in January

to deliver the news was out of the question. They had to tell her over the phone. With both parents on the line, they said they had some difficult information to give her, and they were sorry they had to tell her by phone rather than in person. They told her they had decided to divorce; they had given careful thought to their decision and had tried counseling. They promised to mark all her life celebrations as a family—graduation, marriage, the birthdays of the children she would someday have. Most important, they asked how she was feeling about the information and accepted her tears and anger.

Delivering bad news over the phone, by letter, or by e-mail is at the same time both easier and more challenging than in person. Parents worry if their child doesn't react. "I told my son that his grandfather had a heart attack and is in serious condition. He might not live. And my son just said, 'Well, tell him hello for me.' Then he said he had to study for a test, and he hung up."

Students facing new and difficult situations don't react in predictable ways. If you encourage your child to "talk about it," he'll say something completely inappropriate, or he won't say anything at all. Parents complain, "I don't think he really heard what I was saying." Meanwhile, though, their student has scouted out a friend and repeated every word his parents said with astounding recall. Your child hears you; he just doesn't know how to react.

When you must deliver bad news long distance, plan on checking back with your child. Give her time to digest the information. Let her know that she can call you if she has any questions, or if she would like to talk. And if she reacts poorly, don't judge her. There is no right response to bad news.

QUICK TIPS FOR STUDENTS

- It turns out college is not all about you. You know that everything in *your* life has changed, but things are

changing back home, too. Keep in touch so that when
you go home, you won't be blindsided by your father's
shaved head, the exercise equipment in the family
room, and your mother's new diet, which means no
more potato chips in the house.

- Keep in touch with brothers and sisters still at home.
  They may not say they miss you, but at least sometimes, they do. If you treat them well, they'll watch
  out for your interests and your room while you're
  away.
- If you vent to your family about the woes of your
  world, be sure to tell them when you're feeling better,
  too.
- Give your family the good news. Parents need to hear
  about your successes, and they are among the few
  who will truly, deeply share your pride.

Section 3
College Culture

CHAPTER 6

Credit Loads and GPAs

Adjusting to College Academics

W hen parents ask, "How is school?" they expect to hear a brief report on a recent paper, the outcome of midterm tests, or a list of the classes their student will be taking next semester. They probably would not be happy if the response were, "I only had one class yesterday, so I spent two hours at the coffee shop, watched a couple of videos with friends, and played a cool new computer game with the guy down the hall until two a.m."

The overarching purpose of college, from the parent perspective, is to learn and to prepare for a career path, and the measure of the college experience is the grade-point average. The reality of college, though, is that it is a lifestyle. Academics and out-of-classroom activities blend together for the full college experience. As counselors are fond of pointing out, the most important lesson a first-year college student can learn is how to balance studying, social, and personal time.

Today's students come to campus with little experience in managing their own schedule. The elements of high school life were closely segmented and structured. Classes filled six or seven hours a day. Students had only five or ten minutes between classes plus a lunch break to visit with friends. Beyond those breaks, seeing, calling, or texting friends waited until after school or on weekends. Evenings were set aside for homework or organized activities, and personal time was carved out of any open spots between family obligations and chores. Most free time was spent in front of the TV or computer, but it never seemed like quite enough.

Suddenly the student arrives at college, and supervised school time drops from thirty or more hours a week to eighteen or fewer. An eight a.m. class finishing at nine o'clock might lead into a four-hour break in the middle of the day. A few times a week, the school day may end at two o'clock. An evening class might mean even longer gaps of midday free time, then a return to class after dinner. Every day has a different rhythm, and there is no particular portion of the day designated for homework.

Those students who have led the most organized lives often revel in the opportunity to schedule their own time. Left alone to plan their days, they finally have a chance to listen to music for hours on end, play game after game on the computer, lie in bed and read a novel, or head out to the mall in the middle of the morning to shop. And no one is there to remind them of any obligations.

This freedom comes at the same time students are faced with different teaching and learning methods, higher classroom expectations, the need to make new friends, and greater academic competition than they ever experienced before. It's no wonder the first semester is sometimes disastrous.

ACADEMIC EXPECTATIONS

All his life, Aaron planned to go to the university his parents had attended. The family lived just an hour away from the school, and every year they bought alumni season tickets for football and basketball. As an infant, Aaron was the photogenic baby in the crowd wearing a miniature school sweater, and during high school, most of his wardrobe was made up of T-shirts and caps featuring the college mascot. As a first-semester freshman, Aaron taught all his friends the words to the alma mater, and at football games, he helped the cheerleaders fire up the student section. When he met his parents for dinner after the games, they were delighted to see him feeling so comfortable in the student union and finding his way around all the traditional campus hangouts.

A student earning A-minus to B-plus grades in high school, Aaron expected to do well at college, and his parents were confident that he would be successful. They were blindsided when he told them in January that he had been placed on academic probation.

Aaron's parents, who had met as economics majors in the university's competitive business school, thought that Aaron knew his first priority in college should be his coursework. Aaron, however, had seen only the social side of college throughout his life, and it never occurred to him that college might present more difficult academic challenges than he had experienced in high school. When his parents talked about their college experience, they had always focused on their memories of athletic events, dances and parties, and the spring-break trip they took together as seniors. Only after learning that Aaron's first semester had been three months of playing did they think to talk to him about the hard work and dedication they had both put into college.

"You know, Aaron," his father said, "we *did* go to parties and games when we were in college, but we treated social activities as our reward for studying all week. And there were a lot of times when we couldn't take time out for fun.

"I still remember how I felt one weekend in my sophomore year when I had to choose between going to the last football game of the season or studying for a macroeconomics test. It was killing me because that was the game that would decide whether or not we were going to the Rose Bowl. But I knew I had to do well on the test because I was right between a B and a C for the course. I had to get an A on the test in order to get that B and qualify for the business program the next year.

"I stayed home from the game and spent the morning reviewing everything we had covered all semester. I forced myself to keep studying most of the afternoon and then gave myself the 'reward' of listening to the last quarter on the radio.

"I would have had a good time at the game, but I knew that the coursework came first. There are a lot of choices you need to make about the way you spend your time, and when your four years of college are done, you will need a solid education to get you where you want to go."

GOOD INTENTIONS, BAD ADVICE

It's easy to see why students emphasize their social life over academics. They have been hearing from relatives and all their parents' friends that "College is the best time of your life." When students arrive on campus knowing no one, and every day presents new and challenging problems, it is far from reassuring to think that life will never be better than this. These are times when it's almost refreshing to have a pessimistic codger in the family who will say, "I wouldn't go back to your age for anything. All those doubts, questioning every decision you make, the daily problems? Trust me, kid. Life gets better."

Certainly, parents want their children to have fun in college, but they also want their students to use this time well. They try to provide guidance as their child selects courses, but, with every good intention, parents sometimes provide some of the worst possible advice.

In many cases, parents are thinking back to their own college years, trying to help their children avoid the mistakes they made.

They urge their students to select a prestigious major as incoming freshmen, test out of introductory classes, and get all their liberal education requirements out of the way in the first two years. As a result, students end up feeling bored, overextended, and lost in challenging lab classes or vast lecture courses that are beyond their comfort level. They commit to a major that turns out to be a poor fit, but they believe they must stick with the plan.

In his book, *Making the Most of College: Students Speak Their Minds*, Harvard professor Richard Light notes that first-year students are happiest when they have a mix of large and small classes. During the first semester, students should take at least one class for fun, Light says. Colleges and universities are supporting this idea by offering freshman seminars, small classes taught by some of the best professors, to connect students at the beginning of their college career with some of the schools' top instructors. Unlike large, broad-based introductory lecture classes, seminars focus on a topic and explore it thoroughly, inviting discussion with diverse perspectives. Freshman seminars might offer tips for student success, or they may be cutting-edge science courses on laser technology, an analysis of a presidential campaign during an election year, a study of constitutional law, or a course on happiness. A Minnesota professor, Jim Kakalios, teaches a seminar on the science of superheroes. In his class, Everything I Know I Learned from Comic Books, students test the plausibility of the superheroes and story lines from comic books by using basic principles of physics, chemistry, and biology.

Light also recommends foreign language courses as a way for students to connect with one another in smaller groups that meet on more frequent schedules. Language classes usually meet four or five days a week, and students are required to speak in class, working in pairs or small groups to practice their conversation skills. Instructors ask students to talk about subjects they know well—family, hometowns, how they celebrate holidays, and what they did over the weekend. Students increase their language skills as they learn new words and try to form logical sentences, and they begin to see that mistakes are not fatal. They get to know more about their classmates through their conversational assignments, and they often register together for the next semester's class, extending their relationship beyond a single semester. An extra bonus is that language classes provide background and incentive for study abroad opportunities later on.

GRADES—THE MEASURE OF SUCCESS?

Parents should not pick their children's classes, but they still play a significant role in academic planning and achievement. Students who understand their parents' expectations about studying and grades use those guidelines to set their own goals. Because college is an entirely new academic environment, however, high school standards may no longer apply. The perfectionist who has never been satisfied with anything less than an A might find himself in a classroom where the professor believes that a C is a perfectly acceptable grade, and a C-plus means the student did well. Parents should allow some leeway for slightly lower grades, especially during the first year of college, and promote the concept of "doing your best" rather than "being the best."

Grades alone do not provide a full picture of a student's academic progress, especially during the first year. College work is more intense than most students needed for high school. It takes time to develop the note-taking and test-taking skills, study habits, and time management that college courses require.

The freshman year is a tremendous period of adjustment, and the majority of students will not earn grades that match their high school records. Grades typically drop during the first semester, and a student who has always earned A's and B's is likely to earn B's and C's. The second semester should show some improvement, and grades level off as the student begins to feel more comfortable with college-level expectations.

If you notice that poor marks are coming from one area of studies—maybe your son is doing well in English and history, but the math grades are low—it could be that his high school courses in that one area were not sufficient for this college. Perhaps he registered for a higher-level course than he should have. Possibly his learning style didn't match the teaching style for the class. A pure lecture course, for example, can be very difficult for students who have always been taught through interactive methods. The free-ranging creative writing style that earned an A in a high school literature class may be judged as too unfocused for a college essay. Students who are accustomed to using Wikipedia as their sole research tool might find that their college instructor will accept citations only from "peer-reviewed periodicals," and they don't even know what that means.

Most colleges provide tutoring for students who are struggling with skill-level issues. Although there may be a cost involved, one semester of tutoring can give students a boost not only in the coursework, but also in learning how to study for college-level courses. In addition, disability accommodations are provided for students with documented learning disabilities. Counseling and advising offices or a school's learning commons will offer study-skills workshops, writing labs, note-taking techniques, and exam preparation. Students also can ask a librarian to check their research methods as they begin working on their first college paper.

Most new freshmen hear the message "Talk to your instructors!" Unfortunately, that may be difficult advice for a first-year student to follow. Freshmen are trying to appear confident, and one of their greatest desires is to avoid drawing undue attention to any weakness they perceive in themselves. The last thing they want is for their professor to think they don't understand the assignments. If they go into their professor's office, what could they possibly say that would improve their situation? "If I ask questions, I'm just putting him on notice that I am confused." Nevertheless, all the evidence indicates that students who talk to their instructors are the most successful, the most committed to on-time graduation, and the most likely to complete their degree.

Some advisers tell first-year students to ask *any* question of an instructor, even if the student already knows the answer; conversations and relationships can begin from the most simple and awkward start. Others will tell students to ask a general question such as "How did you first get interested in this field?" Perhaps an easier (and less ingratiating) method is to complete a homework assignment before the due date, and ask to review it with the professor. Instructors are sympathetic to the freshman who is a little insecure about his homework and who wants to head off problems in advance.

Even the best students will come across a course during their college career that seems particularly challenging—it may require skills they just don't have, or it is simply not "their" class. Some students will never be able to pass calculus; the rudiments of organic chemistry might not ever make sense. Sometimes a student just doesn't connect with an instructor. The occasional bad grade is not an indication of serious academic trouble, but a continuing trend of progressively lower grades or an entire semester of below-par performance are sure signs of a problem.

Naturally, parents react strongly when they learn that their student is failing. When you are spending thousands of dollars for your student's college experience each semester, low grades are alarming, especially if they are coupled with the possibility of probation or expulsion. Parents can hardly avoid being upset if they find that they have paid for a year or more of classes that have no value to the student.

When students are suffering academically, most parents will either demand change or advise their student to "try harder." According to students, however, the last thing they need to hear from their parents is "Shape up! Crack down! Get to work!"

"If only it could be that easy!" they moan. "There are a lot of reasons for getting bad grades, and being told to 'crack down' doesn't help."

What's more, if the student is using the wrong study method, applying more of that method is not going to lead to success. On the other hand, when poor grades are caused by poor choices—partying too much, sleeping too little, spending too much time socializing—the solutions are self-evident. The student must adjust his lifestyle. The issue then becomes whether or not he wants to change. Most colleges and universities are intent on providing a good education; their primary goal is not to enforce mature behavior. Neither you nor your student can expect the college to monitor your child's lifestyle and ensure his success if he is not willing to make the effort himself.

There are predictable times throughout a student's academic career when difficulties are most likely to occur. Freshmen may start college with great confidence—after all, they spent all of high school preparing for college—but the first graded paper or quiz can be an eye-opener. "I'm not sure I should be at this school. Does everyone else know what's going on in that class? What's wrong with me?"

For all students, midterm exams create stress halfway through the semester or quarter. Rarely does a student, even the brightest and most organized, go into midterms feeling entirely prepared and comfortable. For freshmen who have never experienced the stress of college exams, the fears are far worse.

From midterms until the end of the semester, the tension slowly grows. Professors set deadlines for major papers or projects right before or right after Thanksgiving break. As a result, students start the week of Thanksgiving with misgiving, and their worries only increase as they try to find time to pack and make travel arrangements. A few days later, heading back to school after the long weekend, they worry that they made little or no progress on their projects—who can study with family and friends vying for attention? The December days leading toward final exams are stress-filled as students try to balance all their end-of-semester responsibilities. Students have accused colleges of blatant cruelty for scheduling finals at the worst possible time of year—just when they must buy and wrap holiday gifts, pack to go home, clean out the minifridge, and empty the wastebaskets for prebreak room inspections.

The process repeats itself during spring term. A relaxed and hopeful start to the semester turns into tense days leading to midterms. Spring break leads into the anxiety of project deadlines. Then, worst of all, final exams come just as warm weather and fresh spring breezes tempt students to abandon their books for last chances at fun with friends before summer separates them.

From year to year, the challenges change. There is sophomore slump, the letdown when students realize that things no longer feel new, different, and exciting. Then second-year students must settle on a major, squelching the dream that "I can do anything I want!" Those who were convinced of their career goals as entering freshmen now are wondering how they can switch to some new interest.

The semester when a student moves from a residence hall into an apartment is a significant adjustment period, and grades often drop. For juniors, classes are more demanding and time intense as students get into their majors. The joy of living with three dozen sorority sisters or sharing an apartment with seven best friends evolves into angry tension, and students realize there's a difference between quantity and quality of friendships. During the second half of the junior year and throughout the final year of college, stress hits as students see the demands of the "real world" creeping up on them. "I need to find an internship. Why did I major in classical civilization? I'm never going to get a job. What was I thinking?"

Times of transition are typically accompanied by academic difficulties, but a drop in grades also may be an indication of personal or social problems. Academic problems can be a symptom of health issues, drinking, or drug dependency. Poor grades may signal problems with roommates or a boyfriend or girlfriend. Students who have been sexually assaulted may be able to project an outward calm, but their grades suffer as a result of the inner anxieties. Poor grades often accompany financial problems. Anytime students are examining their career choice and questioning the direction they have selected, they are likely to suffer lower grades.

As a freshman, Clint's grades were good. His C in physics was balanced by an A in English, and the rest of his introductory courses were straight B's. As a sophomore, though, he had trouble with his math and science classes, and except for elective classes in film production and scriptwriting, his grades were all C or lower.

Although he had always planned to be a chemical engineer, Clint was realizing that he didn't like the sciences as much as he'd expected. English and film studies classes seemed more engaging, and he found himself putting much more effort into homework for those classes, letting chemistry and physics slide. As much as he enjoyed his "just for fun" classes, he was becoming increasingly frustrated with himself as he began to question a future in chemical engineering. How could he give up a prosperous career in engineering for a major in film studies? He was afraid that he was letting passion get in the way of practicality.

Like many students, Clint couldn't bear to tell his parents he wanted to change his major. "They'll be so disappointed in me," he said. "I've always told them I wanted to be an engineer, and they're paying so much for me to go to school here. I picked this university because of its engineering program. I probably could have gone someplace else for film studies and saved them a lot of money."

Students are surprisingly reluctant to talk to parents about changing majors. We continually come across students who stay with a major they no longer care about simply because they can't bring themselves to admit their new interest to parents. Or they change majors, but refuse to tell their family. I have even heard parents, looking for their student's name in the graduation program under the economics heading, confused when they find his name under astronomy. "Well, this is a mistake. They've got him under the wrong major. His degree is in economics . . . Isn't it?"

HOW MUCH CAN A PARENT DO?

There are times when parents *should* step in, but those instances are limited. If the student has a serious illness, is severely depressed, or for some other reason is incapable of making appropriate decisions, parents can contact campus staff to discuss their concerns.

The classroom relationship, however, is between the instructor and the student, and in almost every case, a professor will prefer to talk to the student. Parents don't help their student by calling a professor to complain that a grade was unfair or to explain, "I know how hard he worked on that paper. I read it, and it really doesn't deserve a C."

College is a time when students should be learning to speak for themselves; they should by now be capable of talking with authority figures without help from a parent. If they're not yet ready, this is the time to learn those skills. When you're tempted to step in, take a moment to consider first what your student will learn by doing this job himself. Then ask yourself what would happen if your spouse—or your own parent—made a phone call to complain to your boss about your performance review.

Although parents' influence is limited at the college level, students are not entirely on their own; higher-education institutions have strong support services in place for students. Every college has appeals processes to guide students through disagreements, whether the complaint is with a faculty member, a housing official, or a registration process. At small colleges, staff members know the students and can step in to offer guidance when they see problems developing. At big universities, students may need to ask for help rather than wait for someone to offer it, but help is available.

SAME DANCE, DIFFERENT COLLEGE

Nearly two-thirds of college students today will attend more than one college before receiving an undergraduate degree. For some, transfer is in the cards from the first day on campus—a two-year or community college is designed to start students along the higher-education pathway, then send them on to the next step. For others, however, transfer becomes an option when things don't work out as planned. The student who never expected to miss home so much, the fashion major at a design school who realizes she'd really rather get a business degree, or the health sciences major who doesn't have the grades to get into the selective nursing program she had hoped for—all these students may choose to change schools. And sometimes transfer is not an option, but an edict. The student who is expelled for violating campus policies or who fails to meet academic standards may find himself seeking another route to a college education.

For Michele's parents, who thought they had finished working through the college selection process, it was disconcerting to start over. "She got into her first choice school, and she really liked it there, but at the end of her freshman year she decided she wanted to major in nutrition. Her school didn't have a nutrition program, so we're looking at colleges all over again."

While many of the college search steps are the same the second time around, there are some new factors to take into account. Will the coursework from the first college transfer to the new one? If the credits count, do the classes meet the prerequisites for upper-level courses? If there was a specific problem your student encountered with the first school, how can you be sure the same issue won't arise again?

Transferring should not be regarded as a simple solution to a nagging problem. A bad roommate, lower-than-anticipated grades, missing high school friends, or not feeling connected the first few months are all challenges that can be overcome without changing schools. The general advice is that dropping out midsemester means a significant loss of time and money, and students are encouraged to stay for at least the first full year. Moreover, when specific problems arise, it might be wiser to address frustrations with an adviser or department rather than jump to another school.

Certainly, there are good reasons to change colleges or universities. When students—like Michele—opt for a major that is not offered at their starting school, they have no choice but to find another. If family or financial circumstances or health concerns dictate that the student must be closer to home, or if the student genuinely does not fit in with other students, transferring can be the best option.

But a transfer is not always a seamless process. Even with an associate's degree from a two-year or community college, students can lose credits and fall behind. A student who is preparing to transfer should start with a conversation with the advising office from his first school to find out which colleges and universities are common transfer schools, with a record of successful application of credits. The next step is to meet with a transfer admissions specialist from the college or university the student is considering. The more details students can work out in advance, the more successful the process will be.

One issue typically emerges as students approach the first day at their new school: "Will I make friends?" Michele had a hard enough time leaving her friends from her previous college, and she was convinced that "Everyone at my new school already has all the friends they want." Her parents reminded her that she had made friends before by introducing herself to her classmates and by joining a student group. In her first nutrition class, the instructor asked for volunteers for a community service project, and Michele raised her hand. Within three weeks, Michele had a new group of friends, was doing volunteer work nearby, and had signed on to help with her professor's research project.

GRADUATING IN FOUR YEARS—OR MORE

Most parents expect their student to earn an undergraduate degree in four years. Some career-based programs require a fifth year, but the general expectation remains at four. In fact, however, just over a third of students at public universities graduate in four years. Nationally, just over half of full-time freshmen will receive their degree within five years.[5]

Colleges and universities set up a structure to allow students to follow a formula—typically 15 credits per semester over eight semesters of study—to earn the necessary number of credits to

---

5. "College in 4 years? Try 5 or 6" 2004. http://money.cnn.com/2004/06/21/pf/college/graduation_rates/ (accessed March 21, 2008).

graduate on time. More often than not, though, something will interfere with that plan. An illness, failure to complete a critical paper, or the realization that a class is too difficult might convince a student to withdraw from a class midsemester. A family crisis may call the student back home. One too many withdrawals can lead to delayed graduation. Adding a second or third major will require more credits and more time.

During the college review process, the admissions office had looked carefully at Amber's application. Her high school grades were only slightly above average, but she had performed in the school choir, and she was a student council member and class treasurer. The assessment was that she would have to apply herself, but she should be able to succeed at this college.

The first semester, she registered for fifteen credits, but she dropped her biology class after deciding she was "not awake enough at eight a.m. to be using breakable lab equipment." The second semester, she again enrolled for fifteen credits, but her French III instructor suggested that she withdraw after she failed the first two quizzes. "Since you didn't take French last semester, you've forgotten a lot of your high school language skills. Start with French II next fall or get some tutoring this summer, and you'll be able to catch up."

Although she only completed eleven credits each of her first two semesters, she still couldn't keep up with her courses, and she ended the year with C's and C-minuses.

After talking to her counselor, Amber recognized that she needed to develop better time management and study skills. The study habits that had always worked before were not getting her through her college courses. Cramming for exams might have helped her pass the true-or-false history tests in high school, but the essay exams in freshman political science required a deeper understanding of the material.

Amber's parents began to see that the four-year college plan they had anticipated might not be what was best for Amber. In order to succeed, she would first need to put some time into mastering some of the basic learning skills. A lighter academic load for her sophomore year, supplemented by tutoring and academic counseling, brought her up to speed and improved her grades. She managed to graduate in five years with an acceptable grade-point average of 2.8.

By the time they are eighteen, students should be responsible for managing their own course loads and doing their best to stay on track. When they fall behind by a class or two, though, it becomes increasingly easy for students to conclude that graduating in four years is out of the question. They put themselves on a five- or six-year plan without considering the extra expense to their parents or to themselves. Parents who are footing the bills, then, are dismayed when they learn that their student expects an extra year or more of support.

Ask your child to develop a plan that includes an ultimate time line for graduation and the steps she will take to reach that goal. Students may not be able to identify what their major will be during the first year or two of college, but they should have a sense of when they will make that decision and how long they will take to graduate.

As a parent, you can ask for a periodic accounting of progress toward a degree. The number of credits earned is one guide, but more critical is the number of credits still needed to fulfill graduation requirements. Is the student taking the *right* courses? Just because a student is earning fifteen credits per semester does not mean she will graduate in four years with 120 credits. Some of those classes may not count toward graduation. Every college has seniors with excess credits who still cannot graduate. Students must earn a certain number of credits within their major, and they must take a range of courses outside their major. Signing up for an abundance of elective courses is a lot like consuming empty calories. They fill up the schedule without contributing to healthy progress.

It matters to you if your student is not making progress toward a degree. Students who are attending classes only part-time may not qualify for medical coverage under your health insurance plan. Extra years of school add more than extra tuition; there are also additional student fees, room and board, and, ultimately, delayed entry into the workforce. Scholarships and grants are likely to have a four-year limit, and some loan programs apply only for four years. Tuition reciprocity agreements, allowing reduced tuition charges for students from a neighboring state, have limits as well.

As soon as your student falls behind by a class or two, you should discuss how those credits can be made up, or whether a four-year plan is still logical. Most colleges and universities will accept at least a few transfer credits, so students can take summer classes at a community college or a university near home during the summer. Make sure, though, that your child checks with his adviser before taking transfer courses to be certain the credits will count and fulfill requirements. If your student is not clearly making progress toward graduation, you might decide the sensible option is for him to take a year off, work, and develop a more focused academic plan.

Few of us really want our students to move back home, and the goal is to encourage our children toward responsible independence. While there are cases where some additional time with close family supervision will be helpful, you will want to make sure that's the best solution before you enforce it.

Many students struggle with the conflicting demands of working enough hours to afford college and studying enough hours to do well in their classes. When financial issues are overwhelming, it is hard for a student to balance study time with part-time or full-time work. The decision ends up being a matter of personal and family choice, but in the long run, students might be financially better off taking more low-interest student loans and finishing college in four or five years, rather than extending college an extra two or more years in order to work more hours. The additional interest costs on college loans can be offset by the wages a graduate earns, and earlier entry into the professional world pays off in moving the college graduate beyond an entry-level position at a younger age.

WHEN YOUR STUDENT GOES BEYOND YOU

The day will come when you ask your child about school and find yourself bewildered by the response. "I am so psyched! I've been in the library all day, reading about fenestration of fritillaries. This stuff is amazing!"

When you express confusion, your child will say, with a hint of condescension, "Fritillaries, Dad. You know, butterflies. How can I explain this so you can understand? I guess in the simplest terms, I'm doing a paper about the angle of that feathery stuff on a butterfly's wings. Never mind. It won't make any sense to you."

It's like junior high math all over again, except this time your child doesn't expect you to help. She knows she has exceeded your knowledge base, at least on one topic. This is the reward you get for supporting her all these years and for sending her to college—now she can talk down to you.

If you can show enthusiasm about your child's academic interest, you are contributing to her education. It means a lot to a student when a parent asks for more information and shares the excitement of new knowledge. There is no doubt that it can be challenging to show interest in the sentence structure of the Russian language or the characteristics of geriatric bone density. Your admiration for your student's knowledge, though, can spur her to learn more; in addition, as your child explains the subject to you, she becomes better able to talk about it to others.

Ask questions about what she is telling you, find out why she likes the subject so much, and encourage her to recommend simple books or articles about the subject for you to read. Look up the topic on the Internet. Eventually, she will achieve balance again between all the varied interests in her life, and soon enough, she will come to you for advice on what size lightbulb she needs for her desk lamp. Your status as her personal adviser on all things practical will return, and she'll appreciate *your* wisdom once again.

Progress Toward Degree

Each of the four years of college has its own goals and milestones.

Freshman Year

During the first year at most colleges, students are exploring— or at least sampling—courses in a liberal education. They should be taking a variety of courses representing different subjects and different learning methods. This range of courses lays the foundation for a well-rounded life and for career success, even when the classes are not within the student's major. Classes that teach communications skills—writing, speaking, and presentation— will provide a good foundation for other college courses and for future jobs. Social science classes teach critical-thinking skills, and foreign languages give students experience in listening, questioning, and clarifying information. Ideally, by the end of the year, students will have discovered a few topics that excite them, and they will have at least a quarter of their basic education requirements completed. They should talk at least once with a career adviser to begin the process of identifying working styles, job-related values, and potential career paths.

Sophomore Year

The second year continues the exploration phase as students work on more of their general education coursework. The subjects that initially intrigued them are explored more thoroughly as students sign up for increasingly challenging courses. As they consider areas of study, they should be talking to counselors and career advisers about what the major means in terms of the classes they will need to take and the jobs they can pursue in that field. If career planning courses are offered, students should take one— some career courses are specific to a major field of study; others can help identify career interests. A career adviser can help students find job shadowing opportunities or identify professionals to talk to in fields of interest. Increasingly, sophomores are seeking out short-term internships (often unpaid) to help them assess whether they truly have the skills and interests for a specific career. If they have not previously declared a major, by the end of the sophomore year, students should be prepared to select one.

Junior Year

General education classes should be completed by the end of the year. Students will be taking several classes in their major this year and challenging themselves with upper-division courses. They can talk to a career adviser or the school's alumni group to find a mentor and to explore internship opportunities related to their major. By the end of the junior year, students should have a clear understanding of the range of career options that relate to their major and some sense of the specific career they would like to pursue.

Senior Year

Students will be completing the coursework in their major and finishing any remaining requirements and electives. If a senior project, paper, or thesis is required, it should be planned out by the end of the first semester and completed before the end of the second semester. During the first semester, students should be working with a career adviser to explore employment opportunities or graduate school programs. Exams for graduate school should be taken during fall semester with grad school applications due during the fall or early winter. Students should work with their adviser to make sure all academic requirements are fulfilled and graduation forms are filled out.

All Four Years

A job search is likely to take three to six months, but some of the work can be done long before the senior year. As students take on student jobs, volunteer projects, or internships at any time during college, they can be thinking about the skills they're learning. Although a cafeteria job may seem purely menial, students can develop customer service skills; the employee who is promoted to "line captain" will gain supervisory experience. The student who volunteers to tutor math students at a local elementary school may be learning about children of other cultures or how to motivate underachieving third graders. As students identify skills they're learning, they should include them on their burgeoning résumé. Examples of successful class projects or unique community service projects can be added to a student's portfolio. Most college career centers offer workshops on how to write a letter of application and provide coaching on interview techniques. Students can take advantage of these opportunities throughout their college years and be a step ahead when the right job opportunity comes up.

QUICK TIPS FOR STUDENTS

- You will encounter some disappointments about college. Don't expect college to be a four-year vacation package. Your room will not be like a first-class hotel, the food will not be gourmet, and you can't expect daily entertainment to be provided for you.

- Remember: Your first priority in college is academics. You do get to have fun, but make sure that classes and homework are covered. It's sobering to realize that every course you're taking costs serious money—hundreds or even thousands of dollars. When you skip a lecture or bomb a test, you're actually wasting both time and money.

- During the first two years, take a mix of classes: large lecture, small group, and lab classes; sciences and humanities; language, writing intensive, and speech classes. If your college offers freshman seminars, take one!

- Talk to professors. Some conversation starters: Finish a homework assignment before the due date and ask your professor to check it to see if you're on track. Ask how he or she first became interested in the field. Ask a question even if you already know the answer. Tell the professor, "Everyone says we're supposed to talk to our professors. I'm not sure what to talk about, but I'm here."

- When you're confused, when you have a problem, when you don't know what you're supposed to do next, ask for advice.

- Career planning begins in the first year of college. If you have a major picked out, talk at least once to a career adviser about your long-term plans. If you do not have a major selected, or if you decide you might want to change majors, ask for help in identifying how your interests, work style, and personality might clarify some potential jobs.

CHAPTER 7

How Can One Book Be Worth $92?

Finances Are a Family Affair

Finances are the intersection between family and student, home and college. Love and lifetime history will keep you connected, even when you don't see one another every day, but money ensures that you must talk.

No matter how mature and independent your child is by any other measure, financially he or she still is considered your legal dependent. Almost two-thirds of all students receive some form of financial aid,[6] and the way federal financial aid requirements are set up, parents' income is factored into the package.[7] If your child is receiving any financial assistance, it simply is not possible to draw a clear line between your finances and his as long as he is in school.

Students seem to deal best with money issues when they have

---

6. College Board, "Trends in College Pricing, 2006," p. 2.

7. Students are considered dependent unless they are twenty-four years of age, married, a graduate student, a veteran, an orphan, a ward of the court, or have legal dependents.

a good sense of their family's financial situation. There may be details about your income and expenses that you will choose not to share with your child, but the more information you provide about college expenses and payments, the better he or she will understand the true value of an education and appreciate the contribution you are making.

Unfortunately, it's hard to discuss money dispassionately. When Alan learned that he would be passing through his son's college town on a job-related trip, he arranged his schedule so that he and his business partner could have dinner with his son. The two men picked Joe up from his apartment and went to one of the best restaurants in town. The dinner was excellent, and the conversation was even better. Joe obviously was excited about his classes and his friends. He talked easily with both men about his own dreams for a business career. Alan had never felt quite as proud of his son as he did that evening. Joe seemed so mature, pleasant, and confident—everything his father could have wanted.

After they finished their dinner and were looking at the dessert menu, Alan remembered the financial aid forms in his briefcase, and he mentioned that he would need a copy of Joe's tax statement and tuition receipts from the past year. "We've got to get those forms filled out for your student loans for next year. The good news is, you're going to be a senior, and this is the last time we have to do this!"

As he spoke, Alan could see his son revert back to the sullen and defiant kid he had been at sixteen. Joe slumped back in his chair, checked his watch, and complained that he had to get back to his apartment. Embarrassed that his business partner was witnessing this unpleasant transformation in his son, Alan tried to change the subject and suggested that they have some dessert before leaving. That only seemed to add to Joe's irritation. "I've got a huge paper and an exam to study for. You have no idea how much work my classes are this semester!"

The mere mention of money is a reminder to students that they are still dependent on their parents. Everything that they are accomplishing at college, every vision they have for their future, depends on the continuing goodwill and support of their family. While they appreciate your help and assistance, discussions of finances can bring back in a moment all the unwanted feelings of being a helpless child.

Sometimes parents don't even recognize when they're playing the "money card." When your daughter calls to ask for extra funds so that she can go with her friends to Acapulco for spring break, you might have to tell her that you set aside only enough money for her airline ticket home. "I really can't afford the extra money for you to go to Mexico for a week. I'm sorry."

You may see this as a simple statement of fact, but it's a message of control to your daughter; she's not allowed to make her own decisions because you are in charge of all the money.

MONEY MATTERS

Almost all students will face a financial crisis at some point during their college years. Even those from the wealthiest families run out of cash, and most students dread asking their parents for another handout. Whether they overspent because of an emergency, poor planning, or an unanticipated once-in-a-lifetime opportunity, they balk at having to explain to their parents what happened and why they need more money. Between classes, in the study lounge, and anywhere students gather, we hear them comparing their debts and expenses. Too often, though, a student's focus is on short-term finances rather than the big picture. They panic about getting through the next week or month, although what they *should* be thinking about is how the expenses they are piling up now will affect them throughout the rest of the year and well beyond graduation.

For first-year students, the problems are sadly predictable. Students begin college with a sum in their checking account— in many cases, more ready cash than they've ever had in their lives. Each day presents another chance to meet new people and do new things, but almost every opportunity involves money. Ordering a late-night pizza is hardly worth thinking about, it's just fifteen dollars, split among a few roommates. A new friend recommends a must-have iTunes download, and another ten dollars is gone. Everyone on the hall is going to Six Flags over the weekend, the study group for Spanish class meets at a Mexican restaurant for lunch every Tuesday, and the bookstore is having a great sale on sweatshirts. By November, the checking account is scraping bottom, and the credit-card bill is out of control.

Most parents believe it is their job, not the college's, to teach their children about financial management. Even though they may expect the college to provide guidance and education about other nonclassroom topics such as sex, health, and career preparation, parents say that they will take the lead role on finances. Because every family's situation is different, it really *is* the family's responsibility to make certain that their student has a realistic understanding of their circumstances and a basic level of knowledge about money, savings, and indebtedness.

Jackie's father asked her to jot down daily spending records for the first month of her freshman year as a way of helping him understand what her college expenses would be. "So far, we can only guess how much things will cost, and we might need to make some adjustments." For that first month only, he said, he would like her to let him know each week how much she had spent for personal and entertainment expenses. "But please be careful. I'm hoping we've got enough in the savings account to cover the whole year."

By maintaining a daily record the first month of school, Jackie saw how quickly the dollars could disappear. After the first week, she had spent fully half of her September budget. When she called her father at the end of that week, she explained that she and her roommate had decided to buy matching lamps, quilts, and a rug for the dorm room. She knew when she bought the accessories that her budget would be out of balance, but she had a plan to get back on track. She could begin to make up the deficit by buying juice and snacks from the grocery store to stock her minifridge rather than using the vending machines downstairs every day. Instead of going out for dinner on Sunday evening, she and her roommate agreed to fix soup and sandwiches in their room. At the end of the first month, she reported that she was still behind on her budget, but she assured her father that she would have her expenses in line within a couple of weeks. He didn't ask again for a report, but at the end of October, she told him that her finances were right where they had planned.

Each year in college presents its own financial challenges. Freshmen face hard lessons in managing checking accounts, debit cards, and credit cards. A year or two later, students move into an apartment and find themselves in a financial tailspin. As soon as they settle in, they realize they need to buy a broom and dustpan, trash bags, special cable connectors to hook up the TV and computer, and toilet paper. Rent has to be paid on the first of the month, and it won't matter to the landlord if they haven't had time to transfer funds to the checking account. The plan to save money by fixing meals at home falls apart when the scent of breakfast sausage wafts in from the fast-food restaurant down the block. Missing the bus to campus means hopping in the car, filling up the gas tank, and then paying an extra ten dollars to park for the day.

Budgets fall apart during the junior year when an unpaid internship, which will be perfect on a postgraduation résumé, causes the student to quit her part-time job in the library. A three-week, three-credit study abroad program might cost the same as a January-term class on campus, but the rent still has to be paid on that empty apartment back home while the student is using a credit card to pay for housing in London.

Senior year doesn't offer any breaks. Students who are preparing for graduate school have application and testing fees and maybe a cross-country flight to interview for a fellowship. Job seekers are taking time off work and spending transportation money for job shadowing and interviews. And they must show up in a decent suit and "grown-up shoes," not sneakers or flip-flops. This is also the time when students begin to recognize what their postcollege debts will be and how they will affect their future lifestyle.

Parents and their children often have very different expectations about finances, and they most often confront the differences during school vacations. When Julie came home for semester break, her parents assumed she would replenish her bank account by picking up some shifts at the restaurant where she had worked in high school. Julie, however, thought her parents would continue giving her a weekly allowance during the break period. She was looking forward to three whole weeks of catching up on sleep, visiting with her high school friends, and making up an incomplete from her history class. She hadn't even considered calling her former boss to see if she could work a few shifts.

"Julie, it's not just that your father and I expect you to work," her mother pointed out. "Your financial aid package is based on your contributing some money toward your expenses. You can work during your breaks, or you can get a job on campus, but you need to be earning some income."

THE PAYOFF FOR PART-TIME JOBS

Parents know that college is demanding, and they don't want their student to take on more than he or she can handle. *How many hours of work are too much?* parents ask themselves. Balancing academics with employment is a challenge, and parents need to emphasize that school is the priority. Students who work more than twenty hours a week tend to see themselves as employees first and students second. When exams or major projects come up, students have a hard time reducing their work hours if it means a smaller paycheck at the end of the week.

Having a job helps students organize their time, but for most freshmen, even fifteen hours of work each week can be excessive. During the first semester, a student's emphasis should be on adjustment and self-management. If students need to work that first semester, they are better off taking a position that allows flexibility and does not require learning new job skills. And they need to consider how work will fit into the academic schedule: If an exam is pending, what are the chances they can find someone to trade shifts with? How will the boss feel if they can't come in for a day or two because they have a big paper to write?

Parents and students alike tend to weigh the differences between on- and off-campus jobs by their pay rates, but jobs on campus have benefits beyond wages. Depending on the college, campus jobs might provide practical experience related to a student's major. Lab or research positions within a department provide an in-depth view of the field. Some schools allow upperclassmen to work as teaching assistants, grading papers or leading discussion groups under the supervision of a faculty member. A job that ties in with an academic major benefits students not only by teaching them more about the field, but also by connecting closely with a professor. Those faculty recommendations make all the difference when the time comes to fill out internship, graduate school, or professional job applications.

Campus jobs allow students to work side by side with staff and faculty who can provide valuable guidance and advice on the school and its systems. When Rolf received an overdue library notice on a book he had returned, his work-study supervisor gave him explicit instructions. "Call Bob Givens in the library circulation department, and tell him that you put the book in the return slot on Thursday morning before the library opened. Maybe they sent out those notices before they emptied the drop box. Bob will look it up for you."

Commuter students, especially, benefit from on-campus jobs. The support systems and social opportunities that come with working on campus provide a sense of belonging and a circle of friends. Having a desk or a workspace provides a campus "home" for commuters. "I have a place to drop my books between classes, and I can use the microwave and refrigerator, even on days when I'm not working. Best of all, the people in my office bring in cookies all the time," Tina notes.

NEW RULES FOR THE MONEY GAME

Even if parents began planning and investing when their children were toddlers, they may come up short when it's time to pay the first year's expenses. The cost and financing of college is not the same as when today's parents were eighteen years old.

Thirty years ago, when Tom went to college, he paid for all his expenses himself by working full-time during the summers and saving every penny. He could earn enough in three months to cover a year of tuition and room and board. During the school year, he worked two hours a day at the bookstore to pay for books and earn some spending money. He always figured his own three sons could put themselves through college as well.

As his oldest son approached college age, however, Tom realized his plan wouldn't work. There was no way his son could work enough hours to earn the $17,000 it would cost for his freshman year at a medium-size, in-state college. For all three boys, even with the promise of some financial assistance from the college, the family was looking at a price tag that approached the mortgage on Tom's house.

BASIC TOOLS FOR MONEY MANAGEMENT

You may believe that you have communicated clearly about finances, but your student might not agree. Every time I ask a roomful of parents, "How many of you have talked to your student about finances and credit cards?" about 90 percent of them raise their hands. However, when I ask students, "Have your parents talked to you about finances and credit cards?" only about one-third say yes.

As Keesha explained, "They told me to watch my expenses and not to sign up for any credit cards, but that's not the same as *talking* about finances. They never told me what problems I might have, or why I shouldn't get a credit card. I mean, *they* have credit cards. Everyone does. I wish they had told me how easy it is to let spending get out of control and how expensive it can be when you overdraw your checking account or when you don't pay more than the minimum on your credit card."

Students have a head start on college success if they know how to manage and balance a checking account, understand family expectations about who pays for which expenses, and know how their parents feel about credit and debit cards well before they leave home. Your child already has a sense of how you manage your money—in fact, one of the best predictors of a student's financial problems is her parents' level of debt. Money management, however, is not a topic that can be learned solely by observation or by lectures. Students need practice and skill building. Discussions between parents and their child before school starts provide a foundation, but they won't necessarily forestall all problems.

As a sophomore, Philip carefully rationalized the need for

multiple credit cards: "I had a Discover card for my computer. It was an expensive computer, so I pretty much maxed out that account. I had a Visa for groceries. I made sure I bought all my clothes on my Gap card so I could keep my clothing budget separate from everything else. Then I had a MasterCard for emergencies—my car was having a lot of problems, so that balance was quite a bit higher than I wanted it to be. And I had a Target card, because, you know, you have to buy soap and cleaning supplies and just . . . stuff."

After a year of juggling five separate accounts, Philip caught on that this was not what his parents meant when they told him to manage his finances.

Students need some guidance when they open their first checking account, and they need to understand the penalties for overdrafts. They need a plan for keeping track of debit-card payments, and they need to know what protection there is on their credit or debit card if it's lost. Before they apply for their first credit card, they should know about the fine print on applications and the implications of annual fees and temporarily reduced interest rates. They may be tempted by offers of credit-card points or rewards, not recognizing that an annual fee can undermine any value the points deliver. Many parents start their child with a checking account and debit card in high school or during the first semester of college, then they monitor the accounts. By cosigning for a credit card with an agreed-upon minimum limit—$500 or $1,000—parents have some assurance that their student won't go seriously into debt, and they use the monthly bills to discuss purchasing decisions and the consequences of late payments. A debit card can provide some of the convenience of credit cards without the risk of running up interest charges, as long as the card prevents withdrawing more than is in the account.

Student loans make up the biggest debt that college students face after graduation, but credit cards create the greatest financial problems. Every fall, tables appear on campus or in nearby shopping malls, offering free baseball caps, trendy sunglasses, or coupons for fast food in exchange for filling out a credit-card application. Applicants don't need to prove they have an income; they can simply indicate that they are enrolled in college. Credit-card companies are betting that parents will make sure the bills are paid. Students rarely take time to read the terms of agreement, and most vow they will cut up the card when it arrives. "No way I need another credit card, but check out the free T-shirt! The color's great, and it means I can go another day without doing laundry."

College students believe they can outsmart the credit-card companies, forgetting that financial companies hire the best and brightest finance and marketing majors. In some cases, by signing up for a card, students have agreed to charges they did not foresee; shortly after the card arrives, they receive a bill listing a thirty-five-dollar enrollment charge or a seventy-five-dollar annual fee. They think they can put off a payment by transferring this month's bill to another credit card, not realizing that there is a fee for balance transfers.

Too often, a student maxes out her first, parent-approved credit card, but a new one arrives just in time to pay her cell-phone bill. If the statement from that original card is being sent home, this new one means the student can buy what she wants without her parents seeing the statement and asking any questions.

As the debts mount, the student figures she's doing well to keep up with the minimum monthly payments, but the low introductory interest rate of 8 percent turns out to be only temporary. With $2,000 in credit-card debt at 17.9 percent interest, the interest payment alone will cost $29 a month. Paying $35 a month, it will take more than ten years to erase the debt.[8] That's

---

8. Calculated at www.bankrate.com.

with no new charges. To clear the account in one year, payments will be more than $180 per month. If a single payment is missed, in addition to late-payment penalties, the interest rate is likely to jump even higher.

Credit cards are a part of our national economy, and they are a convenience when used with care. A survey conducted in 2004 by Nellie Mae, a student loan provider, indicated that more than three-fourths of all students have credit cards, and on average, students have four. The typical outstanding debt among college students was just over $2,000.[9]

Most parents say they want their child to have a credit card for emergencies—but their idea of an emergency might be much different from their student's. They recognize that Internet commerce requires payment with a credit card. Parents have pointed out that when their child studies abroad, a credit card is the best way to manage expenses. They brag that by charging their child's tuition and room and board payments, they can accumulate enough frequent-flier miles to book their student's trip home for the holidays. Meanwhile, 20 percent of college students are making no more than the minimum payment on some of their credit cards each month, and another 11 percent are paying less than the minimum amount, putting them in a spiral of debt.[10]

---

9. Nellie Mae, "Undergraduate Students and Credit Cards in 2004: An Analysis of Usage Rates and Trends." United State General Accounting Office, 2005.

10. Nellie Mae, "Undergraduate Students and Credit Cards in 2004: An Analysis of Usage Rates and Trends." United State General Accounting Office, 2005.

Signs of Credit Trouble

The following are common signs of credit-card mismanagement:[11]

- Paying only the minimum amount due on your credit cards
- Charging more each month than you make in payments
- Using credit and cash advances for items that used to be purchased with cash, like gas and groceries
- Your total credit balance rarely goes down
- Being at or near your credit limit and still applying for new cards
- Needing a consolidation loan to pay new debt
- Not knowing the total amount you owe
- Feeling stress whenever you use your charge cards
- Draining your savings to pay debts
- Making bill payments late

EMPHASIZE FINANCIAL INTELLIGENCE

You urge your student to be responsible about finances and to be cautious about his expenditures. Too often, however, students make choices they believe will save money, but that have unanticipated consequences.

Midway through his sophomore year, James tallied up his checking account and realized he was not going to have enough money to make it through the rest of the year. He looked at ways to reduce his expenses and saw that the biggest charge on his debit card every week was for groceries. If he could reduce that amount, he could save a few hundred dollars by the end of the year.

---

11. "Ten Warning Signs of Credit Trouble," www.projectmoney.org/teaching/worksheets.html.

Many students look at food and personal care as the most obvious ways to cut expenses. Certainly, there are ways to reduce the grocery bill or haircut expenses, but meals are not the best choice when it comes to saving money. A steady diet of ramen noodles, while cheap, is not nutritious, and it will end up costing too much in energy and health. Late-night snacks can be cut out of the routine, but groceries are still a good investment. Encourage your student to stick with a good diet and find other ways to trim expenses.

Few teenagers have a realistic concept of living expenses until they pay the bills themselves. They receive an allowance or income from a job, and they know what they can buy with those dollars. They probably don't, however, understand life's basic costs— utility costs, housing expenses, car payments, various insurance fees. They may know those expenses exist, but they don't have a grasp of how it all adds up. They understand best the bills that they themselves have directly affected in the past: The phone bill, in their experience, is all about the calling minutes and ring-tone downloads they charged; they may not have been responsible for the monthly phone plan. They know the exact price of a burger and fries, but the grocery bill is a foreign concept.

Students need to know the overall cost of their college education, but such a big sum, stretching over four years, might seem incomprehensible at first. If you break down the total into monthly and annual expenses, your student can see more clearly the financial impact of the decisions she is making. You will do your whole family a favor by working through a budget with your child each year. Defining your student's role in the finances will empower him by acknowledging the importance of working, saving, and making plans to repay college loans. A solid understanding of the finances before school starts will give your student the necessary background to make good decisions when there are choices to be made.

You can help your child develop financial skills, but it takes time, patience, and perseverance to work through the steps.

- *Encourage—and teach—your child to keep financial records.* You will need the records for tax purposes, and there will be times when your student will need proof of a payment or a receipt for some item. A week after classes begin, if he decides his advanced calculus class is too difficult and he wants to switch to an introductory math class, he will be able to return his calculus textbook only if he can find the receipt. Make sure your child knows that he must keep bank statements, tuition statements, receipts and warranties for all major purchases, credit-card agreements, scholarship records, and loan agreements.

- *Organize a file for financial records.* During the first year of school, a single folder for finances in the college file box might be sufficient. Freshmen can file all major financial receipts and records together. As a general rule of thumb, if a folder becomes too bulky to manage easily, it should be arranged into two or more folders. When a student moves to an apartment, or if he believes that more organization is needed, a separate file box just for financial records will be helpful. Let your student decide if it makes more sense to organize records by month— putting all receipts and statements for a month into one envelope or folder—or by category, such as academic expenses, room and board, communications, transportation, etc. Encourage him to get into the habit of filing receipts and statements faithfully.

- *Be sure your student knows what records are required for tax purposes and for student loan or scholarship applications.* Even if you are paying most of the bills, your student will probably receive the statements and receipts. Discuss how you will communicate about those documents. If you need them for tax purposes, how and when will you get them?

BUDGETING: A BALANCING ACT

In the long run, students learn best through experience—their own and the experiences of their brothers, sisters, and friends. "My older sister got into serious trouble with credit cards, and she had to quit school and get a job so she could pay them off. I am *never* going to let that happen!"

Financial management is critical to becoming a responsible adult. Your role is not to make your child's financial decisions but to give him or her the foundation for making smart choices. Students do have expenses for entertainment, health and wellness, snacks, the occasional new pair of socks, and emergencies. Your student can adjust funds between categories as the semester goes by—"I can save money by having my roommate cut my hair, and then I can afford more art supplies." Making a realistic budget, though, is the first step to making it through the year without racking up unexpected debt.

HOW TO PLAN A COLLEGE BUDGET

1. Figure out your education resources. You can start out with the school's Cost of Attendance—the sum of tuition, fees, and living expenses estimated by the college. It's as good a guess as any, but bear in mind that just because that number is what the college tells you a year of college will cost, no one spends exactly the predicted amount.
2. Next, fill in the numbers that show which resources these anticipated funds will come from—the grants, scholarships,

loans, and cash contributions that the school, the government, you, and your student will each be contributing to your
student's education.

3. Then figure out your college budget expenses. Go through the
   various expense categories, filling in the cost-certain numbers and estimating the rest. Remember that the totals should
   reflect costs for the entire year, including any summer-session
   courses.

4. Finally, figure out how much from each educational resource
   (parents; students; grants, loans, and scholarships) will be
   used for each expense category. Remind your student that the
   expense totals cannot exceed the resource totals. Your student
   will begin to see that his decisions can allow flexibility in some
   of the numbers, and you will have an opportunity to assess
   your student's strengths and weaknesses in budget planning.

A sample budget sheet can be found in Appendix A.

QUICK TIPS FOR STUDENTS

- As with other issues that fall under the heading "Life Is
  Unfair," none of your friends are in the same financial
  situation as you. Don't try to match your spending to
  theirs. Don't feel guilty for what you have or ashamed
  by what you don't have, and don't ever be afraid to say,
  "I can't afford that." College students are not supposed
  to have enough money to buy everything they want.
- Your finances are tied to your parents'. If you are
  receiving college loans, your parents' income is figured into the formula until you're twenty-four. That
  means some of the choices you make will affect their
  financial situation. Talk to your parents about any
  decisions that will have an impact on them.

- Keep your receipts, file them in an accordion file or a file cabinet, and make sure your parents get copies of the statements they need for their income tax.
- Beware of the small print on credit- and debit-card applications—you may be agreeing to an annual fee, an enrollment fee, or overdraft penalties. Make sure you understand the terms and conditions for any credit card you get. Remember: If you don't pay your entire bill this month, you will pay interest next month. And the company will collect its interest payment before it subtracts anything from the amount you owe.
- Watch for deadlines and payment dates on everything. Filling out a scholarship application a day after the deadline is a waste of time—you're not going to get the scholarship. Pay credit-card bills as soon as you receive them. Payments are based on when your transaction is received at the processing center, not when you mail the check and not necessarily the same day you pay online. Late payments mean penalty charges. On credit cards, a late payment might also mean a big increase in the interest rate you are charged.
- One more caution regarding credit cards: That free T-shirt, energy drink, or fast-food coupon that you received by filling out a credit-card application is not really free! The credit-card company is betting that you will pay for that giveaway one way or another.

CHAPTER 8

Sex, Drugs, and Drinking Games

The Social Scene

When newly admitted students talk about the one best thing college will offer, they say "making new friends," "freedom," or "independence." The issues that parents worry most about, though, the ones they can hardly bear to acknowledge, come down to the choices their child will make in three areas: sex, drugs, and alcohol. The wrong decisions on any of these three topics have the potential of changing—even ruining—a young person's life.

As a parent, you probably have been reciting the lectures for years: Don't drink and drive; say no to drugs; and sex can lead to pregnancy and disease. Now, when you mention these topics, your children's eyes glaze over, and you get the look that says, *I know what you're going to say, and I don't need to hear it again.*

They're right—they do know what you're going to say. When it comes to sex, drugs, and alcohol, your children know how you feel. Nevertheless, you *will* worry, and it doesn't hurt to repeat your values from time to time, with positive and supportive messages rather than warnings and threats. In the long run, the best parents can do is offer the background guidance and promote the moral strength their child needs in order to make a *choice* each time the opportunity comes up. We often forget that sex, drugs, and alcohol are not onetime decisions. When your first-year student leaves for college, he may pledge not to drink, but if his roommate offers to share a six-pack of beer some Saturday evening, he may decide to have a couple. That does not mean he has become a drinker. The next time he's offered a drink, he can still say no. Unless your student loses the ability to make that choice, your advice will continue to have an impact.

SUBSTANCE ABUSE—A COLLEGE EPIDEMIC OR JUST KIDS BEING KIDS?

Everyone says it: "College students drink." They know that drugs are available on campus. You've read the news articles, and you've watched *Animal House*. Turn on any college football game on TV on a Saturday afternoon in the fall, and you can pick out the liquored-up fans in the crowd. So what are the odds that your child will get through college without drinking or using drugs? Or maybe you've already accepted the fact that your child will drink at college. After all, by the time kids finish high school, 72 percent admit that they have tried alcohol, and nearly half of high school seniors have used drugs.[12]

"Just don't be stupid about it," parents say. To some extent, parents are simply relieved that it's out of their hands. "There's nothing I can do—it's his choice now. At least while he's living on campus, he won't be drinking and driving. He can walk to the parties."

But everyone also knows that college students are injured or die every year in accidents related to alcohol and drugs. Driv-

---

12. National Institute on Drug Abuse survey conducted by the University of Michigan, 2007, www.drugabuse.gov/Infofax/HSYouthtrends.html.

ing drunk or riding with a drunk driver may be the greatest risk among college students, but a student also might trip and fall down a flight of stairs when he's walking home from a party.

How can you tell if your child is at risk? There seem to be three factors that serve as strong predictors of a student's drinking or drug use:

- The student's alcohol or drug history during high school
- Parents' use of and attitude toward alcohol or drugs
- The culture of the college the student is attending and the friends he socializes with

Student's Alcohol or Drug History During High School

The student who drank excessively in high school is not likely to quit when he goes to college. That's not to say your child is doomed if he partied too much on prom night or smoked a joint that one time after graduation. He might have learned a good lesson when he woke up sick the next morning or had to face disappointed friends or family. A few slipups don't mean he has a major problem.

On the other hand, if your child equates alcohol with having a good time, he will continue to drink in college. If he experimented frequently with drugs in high school, there's a very good chance he will use drugs in college. And if your child got drunk or took drugs on a regular basis in high school, he may have a serious problem.

Unfortunately, some students already have substance abuse problems by the time they arrive at college. The college population represents every possible level of drinking and drug use, from total abstinence to addiction. Some 10 percent of the college population will become bona fide alcoholics, for all the same reasons that adults become alcoholics. About 20 percent will not drink at all.[13] Students, like their parents, vary widely in their beliefs and behaviors regarding drinking and drugs.

Parents' Use of and Attitude Toward Alcohol or Drugs

Some parents are shocked and disbelieving when they get a call saying that their child has been cited for drinking—not because he was drunk, but because anyone cares. "Of course he was drinking. He's a college student." Or they explain, "We let him drink at home. He knows his limits."

When parents drink heavily, especially when they began drinking before or during their own college years, they may expect their college student to drink. Similarly, parents who smoked marijuana in college or continue to as adults don't see anything unusual about pot smoking among college students.

The Culture of the College and Friends

Even the child of abstainers might start drinking two weeks after college begins, simply because "Everyone drinks." Similarly, the student who never considered drug use before college might begin, because he comes to believe that "It's not really a big deal" when he sees other students using drugs.

Peer pressure is at work on campus. Some colleges have a "party school" reputation, and drinking is part of the overall atmosphere. The drink of choice or the places where students go to drink might be part of the unique social atmosphere of the school. Although there is probably some drug use at any college, the type of drugs and the extent of use varies from one school to another. Within a single university, students might be heavier drinkers in one particular residence hall, or there may be more

---

13. Schemo, Diana Jean, "Study Calculates the Effects of College Drinking in U.S.," *New York Times*, http://query.nytimes.com/gst/fullpage.html?res=9E05E1DA113DF933A25757C0A9649C8B63&fta=y.

drug use among students on one floor of a dorm. Studies have shown that student athletes generally drink more than nonathletes, and fraternity and sorority members tend to drink more than non-Greeks.[14] That does not mean, however, that all fraternity members drink, just as there is no reason to assume that everyone in the poetry club is a stoner, or everyone at the party school gets drunk every weekend. What it does mean is that if "everyone is doing it," risky behavior feels much less dangerous.

IT'S ILLEGAL, SO MAKE THEM STOP!

Drinking has been called the number one problem among college students. It leads to poor grades, sexual assaults, fights, vandalism, wasted time, and wasted money. A few beers every weekend may not seem like a lot of money, but it adds up. By some estimates, students spend more on beer every year than they spend on textbooks—and textbooks are expensive.

If alcohol is such a predictable problem, parents wonder, why don't colleges do something about it? Midway through the first semester, Dwayne's father called the university president, demanding, "You have to stop the underage drinking! My son's roommate gets drunk with his friends every weekend, and my kid can't even study in his own room because of the noise. The law says you have to be twenty-one to drink, but the cops have this 'nudge-nudge, wink-wink' attitude, and you just let it continue. What has to happen before you do something about it?"

Colleges are not blindly standing by while their underage students drink. Truly, professors do not want hungover, unprepared students in their classrooms. Residence hall staff would really

_____

14. National Institute on Alcohol Abuse and Alcoholism, 2002, "A Call to Action: Changing the Culture of Drinking at U.S. Colleges," www.college drinkingprevention.gov.

rather not deal with students who are loud, drunk, or disorderly. Every campus has policies regarding underage drinking. Most colleges and universities do not, however, routinely search students' rooms, nor do they conduct random checks for alcohol or drugs. Privacy laws prevent staff members from invading students' personal space without cause; students and their parents would rightly object to searches of innocent students' rooms. Consequently, the quiet student who might have a case of beer in the refrigerator or who is smoking marijuana and blowing the smoke out the window may not be caught. It's the "noise and nuisance" behaviors that alert staff members to drinking and drugs, and those cases are confronted.

HOW WORRIED SHOULD I BE?

Parents of today's college students remember when the drinking age was lowered from twenty-one to eighteen or nineteen throughout most of the United States. Many parents remember celebrating their own eighteenth birthday by drinking legally. But in 1984, federal legislation was passed to phase the drinking limit back up to the age of twenty-one. The reasoning was that alcohol-related automobile accidents were rising, and there was evidence that eighteen-year-olds were passing alcohol along to their seventeen-, sixteen-, and fifteen-year-old high school friends.

While it is now illegal to drink at age eighteen, anyone with a credit card and an Internet connection can order a fake identification card and have it delivered by express mail. If they have a creative friend, a good computer printer, and a laminating machine, students don't even have to wait until tomorrow for their ID. Then again, who needs a fake ID when they know where the keg party is, and the kid down the hall with the beer bong is party central?

The most troublesome trend in college-age drinking is the

emphasis on heavy or binge drinking and drinking games. At both the high school and college levels, the goal is not just to drink, but to get drunk as quickly and cheaply as possible.

It's one thing to consume a few beers while watching a couple of football games over the course of a Saturday afternoon. It's quite another issue when teenagers set out to guzzle a beer in mere seconds, a six-pack in an hour or less. An Internet search for drinking games yields Web sites featuring dozens of games rated by their buzz factor or danger level. The winner is the last person standing; losers are those who pass out, vomit, or black out. Beer pong and keg stands provide a challenge and a fast buzz for the drinker, plus entertainment for observers. Jell-O shots are easy to slide down, providing a quick and painless high. At some schools, a twenty-first birthday means standing on the table to drink a pitcher of beer, setting up twenty-one shots to mark the occasion, or getting a free or cheap drink at twenty-one different bars. Blood alcohol quickly rises to the danger zone.

Students believe that since they're not drinking and driving, they are safe. They're out with friends, and someone will take care of them. They ask one person to "babysit" the group and make sure no one falls asleep on their back, thinking that will protect them from vomit asphyxiation. They choose not to consider the dangers of other types of accidents—fights, falls, hypothermia, and alcohol poisoning. They hear their friends joke about how drunk they got on the weekend, and they pass over the warnings about legal limits of intoxication. "You're not actually going to die from drinking beer," they tell one another. They know plenty of people who took a twelve-pack to a party and came home safe. "Maybe if you drank a couple bottles of whiskey, you'd be in trouble, but you'll get sick from beer and wine before anything really bad happens."

Students don't want to hear lectures about drinking, but they pay attention when they hear statistics that they can apply to themselves. Men listen when they're told that four drinks within an hour will put a 180-pound male over the legal limit for blood alcohol content. Women will take notice when they hear that six beers within an hour could turn fatal for someone who weighs 120 pounds.

Blood Alcohol Estimates

BAL indicates the number of milliliters of alcohol in one hundred milliliters of a person's blood. The following chart estimates the BAL for a 120-pound woman and a 180-pound man, based on the number of drinks consumed in one hour.[15]

No. of Drinks	120-pound woman	180-pound man
1	.04	.03
2	.08	.05
3	.13	.08
4	.17	.11
5	.21	.14
6	.26	.16
7	.30	.19
8	.33	.22

One drink equals roughly one shot, one twelve-ounce beer, or a one-and-a-half-ounce glass of wine. Binge drinking or heavy drinking is typically defined as four or more drinks in a single sitting for a woman or five or more drinks in a sitting for a man. This level has been targeted as dangerous because it is when negative outcomes of drinking tend to show up. Emotions, either

---

15. http://alcoholprev.colostate.edu/bachart.shtml.

positive or negative, are exaggerated. Judgment is impaired, and the risks increase for unplanned sex, accidents, arguments, and fights. Blackouts can occur at a BAL as low as 0.15 percent. At 0.20 BAL, nausea and vomiting is common. At 0.25, physical sensors may be sufficiently numb to result in asphyxiation from vomiting. Death from alcohol poisoning may occur around 0.30, and at 0.40, the brain fails to signal heartbeats and breathing.

Fortunately, it is rare for a student not to survive a night of heavy drinking. She may suffer temporary negative consequences—a hangover, a scraped knee from stumbling into a fence, a wallet left at the bar, or a friend who will no longer speak to her. But there also are the long-term consequences. Students who drink heavily have lower grade-point averages than nondrinkers. They are more likely to miss classes and fall behind in their schoolwork, get in trouble with police, or be sexually assaulted.[16]

Recent research has shown that the binge drinking that students claim as a harmless break at the end of a busy week can do serious damage to the brain. Alcohol use by young adults under the age of twenty-one has been shown to damage the memory and learning areas of the brain, and it inhibits the decision-making and reasoning areas—the very parts of the brain they're supposed to be developing during college.

DRUGS—THE LOW-CAL HIGH

Risky behaviors extend to drug use, and students can creatively justify their use by claiming the highs are less messy (no vom-

---

16. Rose, Patrick, and Edgardo Pimentel, *Benchmarks for Success: Gauging the Performance of College Prevention Efforts* (Southern Illinois University: Core Institute, 2006).

iting, no packaging to toss, "So it's green!") and less fattening ("All those empty calories in beer—no, thanks!"). Marijuana is the most readily available drug on college campuses, and—as with alcohol—students often arrive as freshmen with experience in buying and using marijuana. The Monitoring the Future study conducted by the University of Michigan reports that nearly a third of high school seniors reported use of marijuana during the previous year.[17] Hard drugs, such as cocaine, heroin, and crack cocaine, are much less prevalent on college campuses.

Parents remember their own or their friends' adolescent marijuana use and worry more about the possibility of their student getting caught than about the health issues. Marijuana potency, however, is not the same as it was a generation ago or even a decade ago. Average THC levels (tetrahydrocannabinol, the psychoactive substance) in marijuana have more than doubled since 1983, rising from about 4 percent to more than 9.5 percent, with some samples tested at more than 37 percent.[18] The experience of smokers in the 1970s and 1980s is not what today's pot smokers are getting. Of even more concern are indications of a link between teen marijuana use and increased depression, as well as other serious mental health conditions, anxiety, and suicide.[19]

---

17. http://monitoringthefuture.org/pubs/monographs/overview2007.pdf, p. 5 (accessed July 4, 2008).

18. National Institute on Drug Abuse, Quarterly Report, Potency Monitoring Project, Report 100, December 16, 2007, to March 15, 2008, www .whitehousedrugpolicy.gov/pdf/FullPotencyReports.pdf (accessed June 13, 2008).

19. Office of National Drug Control Policy, Executive Office of the President, "Teen Marijuana Use Worsens Depression: An Analysis of Recent Data Shows 'Self-Medicating' Could Actually Make Things Worse," May

Students generally do not want to take the risk of hard drugs like heroin, crack, or meth, but increasingly they are willing to gamble with club drugs and prescription drugs. They think they are playing it safe using the old standbys—beer or liquor—mixed with relatively common prescriptions, such as ibuprofen, Benadryl, Ritalin or Valium, OxyContin or Vicodin. "These are legal! What can it hurt to wash down a pill with a drink? You get stoned faster, and the high lasts longer." They can even get their health insurance to pay for the pills if they fake symptoms, or there may be a kid down the hall willing to sell some of his prescription for some quick cash. They don't want to know they are creating potentially lethal cocktails, so they don't pay attention to the labels that warn, *Do not mix with alcohol*. They choose not to worry about the blackouts or the lingering effects a day later.

The so-called club drugs, tablets or liquids that have found their way into the party scene, pose particular problems when combined with alcohol. GHB (gamma hydroxybutyrate) and Rohypnol are showing up on college campuses across the country and are associated with date rape. These drugs are clear and odorless, nearly impossible to detect in a drink. With recipes posted on the Internet and available for bargain prices at Mexican spring-break resorts, they are easy to buy or to make and despairingly effective. Victims rarely have the time or ability to recognize the symptoms of the drug, and the traces disappear from the bloodstream within twenty-four hours. When a victim begins to understand what happened, it is usually too late to gather evidence.

Because the purity and strength of these drugs is unknown, their danger is even greater. Mixed with alcohol, they can cause coma and death. And like alcohol, drugs interfere with brain development and can lead to lifelong dependence.

2008, p. 2, www.whitehousedrugpolicy.gov/news/press08/marij_mental_hlth.pdf (accessed June 13, 2008).

Even seemingly safe products like energy drinks can pose risks when combined with drugs or alcohol. The caffeine and sugar in energy drinks, combined with drug and alcohol effects on the body, create a dangerous, but increasingly popular mix.

PREVENTION PARTNERSHIPS

Parents might feel more comfortable knowing that their student's college will notify them if their child violates drug or drinking policies, but parent notification does not *prevent* problems. Increasingly, colleges are hearing from parents after a serious incident, "Someone is supposed to be watching these kids. I trusted you to look out for my child. How could you let us down?"

Even at small, private colleges where staff members do their best to monitor student behavior closely, it is impossible to keep all students from drinking. At a large university where students have much more personal freedom, schools simply cannot monitor every student. Students must take responsibility for their own behavior, and colleges need parents' help in reinforcing that message.

Your messages about alcohol make a difference. Certainly a student's friends will have an influence on her drinking choices, but parents' messages can reduce the impact of peer pressure. A child's relationship with his parents continues to play a major protective role in promoting his development and success throughout college.[20] It is helpful, then, for parents to continue discussing expectations related to alcohol use.

---

20. Schulenberg, J., J. L. Maggs, K. J. Steinman, and R.A. Zucker, "Development Matters: Taking the Long View on Substance Abuse Etiology and Intervention During Adolescence," in P. M. Monti, S. M. Colby, and T. A. O'Leary, eds., *Adolescents, Alcohol, and Substance Abuse: Reaching Teens Through Brief Interventions* (New York: Guilford Press, 2001), pp. 19–57.

The nondrinker can feel alone on a college campus. Drinking and partying are common conversation topics on campus, and the students who roar back into the residence hall early Saturday morning attract much more attention and seem more plentiful than their quiet, sober neighbors. Growing numbers of college students, however, are beginning to assert their right to a clean and quiet living environment. In years past, students who didn't drink or use drugs were willing to accept their housemates' behavior, however annoying it may have been. They bought into the messages that most college students drink, and that drugs were not a problem. Now, though, students who stumble into the residence hall following weekend parties, waking up their neighbors or throwing up in the bathrooms, are much more likely to be reported to hall staff or confronted the next day about their disruptive behavior.

If your student complains about a roommate's or neighbor's drinking or drug use, you can encourage him to talk to the residence hall adviser or hall director. You can also give your child permission to continue to use you as an excuse if friends are pushing him to join the party. Back in junior high and high school, the standard advice was that children could say their parents would not allow them to drink or take drugs: "My mom will kill me if she finds out. And my mother knows everything I do. The woman is spooky." Now the message may include a college angle: "My parents would make me move home if they ever heard I was messing around. I'm having too much fun here to have to go back home!"

This is one area where you can give your student permission to make up stories: "My parole officer said he'd bust me if he catches me doing that stuff again. I want to be a chef, not a prison cook."

College students believe they have perfectly good reasons to drink. Alcohol, they say, helps them relax, talk to new people, and simply have more fun.[21] They rationalize their drinking by claiming stress: "We work so hard that we have to play hard, too." Or they rely on the old stand-bys: "All college students drink." "It's a rite of passage!" "It's a stupid law—what makes twenty-one the magic number?"

Parents can support the college's efforts to control drug and alcohol use by letting students know that all college students do not take drugs or drink to excess. And they can call their student on the excuses: "You should be able to have fun without drugs and alcohol." "Even if you think it is a stupid law, it's still the law, and there are penalties for breaking it." You are justified in letting your student know you will not pay tens of thousands of dollars to fund a four-year rite of passage.

On the other hand, a single drinking incident or a couple of beers at a party are not justification for pulling your student out of school. There is truth to the theory that college students are educable. They learn from their mistakes, and many eighteen-year-olds decide after one serious drinking bout that a blackout is too steep a price to pay for an evening of indulgence.

Although your expectations are important, your student is in that awkward stage between youth and maturity. These are decisions you cannot make for your child. But if you find that your child is partying more than you'd like, hang on to a ray of hope. When students leave college and move into the real world of employment and responsibility, most of them quit their excessive drinking and partying. Once the peer pressure is removed, vomiting and hangovers lose their appeal.[22]

---

21. CORE Institute, 2006, www.siu.edu/~coreinst/.

22. O'Malley, Patrick M., Ph.D., "Maturing Out of Problematic Alcohol Use," *Alcohol, Research, and Health: Focus on Young Adult Drinking*, Vol. 28,

The College Party Calendar

Some of the high periods of drinking and drug use in college are predictable. Although any student might decide to get high on any given weekend, there are times when heavy and dangerous drinking is more likely. Freshmen are susceptible to high drinking rates, especially in the first few weeks of the freshman year. First-year students are anxious about meeting new friends, and going to parties gives them the sense that they are socializing successfully. Alcohol makes them less self-conscious. And, of course, freshmen are reveling in their newfound freedom.

Sophomores generally do a bit less serious drinking, but toward the end of the junior year and into the senior year, dangerous drinking peaks again as students celebrate their own and their friends' twenty-first birthdays.

No matter the student's academic class standing, certain times of the year are more likely to spur drinking:

The first two weeks of classes of every academic term. Parties are where students meet new friends or celebrate reunions with returning friends. Alcohol eases social situations. Students haven't established study schedules yet, so it feels like there's more free time. Homework assignments and deadlines are still in the distance.

Football games and homecoming. Pre- and postgame partying is a tradition at many football schools. Homecoming and Halloween are big party nights, and the stress of midterms is an easy excuse to use alcohol.

Finals. Anxiety and the intensity of studying mesh with

no. 4 (2004–2005): pp. 202–204, http://pubs.niaaa.nih.gov/publications/arh284/202-204.htm (accessed May 24, 2008).

unstructured study days and exam days. Celebrating the last final is a ritual at some colleges. Students coming home for long holiday weekends or semester break frequently drink heavily with their high school friends.

Midwinter weekends and winter or spring celebrations. In cold-weather climates, drinking may be the winter pastime. Mardi Gras and St. Patrick's Day provide excuses for dressing up and throwing a party. Campus festivals often coincide with the conclusion of midterm exams.

Spring break. Escapes to warm locations bring students together from all around the country. The partying is legendary.

The end of the academic year. Students plan gatherings with friends before leaving for the summer. Seniors, old enough to drink legally, are beginning the graduation festivities at the same time they're facing the uncertainty of starting a new job, moving to a new location, facing the postcollege debts. "This is the end of an era," they say, and the nostalgia they're suffering includes memories of college partying.

"I CAN'T TALK TO MY *PARENTS* ABOUT SEX!"

Most of us find it easiest to avoid thinking or talking about either our parents' or our children's sex lives. Although many students don't want to discuss sex with their parents, sex is one of the most important issues of their college years, and they *are* thinking and talking about it—a lot!

When college students talk to one another about sex, they silently compare what their parents have told them with what their friends are saying. They will discover that good people—people they like and respect—have sexual experiences much different from their own. They may decide that their parents do not know much about sex, because they never talked about *this* kind of sex.

As easy as it is to talk to their friends about intimate experiences, it can be exceedingly difficult for your child to talk to you. Few parents know when their child has his or her first sexual experience, but the hope is that the first experience is a choice rather than "something that just happened."

When Cyl was home for spring break during her freshman year, she mentioned to her mother, Joan, that she needed a formal dress. She had been dating her boyfriend for several months, and he had invited her to his fraternity's spring dance. The dance was off campus, at a hotel ballroom downtown. "I don't want you to worry, Mom, but just so you know, we're staying at the hotel after the dance. Honest, we're not doing anything wrong, but Gabe just turned twenty-one, so it's legal for him to drink. It's not like he'll get totally bombed, but we want to be safe, so we're going to get a room. Everyone's getting a room. It's not a big thing."

Although Joan's first instinct was to forbid her daughter ever to return to school, she took a deep breath and said, "Cyl, let's be realistic. You're planning to stay in a hotel room with a young man you like a lot. I think you need to acknowledge that you very well might have sex, or else you need to come up with a specific plan for *not* having sex—like getting a separate room for yourself. Please, don't put yourself in a situation where you end up sleeping together without actually thinking about it and planning for it. I just want you to make sure you talk about it so that you know what it means to each one of you, and you won't have any regrets later."

As Cyl stormed off, fuming that her mother didn't trust her, Joan worried that she had somehow just given her daughter permission to have sex with her boyfriend. A few hours later, however, Cyl came back and acknowledged that her mother was right. "I don't know if you want to hear this, but I think I really do want to sleep with Gabe. He's the nicest guy I've ever met, and I like him a lot. We haven't actually talked about it, but the truth is, I bought a package of condoms a couple of weeks ago, and I've had them with me in case things went too far. You're right—I should talk to him about it, and if it's going to happen the night of the dance, I don't want either one of us to be drunk. I want it to be a good experience."

Cyl was fortunate that her mother was willing to confront the issue. For too many students, sex is unplanned or unwanted, or it's simply not thought through. And that can lead to regret, resentment, or unwillingness to take responsibility.

WHEN GOOD TIMES GO BAD

Sometimes students don't have the opportunity to make their own choices. About 3.5 percent of college women experience an attempted or a completed sexual assault each year.[23] In the vast majority of cases, the assailant is a friend, classmate, boyfriend or ex-boyfriend, or an acquaintance. Women believe they are safe, spending time with a friend, and they are unprepared when the situation becomes sexual. The majority of these assaults take place in the victim's own residence, leaving her with no place to escape to.

Because victims so often know their assailant, their reactions are complicated. They tend to blame themselves, thinking, *I must have made him think I wanted sex.* They experience guilt, wondering if they could have done something to prevent the assault. They are confused about whether or not it was a rape, believing that since they let the person into the room, or they went somewhere willingly with the attacker, no one else would consider it an assault. They even struggle to believe it happened since "He's always been such a nice guy. Everyone likes him."

---

23. Sampson, Rana, *Acquaintance Rape of College Students*, U.S. Department of Justice, Vol 17 (2002), www.cops.usdoj.gov/pdf/e03021472.pdf (accessed May 24, 2008).

Acquaintance or date rape is often minimized as "not a real rape." The victim decides not to report the assault, fearing either that her assailant will retaliate or, by reporting the assault, she may ruin his reputation or her own. She concludes that no one will believe her, knowing that it's "my word against his." If the student who was assaulted is gay, lesbian, bisexual, or transgender, there are additional concerns about being "outed" if the assault is reported.

Acquaintance rape is often compounded by continuing to see the assailant on campus or in the classroom. If the attacker is acting normally, while the victim is churning inside with fear and guilt—unable even to talk about the assault—grades and other personal relationships suffer.

Students especially dread telling their parents about an acquaintance rape. They want their parents to believe they are responsible and safe. Acknowledging an assault may feel like revealing weakness or irresponsibility. They don't want their parents to be disappointed in them; if they think they could have or should have done things differently, they worry that their parents will have the same doubts. Students also know that their rape will affect their parents. They don't want to cause them shame or discomfort.

In many cases, by withholding the information from you, your student is protecting herself or himself (because men, too, can be raped) from admitting what happened. Once the facts come out, the student has to deal with them.

Jenna always had a very close relationship with her parents. "I never understood my friends who wouldn't tell their parents about the parties they went to or the boys they met. I told my parents everything!" But when she was sexually assaulted in her residence hall room early in her sophomore year, she did not tell her family.

It was Jenna's mother, Connie, who finally confronted the issue.

"In retrospect, I should have known right away," Connie said later. "She came home one weekend unexpectedly, and she seemed so exhausted. She asked me to do her laundry and wash her sheets, and she went up to her room and slept. I thought maybe she was just tired—students always seem to work so hard, and they stay up late with their friends. But she slept almost the whole weekend, and when it was time to go back to school, she was so sad. She had always been anxious before to get back, but this time she seemed terribly unhappy—almost clingy toward me and her dad."

As the year progressed, Jenna seemed unsettled. She would call home and cry, fretting about noises outside her room or boys who made comments about her. She no longer talked about friends at school, and her grades were abysmal. At one point, Jenna mentioned to her mother that she didn't drink anymore because once, after she had been partying, she fell asleep and didn't wake up for sixteen hours. When she finally woke up, she couldn't remember anything.

Midway through the second semester, Connie happened to read a newspaper article about a college woman who had been given a date-rape drug. According to the story, some of the woman's sorority sisters noticed that she seemed disoriented and sleepy after only one drink. When she fell asleep and her friends could not wake her, they called an ambulance. The words on the page blurred as Connie began to recognize that her daughter had exhibited all of the same symptoms the article described—confusion, exhaustion, memory lapse, and lingering depression. Had Jenna been drugged and raped?

Connie dug out the orientation materials from Jenna's college and found the school's rape crisis phone number. She talked to the director of the program, who advised her to encourage, but not force, her daughter to talk to a peer counselor. If Jenna wasn't yet ready to deal with the assault, she would not be able to discuss it. If she was ready, she might need only a gentle nudge.

Connie simply told Jenna, "I was looking through some information from your college, and there are peer counselors—students your age—who can talk about rape and sexual assault. It sounds like a good program. They have drop-in hours on Tuesday morning, so you could go in and talk to them. Would you do that?"

Jenna didn't argue or ask why her mother was giving her the information; she simply said she would go. And on Tuesday morning, she went.

Parents' reaction to their child's assault is intense. It feels like an assault on you. Jenna's father was incensed, and he was ready to pound on the young man's door and bodily remove him from the college. Jenna's mother, however, was more intent on taking care of her daughter. She encouraged Jenna to follow the advice of the rape counselor and file a petition through the registrar's office to have her grades for fall semester changed from letter grades to "pass." Connie urged Jenna to move to a different residence hall, where she would no longer have to see where her assault occurred. The support of her family, including both the caretaking from her mother and the fierce loyalty of her father, gave Jenna the courage to work through the steps of the recovery process.

In Case of Rape: How a Parent Can Help

- First and foremost, listen and believe your child when he or she tells you about a rape. Talking about sexual assault is a critical step toward recovery, but it is very difficult for the both the victim/survivor and for the listener.
- Make sure that "first steps" are taken. Be certain that your child is no longer in danger. If the assault was recent, encourage your child to seek medical attention and support. Time is a factor in gathering evidence, preventing pregnancy, and treating sexually transmitted diseases.

Many colleges and universities have sexual assault support programs, and community sexual assault support services are also available.

- Avoid being overly protective or assuming a controlling role for your child. You cannot fix this; there is work to be done, but doing the work is part of the healing process for the victim/survivor. You can, however, encourage your child to seek help, while recognizing that it may take time for your child to muster the energy to move forward. The assault took away the student's power, and it is critical for the victim/survivor to assume self-control again and to know that you support her or his decisions.

- Recognize your own feelings of anger and helplessness. You can find helpful information for yourself by checking your library for resources on sexual assault issues or by talking to someone at your local rape-counseling program. You can also contact the Rape, Abuse and Incest National Network (RAINN), 800-656-HOPE (4673), or check online at www.rainn.org.

- While you can support your child as he or she presses charges or confronts the attacker, it is not your role to retaliate. Your child knows the situation best. In some cases, a victim may not be able or ready to confront the assailant; don't put your child in the situation where he or she is defending the attacker to you.

CYBERSTALKING

Harassment and stalking have long been problems on campus, but the wonders of technology continue to create new forms of harassment. Colleges require students to have e-mail accounts, and those accounts can be used for electronic stalking. Cell phones and text messaging mean harassment and bullying can show up on a cell phone at any time. What might seem like innocent, online flirting or teasing to the sender of a message may feel like intimidation to the recipient.

A freshman noticed an attractive girl one afternoon at a coffee shop and overheard her friend calling her Celeste. She left before he could gather the nerve to talk to her, but that evening, he checked the school's online directory for all the Celestes on campus. He decided she must be the Celeste who lived in West Hall, right across the street from the coffee shop. He sent an e-mail, asking if she had been at the coffee shop at 4 p.m. that afternoon, wearing jeans and an Old Navy sweatshirt and carrying a red backpack. If so, would she be there at the same time the next afternoon?

When she didn't show up the next day, he sent a text message, using the cell phone number Celeste had listed in the college directory. "i will b in west hall lobby 2nite @ 8. cu then."

To Celeste, the messages felt threatening. Someone she didn't know was describing her clothes and her movements. He had been able to find her e-mail address and phone number, and he knew where she lived. She contacted the campus police, who tracked the boy's e-mail address and waited for him in the residence hall lobby that evening. "You have crossed a line," they warned him. "We're not going to take action this time, because we don't think you understood exactly what you were doing. But in the future, don't use the campus directory or your computer account to contact people who don't know you."

Cyberstalking is not always an innocent misunderstanding. Electronic harassment is the newest weapon of spurned boyfriends or girlfriends. When a relationship is going well, students trustingly give their computer passwords to a new love. After the breakup, a savvy "ex" can intercept e-mails or change passwords. It's no longer rare for a student, after ending a relationship, to open up her e-mail account and find threatening notes or hundreds of spam messages. E-mails from a new boyfriend or girlfriend mysteriously disappear. Women and men alike may find that their former friend has subscribed them to pornography listservs or posted their e-mail address on some unsavory Web site.

Facebook, MySpace, and YouTube provide more opportunities for harassment. What seemed like a fun photo or cute video when students were dating can be humiliating when posted with commentary on a Web site for all to see.

Your student's first instinct might be to delete rude messages and hope nothing ever shows up again, but tell your student to save the message and forward it to a campus authority or to the police. If the harassment or stalking is related to campus-managed technology like an e-mail account, the school's technology office should also be notified; the computer services staff will do their best to track messages back to the source. Every college should have a policy addressing electronic harassment. Once the harasser has been identified, cell phones can be programmed to refuse calls or texts from specific numbers. Students can have their e-mail address and password changed, and social networking sites can take down harassing postings.

DO THEY REALLY KNOW WHAT THEY'RE DOING?

College students, as a population, are bright, inquisitive adults who have every resource available to make wise choices. Certainly, they arrive at college having heard the message that abstinence is the only sure method of birth control. In a variety of ways, college health services and residence hall programming offer information about abstinence, birth control, and sexually transmitted diseases and infections, in an ongoing effort to educate students about the risks of casual sex. How could any student possibly end up with a sexually transmitted infection or become pregnant?

All the sex education in the world, however, doesn't alter the fact that college-aged men and women are sexual, sensual beings. They are biologically programmed to desire intimacy, and they are at a prime age for being sexual. Depending on the culture of the school or your child's group of friends, student attitudes toward sex may seem to you to be alarmingly impersonal or even cavalier.

When Louisa walked into the residence hall on the first day of her daughter's freshman year, a basket of condoms on the check-in table caught her eye. While her daughter was filling out forms, Louisa softly asked the student staffing the table, "Couldn't you just put those condoms out of sight until the parents are gone? We really don't need to see that." Later she asked the residence hall director, "How can I tell my daughter it's OK to *not* have sex when you have condoms right there, the first thing she sees on move-in day? How do I get her to believe that not all college students are having sex?"

Various surveys indicate that up to two-thirds of all high school students have had sex,[24] and about 80 percent of college students say that they have been sexually active.[25] While students seem to know the basic facts about sexually transmitted diseases and infections (STDs and STIs), many see the only significant danger as AIDS/HIV. As long as they're hooking up with good, clean college students like themselves, they think they're going to be fine. Condoms will protect them from

24. Centers for Disease Control and Prevention, "Youth Risk Behavior Surveillance—United States, 2005," Surveillance Summaries, June 9, 2006, MMWR 2006;55 (No. SS-5).

25. Boynton Health Service, *2007 College Health Survey Report: Sexual Health*, University of Minnesota, October 2007.

pregnancy and any weird diseases that might be lurking in this partner's distant past. The human papilloma virus (HPV) vaccine will keep them safe from genital warts. They don't think about the HPV strains that the vaccine doesn't affect, and they don't realize that condoms do not protect them from some of the most common STIs. Some infections are transmitted by direct skin contact, oral sex, and mutual masturbation, not just by intercourse. Even more disturbing—even though college students have easy access to condoms and know they offer protection against sexually transmitted infections and pregnancy, only half reported using a condom the last time they had vaginal sex, and fewer than 5 percent used a condom for oral sex.[26] They may know how to be safe, but they don't necessarily use that knowledge.

Some parents would prefer that the message to college students be a one-word statement: Wait. The mother of an incoming freshman criticized the orientation program at her daughter's college because a segment of the program included informational skits about sexuality, pregnancy, and sexually transmitted diseases. "If you tell these kids how easy it is to get and use birth control, you're really just telling them to have sex," she said. "Don't talk about these things, and they won't think sex is an option."

Many students do abstain, and they are increasingly finding support among friends for their choice. In fact, the image of college students gone wild, hooking up every weekend with different partners, is a myth. Over the course of a year, three-fourths of college students report they've had sex with no one or just

---

26. American College Health Association, *National College Health Assessment: Reference Group Executive Summary Fall 2007*, www.acha-ncha.org/docs/ACHA-NCHA_Reference_Group_ExecutiveSummary_Fall2007.pdf (accessed May 17, 2008).

one sexual partner.[27] Nevertheless, whether or not universities (and parents) address intimacy issues, sex will be on the minds of students. The good news is, you still have some influence. Let your student know what your expectations are, and continue to encourage safe choices. And keep talking. Then, if the time comes when your child needs to tell you about a sex-related issue, it will be easier for both of you.

Students struggle with telling their parents if they are planning to move in with an intimate partner, if they are taking a trip with a boyfriend or girlfriend, if there's a pregnancy, sexually transmitted disease, or a dysfunction. They *will* let you know if they're planning to get married. They may tell you if they are gay, but for most gays, lesbians, bisexuals, and transgenders, telling family members is the hardest part of coming out.

Although many students identify their sexual orientation in high school or earlier, it is not uncommon for gay students to recognize and accept their homosexuality during their college years. For some, any feelings of "difference" during high school might have been repressed and attributed to the challenges of fitting into a small community or to the growing pains of adolescence. At college, however, when students have a chance to examine their feelings in a new setting, they may come to realize that the feelings they have hidden or wondered about for years are part of their identity. They finally want clarity. Many colleges and universities have support systems for gay, lesbian, bisexual, and transgender students, and finding a place to ask questions and get answers helps students realize they are not alone. Coming out feels as if a burden has been lifted, the

27. American College Health Association, *National College Health Assessment: Reference Group Executive Summary Fall 2007*, www.acha-ncha.org/docs/ACHA-NCHA_Reference_Group_ExecutiveSummary_Fall2007.pdf (accessed May 17, 2008).

answer to a long-perplexing question, but it brings a few new problems. How will friends and family react?

When Chris told his parents he was gay, his mother felt almost as much relief as he did. She had seen how unhappy and depressed he often seemed, and she had sometimes wondered if he might be gay. She also saw that the cloud had lifted with his coming out. His father, on the other hand, was miserable. He went through every cliché: "You just haven't met the right girl." "It will pass." "Is this one of those college things? You'll change your mind when you get out in the real world." "Did *I* do something wrong? Was it your mother's and my divorce?" "Maybe I should have done more with you when you were growing up. I should have insisted you live with me, not your mother."

Nevertheless, he, too, saw that Chris was growing more confident and content with himself. Although he had trouble accepting that his son was gay, he could not imagine his life without Chris in it. "I'm not exactly happy about this," he told his former wife. "I can't help but hope that he'll change his mind, but I guess that's my problem, not his. Chris really is a great kid, and what I want most for him is to be happy. It does seem like a load is lifted from his shoulders these days."

Whether the subject is pregnancy, a sexually transmitted disease, or sexual identity, your child has probably rehearsed the conversation many times by the time you hear the words, "Mom, Dad, I need to tell you . . ." By revealing the hard truth to the people who love them, students are coming to terms with their situation. Even if they have previously talked to a doctor, a counselor, or a friend, now that they are telling their parents, they are beginning to confront and adjust to the issues.

What your student tells you may conflict with everything you believe and everything you have hoped for your child. You may not approve of your student's behaviors or the situation your child is in. You may be hearing something that forces you to revise how you have always looked at your child. Any objections you voice, however, will not change what your child is telling you. Any suggestions you make will not change the circumstances. These are the times when children need their parents more than ever to help them handle the situation, or at least to keep loving them.

Practice these steps in advance:

1. Listen.
2. Say, "Thank you for telling me."
3. Ask how your child is feeling and if there's anything you can do to be helpful.
4. Say, "I love you." Then be quiet again in case there's more listening you need to do.

QUICK TIPS FOR STUDENTS

Don't Be a Victim of Sexual Assault

- When you're preparing for a date, take care of yourself first. Have enough money to pay for your meal and transportation home, if necessary. Have your cell phone charged and with you. Program a cab company phone number into your directory.
- At parties or bars, keep a friend in sight. Watch out for each other, and check in from time to time to make sure you're both comfortable with how things are going.
- Trust your instincts. If you find yourself in a situation where something feels wrong, look for a way out of the situation—move closer to other people or seek out a safe way to get home.
- Don't ignore sudden feelings of mistrust just because

you have known someone for a long time. You can't tell if a person has the potential to rape based on past behaviors.

- Never leave a drink unattended or accept a drink that you did not see poured. Date-rape drugs can leave you unable to protect yourself, or even know what is happening to you.
- Take assertiveness training and self-defense courses. Passive and submissive behaviors can be dangerous. If you become frightened, do your best to be assertive. Speak loudly and firmly, or yell.
- If you are sexually assaulted, go to a clinic or emergency room immediately. You can decide later whether or not to press charges, but it is critical that you receive medical attention and caring support as soon as possible.

Don't Be a Rapist

- First, be respectful. Anytime you are uncertain whether your partner is comfortable with your behavior, ask! You can simply say, "Are you okay with this?" Assume that "no" means no. What's more, assume that "I'm not sure" means no.
- Recognize that your sexual needs do not give you the right to do whatever you want. Any sexual activity should be mutually desired. If the other person is not capable of making an informed decision, do not have sex!
- Know the definition of sexual assault. If you think a grope or "feeling someone up" is just innocent fun, you could be surprised. In some cases, you can be arrested for these actions.
- Drink responsibly. Nearly every sexual assault on col-

lege campuses follows drinking by one or both individuals. In addition, be aware of how alcohol affects you. If drinking makes you more aggressive, you could be in danger of sexually assaulting someone. Being drunk is not a defense for committing sexual assault.

- If your friend or roommate is sexually assaulting someone, do what you can to stop the assault. You can be charged with complicity if you know about an assault and fail to intervene.
- Be aware that committing rape has severe consequences. For your victim, there can be years of emotional trauma, guilt, and fear. For you, sexual assault can lead to criminal charges, attorney expenses, and prison. For both of you, a sexual assault can result in disease, pregnancy, and social stigma. A few minutes of sex are not worth years of regret.

CHAPTER 9

Study Snacks and
All-Nighters

Health and Wellness

A dining center director polled students to find out which breakfast cereals they wanted in the campus dining centers. The top six choices: Cinnamon Toast Crunch, Lucky Charms, Golden Grahams, Frosted Flakes, Frosted Mini-Wheats, and Corn Pops.

Any college freshmen can tell you about the Food Guide Pyramid. Students know what they should eat, and they have heard more than enough about how a poor diet will affect their health. Nevertheless, it's a fact of college life: Sugar and caffeine form the foundation of the Student Food Pyramid. Students also know the theoretical benefits of a good night's sleep and regular exercise, but sleep and workouts are among the casualties when a final exam is coming up or a paper is due.

A steady diet of soda, candy, and chips provides quick energy, but it doesn't provide the nourishment or stamina for the long haul. Students might manage to stay up long into the night talking with friends or cramming for a quiz, but they make up for the late hours by dozing off during lectures or searching out a secluded library carrel for a nap between classes. With each passing week, they become more susceptible to any illnesses that might be lurking around campus.

A HEALTHY START

As parents look over the list of their child's college dining options, they are swayed by the most extensive meal option. They want their child to eat three meals a day, and the full meal plan is the most economical choice. But why, parents ask, is there no dining option that provides for twenty-one meals per week?

Most colleges offer only two meals on Sundays—brunch and dinner—and increasingly, schools are eliminating the three-meal schedule on Saturdays. So parents select the choice that yields nineteen meals per week, and then two weeks after school begins, their child decides to cut back to the fourteen-meals-per-week option. Her parents are convinced she'll starve.

Very few college students can be classified as "morning people." Typically, they prefer to sleep as long as possible before dashing off to class. Those with 8 a.m. classes don't have time for breakfast; those who sleep past nine o'clock have missed the breakfast line. At best, breakfast becomes little more than a quick stop to grab a bagel, banana, and Coke. If you're hoping to ensure that your student has a decent start to the day, you might make a better investment by buying or renting a dorm-size refrigerator and urging your child to shop regularly for milk, juice, and cereal.

While it makes sense to plan for two meals per day in the dining center, students often protest that they can't possibly eat there that often. "My lab class on Wednesday meets at noon, and the dining room is closed before I get back to the dorm." "It's absolutely required to have at least one burger a week at the downtown diner!" "I wouldn't force a dog to eat dorm food for every meal!"

College dietitians have made great strides in improving food service in recent years, and flexibility has become the watchword in meal plans. Students can select from a considerable range of choices at each meal. Salad bars are standard, and many cafeterias have cereal, sandwich, soup, or pasta bars as well. Vegetarians and vegans can find entrées that fit their dietary demands, or at least they should be able to build a meal around the hot vegetables, pasta, bread, and salad ingredients. Many cafeterias even make ethnic foods available on a daily basis.

At some schools, students can draw down their dining account at an on-campus restaurant—which might include popular chain restaurants—or spend some of their dining dollars at a campus market, deli, or coffee shop. They may be able to use meal-plan money at vending machines. These might not be options that make parents feel better about their child's diet, but they are popular alternatives among students.

Still, students complain. Ethan's mother had dismissed his occasional grumbling about the food until one night, in the middle of the week, he showed up at home just as she was sitting down for dinner. "I borrowed my roommate's car so I could come home for some real food. I'm not going to eat another meal at the dorm!" he vowed. "It's disgusting. I swear, it's the same two choices every night. The vegetables are mushy, the meat is gray, and they even manage to mess up the orange juice. Most of the stuff has no taste at all, and if it does have a flavor, it's foul."

Food was a factor Ethan's mother had been especially concerned about before her son started college. Ethan was one of those high school students who ate steadily from the time he got home after school every afternoon until he turned the lights out and went to bed. She had wanted to make sure he could have second servings and a range of options at each meal. She had even made a phone call to the food service director during the summer, and she was impressed with his description of the dining center. Ethan's complaints didn't make sense, based on what she had heard.

Sometimes, when students complain to their parents about

food, there are other, undisclosed issues. In Ethan's case, the real motive was that he wanted to move out of the residence hall. He had an invitation from his lab partner to sublet the second bedroom of an apartment near campus, but he knew his mother would object. She already had told him she wanted him to stay in the dorm another year. He also knew, though, that he could gain her sympathy by claiming the food was inedible.

Food gets the blame when students want to come home because of a boyfriend or girlfriend, when they want to join a fraternity or sorority, or when they're having roommate problems and simply don't want to stay where they are. It's also an excuse when they don't have friends to eat with and they just can't bear sitting alone.

Using food as an excuse is a brilliant means of persuasion. What parent can ignore a fundamental requirement of life? A kid has to eat. If a student were to complain about the roommate, parents would suggest, "Talk it over. Ask the hall director to help. Maybe it's partly your fault?" But few parents will tell their student to tough it out when they hear she is not eating. What's more, it's almost a form of flattery—your child likes your cooking, and nothing else can compare.

Admittedly, dishes prepared for a college dining center will not taste like home cooking. Because of the range of food sensitivities and allergies among the college population, the recipes are generally not seasoned like home cooking. The student who is accustomed to having real butter slathered on fresh, al dente vegetables will surely find steam-table carrots and peas bland and unappetizing. At the end of most serving lines, though, a spice bar provides salt, pepper, herbs, Tabasco sauce, and the old standbys, ketchup, mustard, and mayonnaise.

Complaints about the food provide students with a social bond. They can connect with one another through shared suffering, and caustic remarks about "mystery meat" or "spaghetti soup" provide easy conversation starters and sometimes lead to a spur-of-the-moment group trip for pizza or dessert.

There are cases, however, where the food genuinely is bad, and students' complaints are the first step toward improvement. An unskilled food service director may be revealed only if students speak out.

How do you determine if the problem is serious, or if it might be the first step in a request to move out of the dorm? Parents can ask their child what kinds of choices are provided: Are there salad and pasta bars? Is there at least one dish that's palatable at each meal? If a student takes an entrée and doesn't like it, can she go back for something else? If your student has dietary restrictions, has he talked to the dietitian about special meals or asked for guidance in selecting foods that fit his requirements?

Although in most cases, the food really is edible, anyone who has eaten in a college dining center understands that the prospect of pulling every meal, every day from a cafeteria line can wear on you. A trip through the serving line can mean making choices from dozens of options—which students demand—but the noise of hundreds of students talking, flatware chinking against plates, hamburgers sizzling, and the occasional breaking glass adds up to a constant din. Each meal becomes a sensory overload. Every now and then, a student needs the break of a solitary meal, eaten in front of the TV, or a quiet restaurant in off-peak hours with a good friend and lazy conversation. If you cannot add ten or fifteen dollars to your student's budget for extra meals from time to time, encourage him to request the cafeteria's brown bag lunch occasionally, just to provide a break from the routine.

ALL WORK AND NO PLAY

Unfortunately, even students who eat three balanced meals a day can suffer physically. We've all heard of the "freshman fif-

teen," those extra pounds that students pile on by opting for spaghetti and bread sticks for every meal, rich lattes at the coffee
shop between classes, and a bag of cheese curls before bed. It is
a college ritual to go out for burritos on Sunday nights, and it's
part of the daily routine to gather in the lounge for sodas several
times a day. It may seem like walking to classes and carrying a
twenty-pound backpack would substitute for a gym workout, but
students can quickly get out of shape.

Young adults are fully aware that exercise improves overall
health, reduces stress levels, and helps prevent weight gain, but
workouts are not necessarily the highest priority at this stage of
their lives. The onetime high school athletes who are no longer
competing in sports abandon their intensive exercise routines as
just another of the many changes that come with adjustment to
college. Those who have never previously given much attention
to working out might not feel much desire to start.

If exercise is ever to become a lifelong regimen, the college
years are key. Health habits picked up during the college years
last into adulthood. Students will never again have quite as many
recreational options; campuses provide a wide range of athletic
facilities, and on many campuses, state-of-the-art equipment
is provided for students at no charge. They can take up activities they've only seen on TV or read about in books. Students
who dreaded the required volleyball matches in junior high gym
might find their niche on a college fencing team. Earning course
credit for lacrosse or horseback riding can provide a new outlook
on exercise, or maybe a class in Latin dance or bowling will make
Monday mornings more palatable.

As with most lifestyle issues, parents cannot force their student to exercise, but you can point out opportunities, ask what
sounds interesting, and encourage participation. Your own
behavior is also influential. When you exercise regularly, your
student sees that you value a healthy lifestyle and that you find

ways to make it part of your regular schedule. You don't need to dwell on the importance of working out, but you can talk about what you saw during your morning walk or mention that you stopped at the gym on the way home from the office. You also can plan hikes and bicycle tours into your visits to campus or schedule a family ski trip during winter break.

WHEN THE FLU BUG BITES

It's a horrible feeling to have your child call home and say, "Mom, I'm sick." Even if she only has a cold, and you know she'll be fine with a bit of rest, you will feel helpless and anxious.

Students share germs in all kinds of creative ways—curling up on the floor with a roommate's pillow, using the computer keyboard in the library, and picking the pepperoni off a friend's slice of pizza. One junior swears that she and all her friends contracted pinkeye by playing with her kitten. You can trust that every student will come down with the flu or at least have a headache at some point during the year.

You know your child, and you know if he tends to overdramatize when he's sick, or if he complains only when he is in serious pain. When you get a phone call asking for help, trust your instincts and rely on your long-standing routines, at least to the extent that long-distance communication allows it. A phone diagnosis doesn't permit you to confirm with a look or a touch just how sick your child is, and your student may not be able to relay satisfactory answers when you ask, "Is your forehead hot? Are you flushed?"

When students call home to tell you they're sick, they are looking for the pampering they received as a child. They want to hear the advice they know you will provide: Go to bed, drink lots of juice, take a pain reliever, and heat up a bowl of chicken soup. They would like you to tell them how long it will be before they feel better. Just hearing the concern in your voice serves as a long-distance hug.

Unfortunately, many students don't want to even acknowledge an illness. Students who are trying to establish independence believe that health problems might mean that they can't take care of themselves after all. One young man suffered for weeks with an ingrown toenail, treating it with a topical ointment and hoping it would get better. He went to the health service only when his toe swelled so badly he could no longer get his shoe on. A young woman with a rash on her buttocks was too embarrassed to tell anyone or make a clinic appointment. *It will just go away,* she thought. After a month of itching, she had to acknowledge that it was much worse. She finally called her mother, only to receive the obvious advice, "Go to the doctor."

PREDICTING PROBLEMS

Cold and flu season hits campus at about the time students are preparing for midterm exams. If shorter days and falling temperatures are not enough to dim the excitement of first-year students, upcoming tests are a reminder that college is stressful. Students start pulling all-nighters and searching for the perfect formula to help them stay awake a few extra hours. In a show of camaraderie, upperclassmen pass along their recommendations to new students: You might be able to sleep through a psych lecture, but never doze off during chemistry lab. Mountain Dew has more caffeine than any other beverage in the study-lounge soda machines, and caffeinated energy drinks are available at the convenience store across the street. The purpose of study snacks is to keep you alert—try mixing equal parts of M&M's, raisins, and roasted, whole coffee beans.

As immune systems are pushed to the limit, students start coming down with any passing illness. Then they postpone treatment until it's "convenient." Homework deadlines and tests are much higher priority than a cough or an ache. By the time they can work a call to the clinic into their schedule, they're miserable and hoping for an immediate appointment and a quick fix.

Freshmen are especially determined to tough out the misery, no matter how sick they may be. The first-year student who comes down with a case of flu midway through the first semester will not want to concede that she can't handle a full class load. She will struggle to attend all her classes, even if she coughs and wheezes all through the lecture. After working so hard to get into college, waiting so long to arrive on campus, and dreaming so much of success, it is unfathomable that the need to sleep could squelch her plans.

Many of the peak periods for health issues are predictable. Students get sick just after they meet the deadline for a major project, and any class that includes public speaking will raise stress levels and lower endurance. Final exam week takes a lot out of students, and a bad cold develops just after they come home for the holidays or for the summer. Within a few weeks after a student moves into his first apartment, he might end up on the edge of malnourishment—the reality of meal preparation is harder than it seemed. And as the senior faces decisions about graduate school or job hunting, anxiety can cause ulcers or tension headaches.

Parents feel torn between the desire to honor their child's desire for independence and the need to protect his health. In most cases, the role of parents during the college years is to support their students as they grow increasingly independent, not to make decisions for them. Unless the student is willing to grant permission, parents will not have access to health information about their child. Although colleges provide forms for release of financial and academic information to family members, they are more cautious about health records. A physician or a psychologist might encourage your son to tell you about a health condition, but she won't be calling you about the diagnosis and treatment options.

ILLNESSES TO WATCH FOR

As difficult as it is to entrust your child's well-being to health professionals you've never met, campus health service staff are particularly skilled in diagnosing and treating those problems that are most likely to affect college-aged students. Some mental and physical conditions are especially associated with young adults, and the nurses and doctors at the college clinic know what to look for. The short list includes mononucleosis, meningitis, eating disorders, and depression. The onset of asthma, diabetes, and schizophrenia can show up in this age group as well.

Mononucleosis: Every year, soon after classes begin, college health clinics expect to see a few cases of mono. Freshmen are especially vulnerable, and they are the most likely to minimize the early symptoms. Adjustment to college, change in diet, and lack of sleep all contribute to weakening the immune system and increasing stress levels. Students who ignore the early symptoms, believing "it's just a cold," end up exhausted and dehydrated, barely able to make it to the clinic for an appointment.

Meningitis: The first thing to remember about meningitis is that it is rare. Meningitis infects the membrane surrounding the brain and spinal cord, and it is usually caused by a viral or bacterial infection.[28] Viral meningitis is painful and often requires hospitalization, but it is much less likely than the bacterial variety to cause serious consequences. It also is not as easily spread from person to person. Bacterial meningitis is more contagious

28. www.acha.org/projects_programs/meningitis/disease_info.cfm#overview (accessed May 25, 2008).

than the viral variety, and it can result in severe long-term health problems or even death.

Students who live in residence halls are statistically more likely than the general population to develop bacterial meningitis disease. Even compared with college students as a whole, those who live in dormitories are at greater risk.[29]

The conditions of residence hall living—close quarters, a population with stressed immune systems, and the tendency among students to overlook simple sanitation—happen to be the conditions that bacterial meningitis prefers. The bacteria spread when students share a soda or a kiss, or through contamination from coughs and sneezes. Its early symptoms mimic flu or colds—headache, fever, rash, sore throat, and nausea. One of the danger signs is a stiff neck and inability to bend the chin down to touch the upper chest. Because meningitis can progress rapidly, it requires a quick diagnosis.

The American College Health Association recommends that students consider being vaccinated against the disease. Not all health insurance policies cover the vaccine, but some colleges will provide vaccinations at no cost or reduced rates. Most parents, when they hear about the risk, urge their students to receive the vaccine.

Eating Disorders: Eating disorders are not confined to first-year students, but they may be exacerbated by the initial stress of leaving home. The complications of so many life changes at once can send students looking either for comfort or for something they can control. Either way, food becomes the focus. When we think of eating disorders, we commonly think of anorexia and bulimia and their effects on women. College men are also affected by these conditions.

---

29. "Meningococcal Infection in College Students," *Internal Medicine Alert* 23, i18 (September 29, 2001): 140.

Anorexia and bulimia are insidious in that victims are so deeply preoccupied by food, diet, and body image that there is no room in their thoughts to acknowledge the need for change. They have a goal in mind, and they are focused on all the minute details that will get them to the goal. Every day they count calories consumed, estimate calories burned, step on the scales to see if they're making progress, and endure immense guilt for any slipups.

Students who have experienced eating disorders during high school are especially at risk when they begin college, but anyone with an obsession about food may develop an eating disorder. In some cases, women in residence halls and sororities have taken bingeing and purging to the level of group activity. They might spend an evening gorging on snacks, then support one another as they justify the logic of getting rid of all those calories.

Eating disorders usually require some form of intervention and counseling assistance, but family and friends face a daunting task when they set out to help. These disorders are complex, and blame or criticism will only make things worse. Until victims want to change, they will find ways to continue their behavior. Unless your child is in imminent danger, the best you can do is point out what you are seeing, express your concern, and provide information on where to seek help.

For more information about eating disorders and the parent's role, check the following Web site: www.nationaleatingdiso ders.org/.

Depression: Clinical depression is often first diagnosed in the late teens and early twenties, but to complicate matters, college students are living a lifestyle that contributes to depression. They are under constant stress, they don't eat healthy foods, they don't sleep regularly, and they don't exercise. They are constantly judging themselves against their classmates, and they can always find someone smarter, more attractive, more outgoing, or thinner. Today's students have exceedingly high expectations for themselves, and few can meet their own lofty goals.

Depression is a concern among college students. You may need to worry if you see evidence that your child is pulling away from friends and family, using drugs or alcohol to excess, refusing to participate in favorite activities, or is feeling especially disappointed or dissatisfied with himself. If he has no energy to go to classes or leave his room, or if he is constantly exhausted, he needs to see a doctor for an evaluation.

Suicide is the second leading cause of death among college students.[30] Clinical depression, along with depression prompted by alcohol or drug use, a financial crisis, academic failure, the breakup of a relationship, trouble with the law, the death of a friend or family member, or issues about sexual orientation can bring on suicidal thoughts. When students recognize that they are not meeting their own or their family's high standards, they can fall into a pit of self-blame and shame.

Nevertheless, the occasional bad day is normal. As much as you hate for your child to be unhappy, students sometimes need to wallow in self-pity and misery for a few days or a week. Before you panic about your child's mood, look for evidence that he is making friends, attending classes on a regular basis, and participating in campus events. As long as your child is maintaining a normal schedule and can talk about activities, friends, and what's going on in classes, things are probably all right.

WHEN THE PROBLEMS ARE TOO SERIOUS TO IGNORE

It's challenging to decide when responsibility should revert to you. In most cases, the safest route is to present options and

---

30. "Suicide and America's Youth," Jed Foundation, www.jedfoundation.org/articles/SuicideStatistics.pdf (accessed May 25, 2008).

allow your child to make the final choices. If an injury or illness keeps a student out of the classroom for more than a week, he might want to consider dropping at least one class so that he can focus on the others. Academic advisers encourage students to think about the kind of classes they are taking, and whether missed classes can easily be made up. Lecture classes and courses that rely primarily on reading and writing tend to be more flexible; some professors will have online notes from their lectures, and students can work with an instructor to complete missed assignments. Language, math, or lab courses, however, rely heavily on in-class learning. It's hard for a student to keep up with the material if several sessions are missed, and it is unfair to the other students in the class to slow down the pace for one student.

Students worry that dropping a class means they will fall too far behind on the college schedule. "If I don't have fifteen credits this semester, there's no way I can graduate in four years." "I can't drop physics—it's the first class in a two-year sequence, and I can only take it fall semester. I'll be a whole year behind."

Certainly, there are downsides to dropping a class, but overworking during a serious illness may result in poor performance in every class. Too many low grades can lead to academic probation; students who don't fully understand the material in the first course of a sequence are likely to fail the next course. A dropped class might require a few months of summer school or even an extra year of college, but if it means success rather than failure, or health rather than lingering illness, the additional time is worth it.

In severe situations, parents do have the right to intervene. If your child is incapable of making decisions, or if you have good reason to believe that your student is suicidal, you will have to step in. Even some of the toughest advocates for student privacy will acknowledge that parents have the right to act if their child's life is at risk. If you have any indication your child is thinking about suicide, let her know that you are concerned, and encourage her to talk to a counselor or physician. If there is evidence that she has made a suicide attempt or is planning to harm herself, insist that she see a health professional. Take her yourself, or ask a college staff member or campus security to check on her if necessary.

For more information about parents' role in college mental health, check the Jed Foundation Web site: www.jedfoundation.org/.

ROAD HAZARDS

Commuter students face few of the obvious health-related adjustments that dorm life creates. They sleep in their own beds, eat home-cooked meals, and avoid the shared germs in residence halls. When they're sick, they even have the caring attention of their family physician, as well as Mom and Dad. That does not mean, however, that commuters are risk-free. Riding on buses and subways puts them in close contact with all kinds of diseases, and students who drive long distances to school tend to eat more than their share of greasy, fat-laden fast foods. The backseat of a commuter's car, strewn with soda cans and candy wrappers, provides evidence of diet deficiencies. Moreover, students who live off campus are less likely to receive age-based health information—those wellness programs that are presented in residence halls, sororities, and fraternities.

Research indicates that commuters are more prone to depression in college than residential students.[31] The commute itself contributes to the stress of school, especially in urban areas, and

---

31. Gore, Aseltine, and Lin Colton, "Life After High School: Development, Stress, and Well-Being," in Gotlib and Wheaton, *Stress and Adversity over the Life Course* (Cambridge: Cambridge University Press, 1997), pp. 197–214.

commuter students usually work more hours than residential students. Their schedules are segmented, and balancing work, home, and school can be exhausting. It's like living three separate lives, and commuters struggle to find enough time in the day to do justice to all the demands. What's more, the frustrations add up as they try to finish homework assignments between classes, only to find the books they need are at home. Or they plan to revise a paper over the lunch hour at work, but then remember their first draft is on their computer at home.

Even with parents on hand to oversee their health, commuter students face considerable risks. Perhaps more than other students, they feel they don't have time to be sick. They push themselves beyond endurance, then multitask in the car on the way to school, eating, drinking, and talking on cell phones while hurrying to get to class on time.

Commuting students are convinced that no one recognizes all the stress and extra responsibility they face. "Everyone thinks my life is just like when I was in high school, but it's not! College is harder, but because I'm living at home, no one notices the change."

Parents of commuters have a better chance than most to see when the demands are greatest and to find ways to ease the pressure. Ginny's mother offered to drive her daughter to campus during midterms and finals, giving her child a chance to study on the way to school and nap on the way home. When she picked her daughter up on the last day of finals, they went to dinner and a movie to celebrate. Neil's parents declared that Sundays meant absolutely no family obligations. He was relieved of all household chores at least one day a week, and his father made the commitment to wash and vacuum his car for him every weekend.

The greatest stress reliever for commuter students is for their parents to recognize that they are working hard and to step in from time to time and give them a break.

QUICK TIPS FOR STUDENTS

- "Prevention is the best medicine." You already know the basics: Eat some fruits and vegetables every day, drink plenty of juices and water, sleep at least seven hours a night, and exercise.

- Keep a cautious distance from friends and roommates when they are sick (but be kind—bring them soup from the dining center and offer to pick up some juice and tissues from the convenience store). During cold and flu season, wash your hands frequently.

- When you do start to feel sick, give yourself a break. Don't try to fight through the aches and pains. Take a nap, drink even more juices and water. Call the health clinic and ask for advice—should you make an appointment to see a doctor? Should you be taking any medication? Then follow their advice.

- Watch for signs of stress. If you notice that you frequently feel anxious or depressed, have trouble sleeping or can't seem to get enough sleep, lose your appetite or can't stop eating, or have persistent headaches or stomachaches, make an appointment to talk to a doctor.

- Colleges usually provide easy access to counselors and therapists. Use the resources!

- Alcohol, tobacco, and long weekends of partying take their toll on health. Look for less hazardous ways to have fun.

CHAPTER 10

Singing in Choir, Studying in Senegal

Learning Outside the Classroom

M ost high school juniors and seniors recognize that they can bolster their college applications by a strong list of extracurricular activities. A balance of sports partici-pation (the swim team), intellectual achievements (the debate team or math club), and community involvement (volunteering at the senior citizens center) is evidence of a well-rounded col-lege prospect. Long-term participation in an activity shows com-mitment, so high school students may continue piano lessons long after they lose interest. Throughout the final year or two of high school, students rush from class to practice to a babysitting job, busy from breakfast until long after supper, with no break on the weekends.

By the time they arrive at college, then, some students are so burned out that they spend their entire first semester holed up in their dorm rooms, watching TV and listening to music. They tell themselves they can't get involved yet because they must con-centrate on their studies. The truth is, they are relieved finally to have a moment to themselves.

Then one day, they emerge from their room, bored by too

much free time and looking for something to do. The options now seem dizzying, and the selection process mystifying. "Student council was kind of fun in high school. How do I get into student government here?" "My philosophy professor said he's the adviser for the chess club. Maybe it would be smart to go to one of those meetings." "It's so amazing to watch the rowing team on the river in the morning. I'd like to try that!"

Experiences outside of the classroom add value to what students are learning in their courses, helping textbook theory come alive. The sociology professor can lecture for weeks about group dynamics, but when students see firsthand how a few intensely competitive individuals can change the personality of the College Bowl team, it all starts to make sense.

SO MANY CHOICES, SO LITTLE TIME

Participation in clubs and organizations can help students clarify their career interests, providing the answers to lingering questions about an academic major. The student who discounted engineering as a career, believing it would mean a lifetime of working in solitude at a computer, finds that collaboration is a critical component in the engineering design process when he joins the school's solar vehicle team.

At the information fair during orientation, Bev tried to point her daughter toward the college newspaper's booth, but Lucie paused to look at the brochures promoting the women's center. "I don't think I want to work on the paper this year," Lucie told her mother. "It was fine in high school, but I heard it takes way more time in college. I'd rather try something different. Remember when I wrote that article last year on family violence, and I interviewed a girl whose family was staying at the crisis shelter? That poster says the women's center is looking for students to be advocates for victims of violence. I'm just going to ask a couple of questions, so maybe you want to go visit some of the other booths?"

Parents look through the lists of student organizations and see a number of groups that seem intriguing, some that raise red flags, and some that raise only questions. "Disc golf sounds like fun." "Why the sudden interest in NORML? Isn't that about reforming marijuana laws?" "How does a student decide between the aikido club, the karate club, and tae kwon do?" Parents can rarely predict which organization might make the most difference in their child's life—perhaps a group that addresses homosexuality, religion, politics, or health and wellness topics.

The most successful and satisfied students invest time and energy in their college. Generally, students join organizations because they have a particular interest, they want to meet like-minded students, or they are looking for personal or career development opportunities. In simple terms, they want to have fun. What they find in student activities are friends, recognition, fulfillment, and personal growth. The college becomes their home because they are making a commitment to some segment of the school through their involvement. They find their niche, their own small community within the larger campus.

All the benefits of campus involvement apply doubly to commuter students. Joining a club or organization helps commuters meet and make friends on campus. The student council office or the gym provides a place to hang out between classes. Membership in a group convinces the commuter that college isn't just a place to park the car and attend class; it's where he belongs.

Jillian's mother noticed that her daughter's entire outlook toward college changed when she joined the gospel choir. "As a commuter, Jillian had trouble meeting people on campus until she made that connection. Rehearsals didn't start until seven p.m., so she had to stay on campus after her last class. Within a couple of weeks, she was going out for dinner with a few of the other singers before practice, and they have turned out to be some of her best friends. Music is not her major, she's actually a computer science major, but she says the gospel group is the best part of college."

The place to start getting involved on campus is wherever the student feels at least a little bit comfortable. Someone who enjoyed band or baseball in high school may not be headed toward a major in music or a pitching position on the college team, but he may still want to practice his saxophone or play ball. He can sign up for the pep band that performs for the women's soccer team or join an intermural sports club.

College activities offer a chance to try activities a student might never previously have considered. A Midwesterner who enrolls at UCLA can join the surf club, and the Mississippi native at the University of Colorado can join the ski and snowboard club. The sense of adventure and accomplishment that comes with learning a new skill or stepping into the unknown makes participation all the more fun.

Students also can find opportunities that don't require a long-term commitment, or in some cases, not even much personal effort. They shouldn't feel that every activity must have a life-altering outcome. A Friday-evening workshop might offer lessons in paper making or pot throwing, but it may never lead to a decision to join the art club. The film society offers weekly entertainment for the entire campus, although only a half-dozen students might be involved in the selection and programming.

Often, a student's personal skills and talents provide an unexpected opening into involvement opportunities. Experience in Web design might be exactly what the law club is looking for in their efforts to update their online image. Artistic ability may be the inroad to the political science club, which needs "Get Out the Vote" posters for the coming election.

Ideally, the first year of college is a chance to sample the opportunities and begin to make choices. Students should try a few different groups with the idea that they are under no obligation to commit long term. The second year is a time to sort through the freshman experiences and determine which groups hold the most appeal. As interests and abilities change, students may find a new group that turns out to be the best fit yet. Sophomores and juniors might begin serving in leadership positions or at least doing more of the active work of the group—helping schedule games and select equipment for a sports club or recruiting new members and organizing readings for the literature club. As upperclassmen, students can shape improvements for the future of the organization and encourage emerging leaders. At any point in their academic career, though, students should have some idea of what skills they are learning, or what they are gaining by being involved with a group.

"YOU'RE INVITED . . ." IS IT AN HONOR OR A SCAM?

Soon after grades were posted from fall semester, Shannon received a letter saying she had been selected to join an honorary society. "You're among the best! Because your grade-point average puts you in the top 10 percent of your class, you qualify for this great honor," the letter explained. Membership costs were "only $65 a year," and Shannon would be eligible for "lifetime benefits," which seemed mostly to be the right to list the organization on her résumé. "You will stand above the crowd when you apply for scholarships, graduate school, and jobs."

Students are flattered by invitations from honorary societies and selective organizations, but the question is whether such memberships make a difference to employers or graduate schools. If the group is affiliated with the student's college major, it probably is a commendable recognition to be invited to join. If it is a national organization, the value of the group depends primarily on the strength of the local chapter. If the local chapter is not active, the "honor society" could simply turn out to be good business for a few enterprising students who collect a scholarship from the membership fees they raise.

When it comes to internships, jobs, or graduate school, listing the name of an honorary society may not make a difference. It will help if the group has a historically prestigious reputation, such as Phi Beta Kappa, and it certainly will be useful if the student can elaborate on his or her contribution as a member. When students can talk about their role in planning or organizing events, serving in a leadership position, or participating in some other active way, the value of their participation becomes clear. Accomplishments—not the name of the group—are the important factors.

Before joining any group, and especially before joining a local chapter of a national organization, students should do some searching to find out about meetings and activities on campus. If no regular meetings or activities are scheduled, the student is unlikely to gain much benefit by joining. Some honorary societies provide community service opportunities, schedule workshops and mentorships, and sponsor national conferences on leadership or career development. A national organization should have a Web site with information about its overall mission and goals. Decisions on joining should be made based on how the group fits with the student's interests, not on the name of the organization and flattery.

SEE THE WORLD . . . BUT LEAVE MY FRIENDS?

At the annual Student Activities Fair, a crowd of eager questioners surrounds the table hosted by the international studies office. A glance at the crowd's appearance, however, reveals more Hush Puppies than sandals, more worry lines than nose rings. It's not that international study attracts only conservatives—the group is made up almost entirely of parents.

Ironically, parents and university staff tend to be more enthusiastic about international study than students are. Every parent has an idea of what study abroad will offer his or her student, and that image usually includes the art museums of Paris, the theaters of London, and the archaeological fields of Italy and Greece. Faculty and staff see international experiences as the ideal illustration of all they are trying to encourage: independence, accomplishment, and problem solving.

For many students, the potential benefits of international study contrast with images of a semester away from friends, an interruption to a budding romance, and the hassles of subletting an apartment in the middle of the year. Those students who decide to take the risk, however, almost always come home with visions of going abroad again. "It was the best thing I've ever done," they rave. "It changed my life."

Short-term study abroad programs allow wary students to sample international opportunities without making a semester-long commitment. In many cases, though, the short-term programs only whet a student's appetite for more. A three-week program, guided by a faculty member from the student's major, often is the prelude to a semester overseas a year later.

Both short- and long-term programs are available that support specific academic majors, allowing students to earn architecture credits through a program in Italy or business credits at a university in Australia. Other programs will offer general education courses, taught in English, in art history, political science, and literature through an exchange program in England, France, or Costa Rica.

A learning abroad experience is an adventure, but the level of adventure your student wants and needs should be discussed before a destination is selected. Students frequently sign up for a program while they're immersed in a semester's work on campus—studying, socializing, working on projects, and taking midterms or finals. Although they do the paperwork and make the decisions, they don't necessarily think through the questions they're asked or research the options as carefully as they should.

So that you and your student understand the program and the purpose of an international study option, discuss the following questions with your student or ask for information from your student's learning abroad office:

- What part of the world does your student want to visit? What does she know about the politics, culture, and climate of the country she wants to visit?
- What kind of predeparture and early arrival information will the student receive? Does someone talk to her about cultural issues and safety? Is there an orientation program when she arrives?
- Who will help her if something goes wrong? What kind of student services does the program provide?
- How will she communicate with her family and friends while she's gone?
- Does she have the language skills to be comfortable there? If classes are taught in another language, the first weeks of classes will be difficult and exhausting. Students who meet just the basic language requirements will struggle; students who are in classes with native classmates rather than other Americans may feel isolated and underprepared.
- How will the cost of study abroad compare with staying on the home campus? What extra expenses, beyond tuition and program fees, airfare, room, and board does she anticipate? If your student has scholarships, will they apply to the study abroad program?

- How long does she want to stay? Will she arrive early to travel or explore? Will she stay after the program ends? Does she plan to travel on weekends or holidays while she's there? Changes in these plans after the student arrives can mean the planned budget will not cover the expenses.
- What classes will she be taking? How many credits will apply at the home college toward graduation? What are the steps she needs to follow to have those international credits applied back home?
- Looking at a future career, are there ways this destination and this particular program will impact her next steps?
- Where will she live while she's there? On a campus, in a family home, in an apartment?

The student's living situation requires more than a brief consideration. The study abroad office at your student's college will have information about the options at each destination, but students should not assume that the terms *dormitory, apartment,* or *homestay* are self-explanatory. A dormitory in Buenos Aires will be very different from what the student has experienced in the United States; it may house students from multiple universities around the city and be a thirty-minute bus ride from classes. An apartment or flat may house only American students, and your son or daughter might never socialize with local residents or speak anything but English outside of class. A homestay gives students a chance to improve their language skills, but the families they stay with sometimes are not the families they imagined. They may find themselves living with a newly married couple just a few years older than themselves; with an elderly couple who have an extra room but not much time for them; a gay or lesbian couple; or a bustling family with five children and two dogs.

Students who select a homestay have the chance to gain the most from an international program, but they must be careful about defining their needs and expectations. Marta, an international programs adviser, recalled a young man she was working with. "My mom is worried I might end up with a family who's not used to feeding a six-foot, one-hundred-and-eighty-five-pound American boy, and I'll be hungry," he told her. "I do eat a lot, I guess, but I suppose I could just plan to buy extra food and keep it in my room." Marta was able to sort through the list of homestay families and find a husband and wife who not only understood the calorie intake of a still-growing boy, but who also owned a restaurant where he could eat dinner every night.

Another student, Marta said, was hoping for a family with at least one young child—but no babies please. She was matched with a family with two teenagers, plus an eight-year-old who delighted in reading children's books to her.

The cost for a semester's study abroad can range from a little less than the cost of a semester at the home college to double that amount. Although you don't want to go deeply in debt for your child's study abroad experience, students should not try to make do on a completely bare-bones budget. The student who lives in London for three months and cannot afford an occasional half-price theater ticket or train fare for a day in Brighton will be frustrated by missing some of the obvious benefits of the trip. One of the common problems for students, though, is piling up credit-card charges while they are abroad. They learn that their college in Paris is just a fast-train ride from Brussels or the Riviera, and every weekend they're on a train for a new destination. Since "this is the chance of a lifetime," they buy a ring in Amsterdam or a watch in Germany.

Clear communication about finances is critical before your student leaves home, and parents should be alert to evidence of overspending. You can't blame your child for wanting to buy holiday gifts or a memorable souvenir overseas, but the debts that mount up while he's gone can take years to pay back.

Study abroad has particular benefits for commuter students. Beth lived at home during her freshman and sophomore years, but the first semester of her junior year, she signed up for a program in Spain. Besides giving her a chance to work on her Spanish credits, this was the first time she had lived with students her own age. "It was hard at first to live with a houseful of other students," she said, "but it was so much fun to go out with them, or we would just sit around and talk for hours on end. The whole experience of studying abroad was great, but living with other students was, for me, the best part of the program."

THE LONG-DISTANCE GOOD-BYE

Even those parents who have sent their child to a college or university halfway across the country will find it hard to put their student on a plane to go overseas for four months. All her belongings must be reduced to what she can carry. You didn't get a chance to scope out the campus this time; you have no idea what kind of living conditions he will have. What if something goes wrong? What if he needs you?

Clarise's mother always imagined her daughter would go to Paris—after all, she was getting a minor in French. She was taken by complete surprise when she heard that Clarise had signed up for a program in Senegal.

"Senegal?" her mother asked. "I don't even know where that is. Why would you want to go there?"

"My roommate's sister went last year, and it's a great program, Mom. The classes are taught in French, so I'll get a lot of language practice, plus you do a six-week internship while you're there. I'm thinking I want to get a master's degree in public health after I graduate," Clarise explained, "and the internship should help me get into the grad program I'm looking at."

An Internet search provided Clarise's mother with reassurance that the program in Senegal was accredited and had an excellent reputation. Her daughter would have advice and assistance from study abroad staff in case of any problems.

International acts of terrorism in recent years have made parents cautious about study abroad. A mother called the day after seeing reports of violence in the African country where her son would be studying: "I saw the news reports about flare-ups in Kenya. My son is supposed to go there next month. How do I cancel him out of the program?"

Colleges and universities promote international study as one of the most important ways to increase global harmony. American students who spend time in other countries come home with a better grasp of the connections between cultures and economies around the globe. But is it safe?

Advisers of reputable programs do not recommend study abroad in any area deemed dangerous, and they will provide thorough background information on the culture and political climate of the area students will be visiting. Staff members are on-site to talk with students about local and international issues and to provide assistance in case of an emergency. They will instruct students on how to maintain a respectful demeanor and a low profile, and they will talk about reasonable safety precautions wherever they study.

Parents can worry themselves sick over all the possible (but unlikely) problems, but a bit of careful planning will take care of most troubles.

- Make sure to confirm current travel safety information at www.travel.state.gov and health information at the Centers for Disease Control, www.cdc.gov.

- Be sure your student is aware of the medical requirements advised by his study abroad program. Program advisers should be working with students on immunizations and other preparations appropriate for the destination.
- Be certain that your student will have health insurance coverage overseas. Some insurance policies will not cover international medical care or emergency transportation back to the United States. If the study abroad office provides an insurance policy, compare it with your own to make sure your student has good coverage. Ideally, your student will have a policy that covers family emergency transportation (to allow a family member to travel to the destination in case of serious illness or accident) and emergency medical evacuation (to bring the student home if necessary).
- Have your student assign power of attorney to you or another responsible adult for the time he or she is overseas. It's hard for students to give up their newfound status as an adult, even temporarily, but power of attorney allows you to take care of those transactions your student may not be able to handle from afar—financial aid, banking, insurance, and income tax filing.
- Be sure your own passport is valid and up-to-date. In case of an emergency, you will not have time to renew or apply for a passport.
- Make arrangements for discount rates on international telephone calls. A minor problem for your student, such as lost luggage, can result in lengthy phone calls and astronomical phone bills. Some long-distance phone services provide inexpensive rates for collect

international calls. Be sure that you and your student understand the calling procedures and limitations in advance. Many discount programs will cover your child's calls to your home phone number, but not to your work phone or other numbers.

Although parents worry most about international incidents while their student is abroad, the greatest dangers students face come from their own poor choices. A nineteen-year-old can drink alcohol in most countries, and the freedom of finally being able to drink legally leads to excess. Europeans and Asians, however, have little tolerance for drunk Americans. Students can find themselves in trouble with their hosts or confronted by police for alcohol abuse.

Students who are arrested for drug use while abroad can end up in jail, facing court procedures in a legal system and language they do not understand. Before they go, students will hear from their study abroad advisers about the laws in the country where they will be, but students don't always heed the warnings.

Academic failure is also a factor. Students believe their work will be judged less critically when they are studying abroad. *The professors know we're not going to study*, they think. *They'll take into consideration the fact that we're here for the total experience.* International universities have somewhat different teaching styles, however, and a student may find his courses more difficult than at home. In addition, the temptation is strong to skip classes. After all, *When will I ever have the chance again to go to Oktoberfest in Munich?* the student thinks as she cuts classes to travel. A week later, walking past a travel agency, she sees a sign that announces BARGAIN RATES TO MALTA! and plans another trip. Classes become low priority among all the tempting alternatives. But low grades on a study abroad program will show up on the home-school transcript. Students need to consider that a prerequisite for a future class, admission into a graduate program, scholarship qualifications, and future jobs can all be affected by poor performance in an international program.

DEALING WITH THE UPS AND DOWNS

After Naomi received her acceptance letter for a summer study abroad program to Turkey, she called home to tell her parents the exciting news. "This is going to be awesome! I can't wait. I wish I could leave tomorrow!"

A week later, she was on the verge of dropping out of the program. "I can't go to Turkey! It's about a hundred and ten degrees there in the summer. I don't much like Turkish food, and I'm not sure they treat American women very well. What was I thinking?"

The mood swings that students undergo before they travel abroad are only a precursor to the emotional fluctuations they will suffer during the first few days after they arrive. Studying abroad can be exhausting. By the time your daughter figures out the phone system or finds an Internet café where she can finally send you a message, she is likely to be tired, homesick, and depressed. Just as you did during those first phone calls home during the freshmen year, you will hear about all the horrible experiences she is suffering. You will want to rush to her side or transfer funds for a return ticket right away.

Keep in mind, though, that your child has already made some significant strides. She did, after all, figure out how to use a phone or computer to contact you. That probably meant that she first had to find a shop that sells phone cards or use foreign currency to rent a mobile phone, or she had to find that Internet café and figure out how to pay and sign on to an account. The small accomplishments that meant little or nothing back in the United States feel like major achievements in a new land.

When they are in a new setting, students establish routines quickly to help them feel more comfortable and in control of their environment. They are compulsive about checking for their keys before they leave the house in the morning. A daily trip to the greengrocer to choose fresh vegetables becomes a ritual. They will make special efforts to board the same bus each day in order to see a familiar face in the driver's seat.

As life falls into a pattern, they begin to feel more competent and secure. With every new success, they gain confidence. They learn that local residents can understand them, even if their grammar and diction are not perfect. Instead of the embarrassment they suffered when they first tried to order a cup of coffee, they can now laugh at themselves when they realize they just asked the price of a library, not the cost of a book. They dare to make mistakes, and they find ways to correct their errors.

When students return from study abroad, they are likely to face culture shock as they readjust to life at home. They have new thoughts on what is truly important. They may resent the Gap stores where they once bought all their clothes; now they cling to the shawls or skullcaps they picked up on market day in the village. They scorn the evening TV newscaster, challenging his comments about world politics. They talk for hours on end about the people they met and the places they visited—or they sit sullenly in front of the computer, writing poetry or blogging about their time abroad.

Students are changed by international travel, and they typically believe that friends and family cannot possibly understand what they have gone through. They are more critical, more serious, and more reclusive for a time. Negative comments about home and American culture are common when students first return, but they will subside with time.

You can help make readjustment less difficult by looking at the photos with your student and encouraging him to talk about his experiences. Ask about those routines your student established: What foods did he like? Who were the people he saw daily? Where did he go to study? As you listen, you will see how your child has changed and grown.

STUDY ABROAD—AN EDUCATION FOR THE FAMILY

Your interest in your child's destination can make the journey more exciting and more educational for your student. As Mother's Day, Father's Day, or your birthday approaches, suggest that the gifts you most want are a map and a tour book of the area where your child will be. You can use the map and guidebook to learn about the area before she leaves, and while she is abroad, you can pinpoint where she is living and traveling.

When students are overseas, especially in a country that is very different from home, it can be almost impossible for them to figure out how to talk about their experiences. When students call home, parents help by asking questions that put information into a familiar context. "I went to farmers' market in town this morning, and I was curious—are there outdoor markets in your village? Where do you buy vegetables?" "I'm sure there are no Baptist churches where you are—have you learned anything about how people worship?"

The more you know about your child's destination, the more you will want to explore it for yourself. Seeing your student function in a different culture can be one of the most gratifying experiences of parenting a young adult. Knowing that your son has mastered the train system of Russia or your daughter can read a ferry schedule in Greek is heartwarming proof of your child's intelligence, maturity, and independence. When you share some of your child's experience, it becomes more real and comprehensible to you—something you and your student can talk about and relate to in the months and years to come.

If you decide to visit your student during her international experience, however, assure her that you will not interrupt her academic schedule. Most study abroad programs require students to be in class or working on projects a large part of the time. If she meets you for tea after class, she may need to spend the evening doing homework. And students need time with their classmates—as study abroad participants, they are all working through the same issues, and the support they offer one another is invaluable.

Still, a well-timed visit from parents can be welcome, especially when students are aching for the sound of a familiar accent or wishing they didn't have to miss the holidays at home. By following a few guidelines, you can make a family visit rewarding for you and your child:

- Do not visit during the first few weeks of the program. Students need time to adjust and adapt to their new surroundings. Also, avoid visiting during the last days of the program. Exams, packing, and spending time with friends will fill their days as the program draws to a close.
- If you can schedule your arrival for a weekend, your child won't immediately have to choose between you and classes. Be prepared for role reversal while your child takes the lead, showing you where things are and how things work.
- Keep in mind that you may be on vacation, but your student is not. Don't spend more than a few days near your student, and don't take up all his time any day you're there. Take this opportunity to do some exploring on your own.

- If you plan to tour with your child as a follow-up to his international study, let him finish the program before you arrive. And be prepared for some letdown after he has said good-bye to his classmates or hosts.

Domestic Alternatives

For the student who is not comfortable with the concept of international study, many of the same benefits are available without crossing an ocean or even using a passport. National college exchange programs let students spend a semester or a year at another college within the United States. The Oklahoma State student who always wondered about New England can spend a year at the University of Maine and get the best of both schools. Students can learn about different cultures by doing an internship on a reservation in New Mexico or a work project in Harlem; they can study French in Quebec or Spanish in El Paso.

Students also can explore the unknown in their own backyard. A student attending a school in a large city can tutor recent immigrants who are learning English; a whole new culture, just a bus ride away.

LEARNING BY DOING: COMMUNITY SERVICE

Your son mentions that he is earning credit in his nutrition class by packing box lunches for an AIDS organization, and you can't help but wonder: Whatever happened to lectures and exams? Your daughter calls home to say she's raising funds for the homeless by living for a week in a refrigerator carton. She's probably thinking this will be a great time with good friends for a noble cause. You're probably worrying about her safety, her studies, and her sanity.

More and more, colleges and universities are incorporating

service learning and community projects into the curriculum. A pre-law class might include helping Somalis study for a citizenship test. An accounting course might involve setting up a budget for a nonprofit community organization. A women's studies class might ask students to interview women who are involved in local politics.

A good service learning project will not only provide opportunities for students to examine real-life situations, but it also will include discussion and reflection on what students are observing. As a student's idealism faces off against some of life's reality, an instructor or adviser should be talking to him about his impressions and emotions related to the project. Frequently, students are asked to write a journal of their activities and reactions, and those impressions are shared with the instructor and classmates. The responses from other students can be particularly reassuring and supportive as individuals recognize that their responses are not so unusual.

If your student tells you he will be doing a service learning project, there are some points that he should be able to discuss:

- How do students get to the site? How will they get home?
- Is there supervision at the site? What kind of support and guidance do students have from a faculty member or adviser? If there are problems or questions, who will students talk to?
- What are the goals of the project? What is the student role in the project?
- What is the outcome (a report, a journal, a proposal for change)?

For more information on service learning, check www.service learning.org.

QUICK TIPS FOR STUDENTS

- As they told you at orientation, join something! Try one safe bet—something you liked in high school. If you enjoy sports, check out what's available at the campus gym; if you were in the orchestra, find out if there's an ensemble group you can join. Also try one completely new activity. Can't find what you want? Ask your academic counselor for a suggestion, or ask your hall adviser if there's something you can volunteer to do in the dorm.

- If the group you join isn't as interesting as you thought, quit. If someone tries to pressure you to stay, make your decision based on what's right for you.

- Don't overcommit. It is important to be involved, but it's easy to get sucked into too many activities. Classes come first, then save time for studying and for being with friends. Clubs and sports should be fun, not add to the stress in your life.

- Service learning projects give you a chance to use the information you're learning in class, and they help you become comfortable in the community. There are great benefits to getting off campus and meeting the people who live nearby.

- Think about studying abroad. Most students discover it's the best thing they've ever done. Yes, it's hard to leave your friends, and there's the problem of leaving your dorm room or apartment for a semester. But you won't be the first person to study abroad, and someone on campus can give you some ideas for dealing with the details. Before you sign up for a program, get lots of advice, talk to your study abroad office, and check in with your academic counselor to make sure you stay on track to graduate.

CHAPTER 11

"You Pierced *What?*"

When Social Choices Clash with Family Values

In early November, Sharon drove to campus to bring her daughter home for a weekend visit. When Carla came to the dorm lobby to meet her, Sharon had to look twice to recognize her, and she worked hard not to show her dismay. She had not seen Carla in two months, and she had no warning that her daughter had dyed her hair ink black with purple highlights. Worse, it was now chopped short on just one side, revealing a row of silver hoops lining her right ear. Carla was wearing a long black skirt that looked like it had seen years of wear, although it had never been part of her high school wardrobe. The cute, brightly colored parka Sharon had bought before Carla went to school had been replaced by a shapeless floor-length wool coat, and Sharon could track her daughter's footsteps by the clopping of her heavy, thick-soled boots as she dashed down the hall to say good-bye to friends.

The ride home wasn't at all what Sharon had been looking forward to. She had imagined a long, pleasant conversation about Carla's classes and campus life, but as soon as they got into the car, Carla announced she needed a nap. "I had two tests and a paper due today, so I didn't get much sleep the past couple of nights." Then she slumped down in the seat and closed her eyes.

When they arrived at home, Sharon fixed a quick dinner. As she offered Carla a taste of the pasta sauce, she spotted a round, gold stud piercing her daughter's tongue, and she flinched with disgust. All her questions came out in one loud burst of angry disapproval. "What have you done to yourself? Have you punctured every part of your body? These clothes—where did they come from? And that hair! Don't you have any self-respect?"

Although Carla's new look was a huge surprise to her mother, it didn't seem particularly dramatic to Carla. After the initial blowup, Carla reminded her mother that she began college with two piercings in each ear, and Sharon had signed the permission forms for those. Adding six more to one ear didn't seem like such a big issue.

During weekend trips to campus-area thrift shops with some friends, Carla had gradually built up a new collection of clothes. "And they hardly cost anything at all. You can get real bargains at thrift shops, you know." The hair was a Halloween weekend makeover, and she decided she liked it enough to keep it for a while. "It's hair. It grows out," she reminded her mother. She admitted that the tongue piercing might be significant, but compared to the people she lived with, it wasn't all that unusual. On her floor in the residence hall, Carla said, there were at least four kids with eyebrow piercings, "everyone has a pierced navel," and a couple of students had pierced lips. "Mom, some kids have piercings in body parts you wouldn't even think *could* be pierced. And don't worry about my tongue—after I freak out my high school friends, I'm taking the stud out and letting the hole grow over. It's kind of weird, feeling it in my mouth all the time."

NEW FORMS OF REBELLION

As you look at the crowd during Parents' Weekend, it's no longer a surprise to see mothers with an ankle tattoo or a small diamond nose stud or fathers with pierced ears. During their own college years, parents who fit the Generation-X label rebelled against their own parents' standards by getting tattoos of a rose, a Chinese symbol, or a Celtic cross. Nose rings and navel piercings may have shocked college parents in the early 1980s, but a good many of today's parents helped their daughter select her first tattoo or took their son for his first ear piercing. Nevertheless, a college student's tattoo or body jewelry may still be a surprise and disappointment—not necessarily because the student had it done, but because he didn't call home first to talk it over.

Certainly, there are plenty of parents who would consider any body art or dramatic change in appearance to be a significant act of rebellion, but a poll of parents indicates that, for some, it's more a matter of nuance. They would be more upset if their child got a tattoo or piercing from a less-than-sterile shop, selected a piercing or tattoo that might interfere with a job search, or got "more piercings or tattoos than she already has." For others, an act of rebellion would run more along the lines of refusing to communicate with the family, smoking, drinking, doing drugs, or rejecting family values.

The current generation of students is less likely than their parents' peers to actively rebel against the family or society. Still, they think it's fun to try out new appearances, to use their body for artistic expression, or to experiment with an unusual hair color or makeup schemes. While any significant changes in appearance or attitude could be an indication of shifting values, different groups of friends, or even drug use or onset of a mental health condition, consider the big picture. Is your student still communicating with you? Is he doing well enough in school? Is she involved in activities and excited about college? If the answer to these questions is yes, just keep talking with your child—and keep in mind that you may not be so innocent yourself. As one mother noted, "I had a reunion last year with a bunch of my college friends, and we all went home afterward with matching tattoos. Apparently peer pressure can affect you at any age."

ADJUSTING WHEN YOUR CHILD COMES HOME

For many students, the first year of college is as much about experimentation as it is about education. In high school, students may have avoided anyone who seemed strange. Now, living alongside dozens of new people, they find the differences engaging. They decide that the star athlete who, a year ago, would have seemed so arrogant is actually a lot of fun, and the eccentric who once might have seemed so unapproachable has a wonderful, wry sense of humor.

In some ways, it's like junior high all over again—a chance to meet new people and try on different personas to see what fits. A student can adjust his image entirely from one day to the next, dressing in artsy black for a poetry slam on Tuesday evenings, wearing a business suit for an internship in town on weekday mornings, and painting his face in school colors for the game on Saturday afternoon. And in each transformation, he can still be himself and still be surrounded by supportive friends.

Major family issues crop up during the first visit home after a student goes to college, over winter break when the student is home for more than just a long weekend, and the summer following the freshman year. Both you and your student will have your own expectations of how the weekend or the vacation visit will go, and your ideas will conflict. You might have made plans to stop at a nice restaurant for dinner to break up the ride home, but when you get to the dorm, you see that your son and his roommate are just finishing off the last of a three-foot submarine sandwich. You have invited Grandma for dinner, but your daughter has made arrangements to go out with a friend from high school. "I absolutely have to talk to Angie. We haven't seen each other in months. I promised I'd call her the minute I got to town."

You have been looking forward to having your child home again, but after a few days, you find yourself incredibly annoyed at her behavior. "She hasn't picked up a single dish, she doesn't have time to help with anything around the house, and she's completely self-absorbed. She acts like God's gift to the family. How did I raise such a spoiled princess?"

Meanwhile, your student is baffled by her emotions at being back home. The family is not like she remembered. Things feel different, because things *are* different. She notices that you seem to be closer to her younger sister than you used to be, and her brother is talking about neighbors she's never even heard of. Or you moved the big TV into your bedroom and the little TV into the kitchen, so if she wants to watch a program, she has to sit at the breakfast counter.

She refuses to revert to the teen rules of reporting where she's going and when she'll be home. You want her to fit back into the family; you don't have any intention of treating your child like a guest in her own house. She, however, wants you to convey that her visit home is special. "You said you missed me. I thought you'd be glad to have me back! I didn't know you just wanted somebody around to do the dishes for you." And you, meanwhile, don't understand why the only things she seems to appreciate about being home are the bathroom, the refrigerator, and the television remote.

For families that haven't seen their student in a while, the changes can seem abrupt and dramatic. It is hard to figure out how this person could have become so different so quickly, let alone understand that she may yet change back.

Avoiding the Mishaps of the Student Visit

- If you will be picking up your student from school, clarify what time you will arrive and what time you expect to start home.

- Talk to your student about how much he plans to bring home. You might be thinking it's just a brief visit, so he should be able to fit everything into a duffel bag. He might have saved up a month's worth of laundry, and he may be planning to bring home his laptop, sound system, game system, all his DVDs and CDs, not to mention all the chargers for all his electronics. "I can't live without this stuff for the whole four days of Thanksgiving break!"

- Allow some time for helping your child pack the car, as well as some extra time for students to say their good-byes.

- Since the days leading up to school vacations are usually hectic, don't be surprised if your child sleeps all the way home. You'll seem like the best parent ever if you bring along a blanket and pillow for the car. Once she gets home, she might sleep more than seems normal. There are valid reasons why students spend long hours in bed: they are exhausted by dorm life and exams; it feels comfortingly safe to be back in their own bed, in the security of their home and family, and retreating to bed is a way to gradually work back into the rhythms and pace of being home.

- Talk in advance about family obligations and how you will handle use of the car, curfews, and information sharing. Explain the reasoning behind your rules. Many parents find it's easier to say when they expect their car home rather than when they expect their child home.

- Discuss your expectations regarding doing your child's laundry, what daily household chores you want help with, and any family or holiday plans. If you ask what plans your student is making, explain that you want to know so that you don't make arrangements that will conflict with his schedule.

- Recognize that some of his disagreeable behaviors are not a rejection of you and your values, but they serve as a way for him to communicate his independence.

ADJUSTING WHEN YOUR STUDENT COMMUTES

If your student lives at home and commutes to school, the evolution is no less troubling for commuter families—it may be even more difficult because the whole family will be living with the adjustments on a daily basis.

Like Carla, Janet's son took to buying clothes at thrift shops during his first few months at college. Instead of his former standard outfit of jeans and a sweater, he was now wearing dark, turtleneck shirts and black pants. One weekend, he hauled several boxes of his old clothes down to the basement.

"I don't have room for these clothes," he said. "I'm moving my bookshelves into my closet. I found a couch at a yard sale, and I'm putting it in my room. I need my own space to study."

It wasn't so much the clothes and the redecorating that bothered Janet. Her son had been a fairly traditional high school student—participating on the track and cross-country teams, involved for two years with the debate club, playing trumpet in the school band. Now it seemed like he had no interest in sports, and all he talked about were music and movies. When she heard him on the phone with his friends, the conversations were all about musicians and film directors. He began coming and going at odd hours.

One night she wasn't sure whether he had even come home. When he showed up for dinner the following evening, Janet confronted him. "You can't stay out until all hours like this! This is still my house, and as long as you live here, you have to follow a few rules."

"Mom, I'm an adult," he said. "Most kids my age don't see

their parents from one holiday to the next. You can trust me. I don't want to have to keep you posted all the time."

It's not living away from home that changes college students. All their lives, children gradually move away from their parents. College coincides with the time in a child's life when he is taking bigger and bolder steps on his own. A young adult's separation from his family is a natural and necessary step in the growing-up process.

While it's true that you have the right to establish the rules in your own home, you also need to recognize your child's increasing maturity and all the obligations in his life. A student's social commitments are interwoven with work and school. Study groups, going out with friends, and dating are all part of the package.

When your student lives at home, you expect to rely on him for a few basic family responsibilities. A family dinner on Sunday seems to you like a tradition, not an imposition. From your student's standpoint, it feels like one more obligation in an already overplanned schedule. Nevertheless, while you must sometimes accept the demands on your student's schedule, you can also request some family participation and basic respect.

CULTURE CLASH

Education is not only about gathering facts and theories. It's also about integrating lessons into life. Students are opening their eyes and their minds to the ideas and lifestyles of the friends they're meeting, the professors they're hearing, and the authors they're reading. Inevitably, they will begin to see their own experiences and their family's values in new ways.

The beliefs and practices that they have always taken for granted are challenged during the college years. Whether the doubts students express are about the religion they were brought up in, the family's politics, or their parents' economic status, parents can hardly help but feel threatened. It is painful to have your child question or challenge your beliefs, and it is frustrating to see her take on behaviors you had not expected.

Scott Slattery, a counselor and psychologist at the University of Minnesota, suggests that parents treat their suddenly unfamiliar student as they would a foreign exchange student.

"If you had a student visiting from Eastern Europe or northern Africa, and he wore strange clothes or had an unusual hairstyle, you probably wouldn't be offended," Scott says. "You might think it was all quite interesting. You would probably ask about some of his habits or appearances."

Scott suggests that parents try the same approach with their student. "Talk about what you're noticing and ask your child, 'Is it common where you live to sleep during the day and stay up all night?' 'Do a lot of people have tattoos like that?' 'Does the symbol on your necklace have a particular meaning?' "

Just as you would probably explain your culture and your family traditions to an exchange student, Scott says, you can remind your son or daughter of the way things are in your household.

"Tell them, 'Here, we all go to bed before midnight. You'll find it's a lot easier to sleep between eleven or twelve at night and seven in the morning, because that's when we sleep. And since everyone here helps with chores, we'd appreciate it if you would take care of the breakfast dishes sometime before noon so the kitchen will be clean when we make lunch.' "

College students are not slow-witted. They'll pick up on the sarcasm, but they'll also appreciate that you are asking about their appearance or reminding them of family routines rather than either accusing them of doing something wrong or stoically pretending that nothing has changed.

Students do change over the course of their college years. They are going through a process of confronting their past, present, and future. They are questioning who they are, testing new directions, doubting their abilities, and discovering impressive qualities in themselves. All young adults examine their self-image, and most will make at least some changes based on what they are learning about themselves.

The Five *W*s of the College Years

Throughout college, but especially during the first year or two, students are asking questions that families find uncomfortable. As hard as it may be for you, this is work your child must do. Students are looking for the answers to the Five *W*s: Who, Where, What, When, and Why.

- **Who am I?** Students are engaged in the normal, but painful, process of separating the self from the family. During the college years, it is not unusual to try out different behaviors and beliefs and examine the values they were raised with. Questioning is part of the process of assimilation that must occur for their values to become embedded, to make the change from what they've always been told to what they truly believe.

- **Where do I belong?** College students start to think about how their family's social position, culture, and income influenced their upbringing. They wonder how these realities can affect their own position in the future and what they can do to change their destiny.

- **What will I do with my life?** Students recognize that by the time they leave college, they will want a sense of what comes next. Some students come to college with a clear and unbending vision of their future, but most need to figure out what it means to apply their values through their work and actions.

- **When does it all begin?** When do I grow up? Students express a constant desire for whatever comes next—the next semester, the next stage in a relationship, or the next phase of life. They are waiting for the moment when everything finally will feel complete, when people will consider them as adults at last. That was supposed to happen when they got to college, but now they find that college is just more preparation.

- **Why?** The three-year-old's constant "why" reemerges in college. Students will pick apart a relationship, a plan, or their past and analyze it almost to the point of obsession. This is part of the growth process, and it is connected to the fear of making a mistake with their newfound responsibilities. They are seeing old, familiar ideas in brand new ways, which can be disquieting. They struggle with the idea that life is not just black and white, right or wrong, but that there are many shades of gray, along with primary colors, pastels, and all kinds of tints and hues.

Each time your student comes home, and especially during the first year, you will need to figure out how to fit your family back together again. It can be a slow, grating challenge as you try out the old roles and realize they no longer seem comfortable. Then again, rather than a slow adjustment phase, you may run head-first into a major collision with your newly independent child. More than one family has seen their student come home over spring break and in short order accuse his parents of hypocrisy.

"You send a check to the Sierra Club every year, and you claim to be such an environmentalist, so why do you have to drive that SUV around town? You seem to think that everyone else in the world should conserve energy, but you get to pollute the whole valley."

As uncomfortable as it is to have your child challenge your beliefs and behaviors, your explanation is important to him. In this case, your student is probably not saying you should stop sending that check to the Sierra Club, nor should you get rid of the car. He probably likes driving it as much as you do, but he may genuinely want to know how you have managed to put these seemingly disparate behaviors together. Maybe you respond by admitting that you wanted a truck all your life, but you could never have one because you needed a family vehicle; your son might come to see that having this midsize SUV is a compromise that allows you to quietly fulfill your long-held fantasy without getting a full-size, two-seater pickup. Or you may acknowledge that you always worried about your children's safety in your previous car, and in this one, you feel like your family is more protected; this gives your son a glimpse of his parents' priorities. He still may disagree with your rationale, but it helps to see how you reach your decisions.

You may feel like your child is rebelling against everything you ever taught her. You probably won't understand where his new ideas came from and how your child reached his decisions. Even though your child is questioning the way she was raised or the things you believe in most deeply, she has heard your lessons throughout her life, and she is taking your words into consideration. She will not completely reject out of hand everything she's ever learned.

Those of us who work on campus frequently hear students say, "My parents think . . ." or "My mom says . . ." or "In my family, we always . . ." Students know their parents' opinions, and they care what their family thinks. The student who lights up her first cigarette is thinking, if not saying, "My dad would kill me if he knew I was smoking."

Every college student makes choices his parents would criticize. Nonetheless, you can trust that by the time your child reaches eighteen, he or she knows what you believe. Your words will pass through his mind as he makes his decisions. And even if family values drop out of sight for a while, they usually reappear by graduation.

WHO IS THIS KID, AND WHAT DID THEY DO WITH MY *REAL* CHILD?

When parents leave their students at college, one of their great fears is that their child will change *too* much. They expect their child to become more mature, to grow in intellect, to gain a focus on life. It can be hard, though, to think of all those changes happening when you are not around to watch the progress.

Throughout high school, Miguel had been cynical about athletics and most of the typical after-school organizations. He and his friends scorned the student council members and class officers; anything resembling school spirit irritated him. His own extracurricular activities revolved around drama club, debate, and the school play.

At college, though, his outlook changed dramatically. At his small liberal arts college, he joined the newspaper staff, volunteered to give tours for the admissions office, and signed up for training to become an orientation leader. As a sophomore, he was elected to the student assembly, and the next year he ran for student body president. When his parents visited him on campus, he seemed to be admired by everyone, and he was obviously flourishing.

College can bring on a complete personality reversal. Miguel's parents were impressed with all the growth they saw in him, but they couldn't help but wish they had been a part of it. It almost felt like they might have been the reason he was so cynical all those years; as soon as he moved away from home, he became energized and excited. It was not his family that made the difference, though. In the small-school atmosphere of Miguel's college campus—rather than the huge and highly programmed high school he had attended—he saw that his efforts could make a genuine difference.

Sometimes the changes go the other way. Students can get lost in the freedom of their new way of life. Instructors don't take attendance, and if students don't turn in a paper, no one asks for it. There are few rules, and with a bit of ingenuity, most of them can be broken. And every college student has lapses of judgment. Your daughter gives a hundred dollars to a stranger because he has a sad story; your son loses his backpack; your daughter leaves the apartment unlocked, and her violin is stolen.

The college years are a staging ground for adulthood. In most cases, mistakes are made within the relative safety of a supportive environment, and there are people around to help students pick up the pieces. Not every problem is easily remedied, however—the unplanned pregnancy, the run-in with the police after a night of drinking, or the inappropriate behavior that leads to a charge of sexual assault.

Sometimes it's even hard to understand what rules were broken. Once again, technology adds both to life's comforts and discomforts. Students are being sanctioned for online stalking and plagiarism, and they're sued for online theft. What seems like an innocent Internet search for a couple of new songs turns into illegal downloading, and those music tracks come with a loss of Internet access.

When students make mistakes, their reaction may be to give up and drop out of school rather than work to find a solution. Parents, meanwhile, feel the need to step in and fix the problem. Colleges routinely hear pleas from parents saying that "He's only a kid! Can't you let this go?" Whether it's underage drinking, plagiarism, or lighting a Dumpster on fire after a basketball victory, there are families asking for leniency, just this once and just for their child.

People over the age of eighteen are adults who are responsible for their actions, and they must be prepared to face the consequences when they make mistakes. This is part of the maturing process. Colleges, like society, enact rules and policies in order to ensure a safe and fair community for everyone who lives, works, and studies on campus.

When a student makes a significant mistake or breaks the rules, family members have to decide if they can help—and realistically, whether they even should help. It may be the hardest thing you've ever done to tell your student you cannot intervene, and you will not fix the mess he's in. It may also be the best thing you can do. When students think their parents will continue to protect them from the consequences of their behaviors, they do not feel a need to grow up and accept responsibility. Facing the outcome of a serious mistake is a painful process, but facing it is better than doing nothing—and much better than repeating the mistake.

Some eighteen- to twenty-year-olds simply do not belong in college. If that sounds like your son or daughter, you will want to work with your child to think about what comes next. You don't have to, and should not, support a college education if your student is not going to take advantage of it. Most colleges are willing to defer enrollment if a student decides to take a break for a semester or two. Advisers and counselors will often encourage a student who is having academic problems to take some time off. Work or travel experiences can help students identify interests or decide on a major. If a year off helps a student mature, focus, and develop a commitment to education, it's time well spent.

Nearly every student makes at least some changes during the years between age eighteen and twenty-two. As the years pass, though, that stranger begins to look more and more familiar.

The daughter who blasted her religious training usually ends up getting married in the church where she received her first Communion or the synagogue where she had her Bat Mitzvah. The son who questioned his family's politics ends up voting for the same candidate as his father. Children call home to ask for their grandmother's holiday recipes, and eventually they want all those books, toys, and clothes they stuffed into the attic years ago.

However, the turnaround doesn't happen quickly, and it usually doesn't yield a totally satisfying outcome. Your children will be different from you, just as you are different from your parents. You probably rejected some of your own parents' practices and values, and few parents are entirely pleased with all of their children's choices.

You're still going to enjoy watching them as they start their careers and move on with their lives. In the meantime, focus on the positive. Most parents, when they stop and think about the differences they've seen since their child started college, say that he or she is more independent and mature, more intelligent, and more appreciative of home and family.

QUICK TIPS FOR STUDENTS

- Before your parents come to campus for family weekend or before you go home for a visit, take a quick assessment: What has changed about you since the last time your family saw you? Do you look different? Are you dressing differently? Do you have new habits or have you accepted a new core belief that your family is not expecting? Give them a call and let them know in advance. It's a challenge for parents when they're dishing up the Saturday-night stew to hear their son announce, "I'm a vegetarian. I won't eat that stuff." You'll help your family adjust, and while you still may face some conflict, it's likely to be milder than if they had no warning.

- Expect and respect new family patterns. You have changed since you left home; don't be surprised if your family has, too. With you gone, maybe your parents decided to change their diet, adopted a cat, or started going to the gym every night. If there's something that really bothers you, mention it, but don't consider their changes as a personal insult. Look for the benefits and tell them when you notice something you like. They'll be amazed by your maturity.

- If you have a problem—you've overdrawn your debit account, someone stole your cell phone, or you're failing chemistry—tell your parents. Remember when you were in high school and they told you, "If you get in trouble, I'd rather hear about it from you than from someone else"? They still feel that way.

- If there's a big problem, put yourself in their care. You don't need to come up with the perfect way to bring up the topic: Just say, "Mom, Dad, I need to tell you . . ." (And it doesn't hurt to tell them, "I'm scared.")

Section 4

Focus on the Future

CHAPTER 12

Moving Out, Moving On

Leaving Dorm Life Behind

After Peg helped her son move into the residence hall at the beginning of his freshman year, she drove home feeling overwhelmed with pride. Logan, now a quiet and mature young man, was starting a new life at a prestigious East Coast university. They had talked about the challenges he would face, and he was determined he would succeed. Good grades and recommendations from professors would get him into a top medical school someday. Peg would be paying back college loans for years, but Logan had a bright future.

Six weeks later, she got a phone call early on a Saturday morning. Logan was yelling to be heard over the pounding bass of music in the background. "Mom! Guess what! I just got invited to pledge a fraternity, and I'm moving into this big old house with forty-two of the greatest guys I ever met! This is the best!"

Today's college parents probably formed their opinions of fraternities and sororities many years ago. In the social-conscience atmosphere of the late 1960s and '70s, many college students concluded that fraternities and sororities were elitist and exclusive. Membership was a highly selective process, and more students were rejected than initiated. That reputation was both championed and challenged in the 1978 movie *Animal House*, and during the eighties and nineties, the popular image of fraternities declined to a picture of degeneration. As the 1990s drew to a close, many chapters were reduced to renting out rooms to nonmembers, just to keep their houses afloat. Hazing and the well-publicized outcomes of wild parties, including injuries and deaths related to heavy drinking, turned the tide against the so-called Greek societies.

Despite the continuing media depictions of fraternities and sororities as breeding grounds for both elitist attitudes and drunken orgies, in real life, fraternities and sororities have been fighting back. At their best, Greek chapters are a tremendous asset to the campus and the community. Ideally, upperclassmen look out for new recruits, mentoring them through the first years of college. Philanthropy and campus involvement are requirements of membership, and Greeks often take the lead in college events like homecoming and student elections, as well as community activities such as food drives, trash pickups, or tree planting. Members are expected to maintain good grades; the chapter elects an academic officer who ensures that students attend classes regularly, study diligently, and understand that graduation in good standing reflects well on the entire house.

At their worst, however, fraternities and sororities continue the *Animal House* saga. On a few campuses, neglected fraternity houses have been condemned and closed down, chapters have been banned, or the entire Greek system has been eliminated.

How do you, as a parent, differentiate between the good and the bad chapters? How can you know if the fraternity or sorority your child wants to join will be a positive influence or a negative one?

When Tracie called home to tell her parents she had been invited to pledge a sorority, they were worried. "I've heard about the parties and the problems," her father said. "Tracie is saying this is a science and engineering sorority for women, and the girls who live there are good students. She says they'll help her when she has questions with classes like physics and calculus. But I'm not happy about the whole fraternity and sorority scene. It seems like trouble."

Parents can do their homework, researching the national organization's Web site by searching online for the name of the group. They can also check the college's Web site to see if additional information is available on the local chapter. The dean of students or a student activities adviser on campus should be able to tell you if the chapter has had significant problems, if it is on probation as a student group, or if it has a positive reputation. You can ask for the chapter's grade-point average and find out if information is available on the group's financial status or the condition of the house. A low-average GPA, members who are not paying their dues, or a house that needs significant repairs are all indications that the chapter could be struggling.

The best indicator of the character of the fraternity or sorority, however, is your own student. Greek chapters are small communities; members decide whom they will invite to pledge, and they want to maintain the atmosphere they have created. Fraternities and sororities have a good idea, when they ask new pledges to join, that the student will fit into their chapter's culture. If your son or daughter is a conscientious student who speaks out for social justice issues, he or she is not likely to be invited to join a group that spends Monday through Wednesday recovering from weekend binges.

Commuter students don't often think about joining a fraternity or sorority, but belonging to a chapter can address many of the challenges commuters typically face. Membership often does not require living in the house, but commuters find they have a group of supportive friends, along with a place to study between classes, to eat, and to socialize. And the commuter who decides to move closer to campus has a room waiting.

Fraternities and sororities can be viewed as an extension of the college residence hall. As in the dorm, students live together in a close community; the difference is that they select their own residents, and they regard one another more as family than as housemates.

This call for comfort—wanting to be with a caring and supportive group of friends—is a natural response to the upheaval of college life. A student might choose a large university because of all the possibilities it offers, but she still wants to go home at night to a safe and familiar spot with "people like me."

Still, college should be a time to learn about diversity and difference. Any number of campus programs will be available to expand students beyond their comfort zone in a carefully constructed, learning atmosphere. Even if your daughter chooses the safety of a sorority, she should strike out to experience some of the new and different adventures that college offers.

"2 BDRM, OFF-ST PKG, NR UNIV"

At some point, you can expect your child to announce, "My friends and I are getting an apartment. We looked at some places that are just a couple blocks from campus, and it's going to be way less expensive than the residence halls. I just thought I'd let you know. Okay?"

Sometimes the message is a bit more ominous:

"I missed the reapplication deadline to live in the residence hall next year, so I don't have anyplace to live. There's a guy in my math class who needs a roommate for fall semester, so I'm thinking I'll take a look at his place."

"I absolutely cannot stand my roommate another week! I'm moving out of the dorm and getting an apartment. I've looked through the want ads, and I'm going to check out some places this afternoon."

For commuter students, the announcement is accompanied by a calculation of the hours they can save by living closer to campus, the money the will save in gas or bus fares, and the academic benefits of living closer to the library.

Frequently, families first hear about an apartment midway through the freshman or sophomore year—long before they are ready for it. Parents feel safe when their student is living in a residence hall. They believe their student already has sufficient independence, but guidance is comfortably nearby. In the residence hall, their child is setting his own hours, working out lifestyle decisions with roommates and neighbors, and making his own choices about what he will eat or how much he will study. For commuter students living at home, curfew rules and chore assignments have been relaxed to accommodate student life. How much more independence does he need?

Thinking about an apartment, parents once again revert to worrying about safety and their child's ability to take care of herself. They question the financial benefits, and the issue becomes all the more complicated when lease confirmation requires first and last months' rent plus a damage deposit. Your child is hoping you will hand over hundreds of dollars that were not in your budget, and your reaction is, "If you think you're mature enough to have an apartment, maybe you should be mature enough to come up with the money yourself."

From a developmental standpoint, apartment living is an important step in learning to share responsibilities, identify priorities, and resolve conflicts with others in a relatively safe environment. These are all skills that will transfer to intimate relationships, marriage, and the world of work. The presence of roommates who are also college students continues the security and supportive atmosphere from the residence halls; young adults can work through life's difficulties in partnership with friends who are going through the same experiences and life stages.

In recent years, increasing numbers of parents have considered purchasing a condominium or a home near campus as investment property, especially if they expect more than one child in the family to attend the same college. Very few students are prepared to handle the responsibility of home ownership, though, and for a freshman, it's especially hazardous. With all the adjustments a first-year student faces, adding cooking, cleaning, housework, yard work, repairs, and the occasional household emergency is too much. Moreover, the freshman who lives off campus and does not have the supportive guidance of either residence hall staff or his parents is unlikely to join organizations or meet the friends who will connect him to his college.

An apartment represents independence, but not every student will be ready for an apartment when he starts his sophomore year, or for that matter, when he begins his junior year. The steps from dependence to responsibility are predictable, but they don't always fall in a straight line. If this is the first you've heard about an apartment, you may have cause for worry. Moving into an apartment should not be a snap decision. Peer pressure can cause students to link up with roommates they don't know well: "Everyone's getting apartments for next year. I don't want to be the only junior living in the dorm. I need to find three people to move in with. I'm just not sure yet who to ask."

It's not quite enough for you that your son or daughter is convinced everything will work out. You want to feel comfortable about this decision, too. There are some obvious clues to indicate whether or not your child is ready for an apartment:

- *During the past year, has your child made good choices?*
  Are you confident that she can manage her finances?

Are you comfortable with the friends she has made? Can she balance social, personal, and academic demands?

- *Ask your child why he wants to live off campus. Are you satisfied by his answers?* Most students say they can save money by living off campus. Rent costs may sound less expensive than room and board in the residence hall, but be sure he has considered groceries, transportation costs, utilities, and parking.
- *Are his budget estimates reasonable?* In most college communities, on- and off-campus expenses tend to be comparable, but an apartment might mean a twelve-month commitment.

Students who say they will study better in an apartment, or they can't bear the noise or the food in the dorm for another year, might be surprised to find that life is no better in an apartment. If, however, your child says he is ready for an apartment, he wants the responsibility of his own place, and he recognizes that he will be taking care of himself, he is ready for the next step in the growing-up process.

Although even the best preparation cannot prevent every problem, it will help to discuss apartment issues long before your student is ready to sign a lease. During holiday or summer breaks, parents should be talking with their child about general guidelines for apartment life. Maybe you don't want your daughter living on the ground floor in a building with no security entrance; perhaps you want your son to live within walking distance of campus because he will not have a car. And you can ask your child to fix some meals and clean the bathroom at home as reassurance that he has the life skills necessary for apartment living.

If you still find yourself worrying about your student's leaving the protection of the residence hall, think about what your underlying concerns might be and whether they are realistic:

- *It's too much responsibility. She won't have time to study.* If your child has made an effort to develop good study habits, she will probably maintain them.
- *She won't eat well. She'll get sick.* Let her know this is a concern, and ask what she and her roommates plan to do about meals. You *should* be concerned if she says, "There's a taco joint right next door. We figure we'll eat there every day." On the other hand, you can stop worrying if she says she will sign up for a once-a-day meal plan at the dining center, or if she has a food service job lined up so that she can eat some meals on campus. If your student has done some thoughtful planning about food, and if she knows how to cook, she will be fine.
- *I'm worried about sex. I think he's getting an apartment so he can have his girlfriend over.* If students want to have sex, they will. An apartment might provide more privacy, but living arrangements are not the deciding factor in whether or not students have sex.
- *I've heard about the house parties near campus. I don't want to pay all that money for an apartment just so he can have drinking parties every weekend.* Like the sex issue, students who want to party will find a way. It's true that most students will occasionally want to host a party. At least some of the charm of having an apartment is being able to entertain friends, but responsible students are not going to risk their damage deposit or invite the possibility of eviction by throwing out-of-control parties. You *should* be concerned if your child rents an apartment that has earned a recurring

reputation for parties. The apartment building across the street from the football stadium or the run-down house in the block behind fraternity row might be a poor choice. If you know that your child routinely drinks too much on weekends, and he decides to rent a place that already reeks of stale beer, this apartment will not help him become a better scholar.

Renting an apartment is a significant step, and many parents still prefer to review the lease or even check the apartment before the student signs anything. Seeing the apartment is not always a possibility, especially for out-of-town parents, but the more you know about the lease, the apartment, and the roommates, the more comfortable you will feel.

A point to keep in mind, though: When you consider that an apartment usually combines two to five roommates, the "helpful advice" of anywhere from four to ten parents is completely overwhelming.

PREREQUISITES FOR APARTMENT LIVING

When students move into an apartment, a whole new set of skills are required, including paying their bills on time. Even if their parents are continuing to support them, the bills will be in the students' names and will go to their address. There is no longer a residence adviser on the premises to provide helpful advice or mediate roommate disputes. Before signing a joint lease with other students, students need to talk about the limitations or minimal standards each roommate requires:

- How much can they afford? Roommates must decide jointly how much rent they can pay. Within a residence hall, everyone shares the same living conditions, and socioeconomic differences may not be an issue. A student from a wealthy family, however, might expect to move into a luxury apartment right across the street from the recreation center, while her best friend can only afford the upstairs of an old house eight blocks away.

- What kind of an apartment should they look for? Does it matter if they pay a bit more for a furnished apartment? Are roommates willing to share a bedroom? How many roommates will be living together?
- What transportation issues might arise? Will one or more of the roommates have a car? If only one student has a car, is she willing to run all the errands, take her roommates to school, and be on call for unexpected trips? Can her roommates use the car? If more than one person has a car, who gets the reserved parking spot?
- Are all the roommates equally committed to the rental agreement? Until now, students have rarely been faced with a legal commitment to another person. When they sign a lease, they are legally responsible to fulfill certain basic requirements. Depending on state laws and local ordinances, that responsibility may be formally tied to another person; in other cases, only one student signs the lease and must trust the others to pay their share. The rent must be paid, in full, by a specified time each month. Tenants are required to maintain minimum levels of cleanliness. They can't just walk away. If a student decides next week that he would rather live with other friends, or maybe he won't come back to school next year after all, he's stuck. Roommates have to know they can rely on one another for the required finances.

Even the best-prepared roommates might find that apartment living delivers some major disappointments. The rose-tinted image is that "having your own place" will mean time spent fussing over gourmet meals, relaxing on the balcony, or—in the more upscale student apartments—hanging out in the exercise room or at the pool. Like that first semester during freshman year, though, students face a significant transition when they move into an apartment.

Meal preparation and cleaning are extra tasks added to an already busy schedule. Roommates need to talk about the division of household chores before they commit to a lease. Some students are good cooks, some are meticulous housecleaners, and some are willing to do the real dirty work. Others turn out to be pretty much useless.

Emily was the only cook in her apartment. With no classes scheduled after 3 p.m., she agreed to take on the task of fixing dinners for her roommates, and she offered to have a full and balanced meal on the table at six-thirty each night. In return, Dina was willing to do the dishes and clean the kitchen, and Tammy said she would clean the rest of the apartment. Within a few weeks, however, it was clear that things weren't working out. Tammy came home hungry at four-thirty every day and ate a couple of sandwiches, so she wasn't interested in dinner. Dina didn't see the sense of washing dishes every night when there were still plenty of plates, bowls, and cups in the cupboard. Once or twice a week was often enough to clean the kitchen, and if the milk residue in a glass was too hard to clean out, it was simpler to toss the glass into the trash than wash it.

Before long, Emily declared she would no longer cook meals for her roommates. "With all these dishes stacked on the counter, there's no room for food preparation. Tammy doesn't eat dinner, but she's right there in my way while I'm trying to cook. It's just not worth it. Let's all buy our own groceries, fix our own meals, and be responsible for washing our own dishes. And, Dina, I am not going to wash your dishes—if you leave them on the counter for a week, that's your problem."

The work involved with housekeeping, along with the room-mate conflicts, takes its toll. It is not unusual for grades to suffer when students move into their first apartment. Students typically notice they're having academic problems midway through the first semester. Unfortunately, the wake-up call may come in the form of a shouting match among friends, and it might not come in time to rescue the first semester's grades. If you detect a drop in your student's academic progress, ask what she thinks went wrong and what she is doing to keep the same problems from happening again.

In most cases, after the initial glow of a new apartment has passed, homemaking and academics become incorporated into students' home life. They work out an acceptable division of labor among roommates, and when they come home from class, they crack the books. Most students end up fending for them-selves—when they're hungry, they open the cupboard and grab whatever food takes the least effort to prepare. A microwave meal can be ready in minutes, which is about all the time a stu-dent can spare between midday classes. Standard fare for the col-lege diet is pasta with ready-made sauce, rice topped by a can of soup, or ramen noodles. Tacos, spaghetti, hamburger dishes, or fish sticks are about as fancy as it gets. A balanced meal means throwing a handful of frozen corn into the rice and beans while it's heating. Students are more likely to debate the nutritional merits of cereal for supper versus brown rice with soy sauce than to compare lasagna recipes.

Soon enough, students figure out how to read while stirring the macaroni and cheese or balance a peanut-butter-and-jelly sandwich while working at the computer. In fact, after students graduate, most find themselves bewildered by all the free time when all they have to do at home is the housework. "It's great to be done with school, but now I don't know what to do with myself in the evenings. I can't believe I miss homework! I need assignments and deadlines. I need someone to tell me which books to read. I think I want to go to grad school, because I don't know what else to do with all this time on my hands."

FRIENDS, ROOMMATES, OR LOVERS?

"One male or female roommate wanted, nonsmoker, to share two-bedroom apartment near campus."

You remember being twenty years old, and you know that young adults are thinking about sex. It's no wonder you panic when your child announces that "Ted, Sally, and I found this great place to live next year."

Mixing genders in an apartment still feels inappropriate to parents. How can college-aged students *not* become intimately involved when they're living together? Even the most platonic intentions are too easily set aside when twenty-year-olds share a bathroom and sleep in adjoining rooms.

The questions are: What will the relationship be? And are you—the parents—comfortable with this arrangement? As long as you're paying the rent, you can set a few limits, and many parents insist that their student live with others of the same gender.

Still, it can work well to have men and women share an apartment, as long as they approach the arrangement with a sense of reality and friendship. After spending freshman year in a mixed-gender residence hall, where students shuffle down to breakfast together wearing baggy sweatpants and slippers, without benefit of makeup or a shower, it's really not a big step to a nonsexual relationship in adjacent bedrooms in an apartment. When they select their first apartment mates, students usually pick friends, not lovers.

Moving in with a romantic partner is a step that most students approach very cautiously. Living together represents a commitment. Students know that a breakup can leave them with serious and difficult decisions about whom to turn to and where to live. While students might select roommates in a relatively nonchalant manner, figuring that it's only for a year, they don't savor the prospect of living with a former lover if the relationship goes bad.

APARTMENTS: THE GOOD, THE BAD, AND THE REALLY UGLY

The standards of student apartments vary immensely, ranging from old houses that have seen decades of use and abuse by college students to luxury high-rise apartments with built-in washers and dryers, separate bedroom-bath suites for each roommate, and a concierge in the lobby. Wherever students choose to live, they want to mark their new territory as their own. By decorating, deciding where to place their belongings, and establishing a routine in this new setting, they make it a home. Parents tread carefully when they venture into their child's first apartment. Do you ignore the obvious problems, or make the obvious suggestions?

Rose refused all offers of help when she moved into her first apartment, saying that she didn't want her mother to see the place until she and her roommate were settled in. Two weeks later, she called and invited her mother to come for dinner. "I can't wait for you to see what we've done! We hung some pictures, and I bought a plant! I even made new curtains for the kitchen. You'll love it."

As hard as her mother tried to focus on the decorating, though, she couldn't ignore the stained sofa in the living room, the dangling light fixture in the hallway, and the constant drip of the kitchen faucet. "You've done a wonderful job here," she told Rose midway through dinner. "The curtains look great, and the plant is a nice touch. I think, though, that the landlord needs to hear about that faucet and the hall light. And can you find out if they can replace the sofa, or at least pay for a cover for it? It's pretty bad."

"No, Mom, we don't dare complain! Do you know how lucky we were to get a place this close to campus? We want to live here next year, too, so we can't have the landlord thinking that we're troublemakers."

Students learn valuable lessons by living on their own, including what rights they have and how to get things done. Many young men and women have never had to solve problems or assert their rights without assistance from a parent, coach, or teacher, and they may not be prepared for the unexpected events that are sure to come up. One student called her father late at night, nearly hysterical: "Dad, there's a mouse in our apartment! What are we supposed to do? This is gross! A mouse. I can't stand it!"

"Laurel, it's not the end of the world," he told her. "No, you don't want mice in your apartment, but it's not going to actually hurt you. In the morning, you can call the apartment manager. They'll give you a trap or some poison to put out. And the important thing is that you probably need to clean your apartment. You usually get mice because there's something for them to eat. Sweep the floor, vacuum the carpet, and check the cupboards for any open food or boxes of food that a mouse could get into. And don't worry. It happens."

The concerns you felt when your child first announced plans to move into an apartment—that she was not ready for this step, that it was too much of a commitment—may continue throughout her first year of off-campus living. Most students will face at least a few problems as they learn to deal with the world of leases, landlords, and independent living. They will still want their parents' advice and the occasional practical help, though. They will send a text message from the grocery store to find out what ingredients they should buy to make your famous omelet. Or they'll call Saturday evening to tell you, "I bought an entertainment center. It was a real bargain, but I just realized, I don't have any tools. Can you come up this weekend and help me put it together?"

Your time—and any duplicate cookware, wrenches, or patio furniture you might have lying around—will be happily received. Your son or daughter will be grateful for a gift box of packaged foods in the mail or the occasional bag of groceries or reheatable meals when you come to visit.

A twelve-month apartment lease most likely means your child will not come home for the summer. Although most students go home for the summer following the freshman year, the numbers taper off after the sophomore year, and it's typical for students to stay near campus or find work somewhere else after their junior year. By the time students move into their own apartment, they no longer have any doubts that college is their home. Even if you live only a twenty-minute drive away, and even if your student is in your laundry room every weekend washing and ironing clothes, having an apartment means he has moved out. Your child still needs you! Just not as much, and not in the same ways.

QUICK TIPS FOR STUDENTS

- If you go through fraternity or sorority rush, be yourself. Greek chapters are looking for pledges who will fit into their house. If they don't see the real you, you could be setting yourself up for a miserable match.
- Joining a fraternity, sorority, or any other group

should not require you to do anything to endanger yourself. If you are asked to drink excessively or to perform any acts that feel uncomfortable in order to become a member of any organization, decline. You can find better friends.

- Moving into an apartment is a natural progression from residence hall living, but it calls for more responsibility. Do some solid research before committing to a lease, and be sure you know what is included in the rent and what extra expenses you will have to pay. Are water, heat, and electricity provided? What about phone rates and computer hookups? Cable TV? How will you get from your apartment to campus? If you will need a car, will you have a parking space? Does parking cost extra?

- Consider the up-front costs of an apartment. If you must pay first and last months' rent and a damage deposit in order to confirm the lease, do you have that lump sum on hand? Do all roommates have their share of the deposits?

- If anything seems unclear about the arrangements you're making, the apartment you're planning to take, or the terms of the lease, ask for time to think it over. You should be able to see the exact apartment you will be renting, and the lease should stipulate the rental amount for the entire length of the contract. Be cautious if there are stipulations for the rent to be raised at the discretion of the manager. In some leases, a single noise complaint could increase your rent or even be grounds for eviction.

- Talk with your roommates about how you will handle bill paying, how you will divide up household chores, and how you will deal with disagreements.

- Practice your housekeeping skills. Make sure you

know how to cook, clean, and take care of minor household repairs. Hint: Your parents will be much more receptive to the idea of an apartment if you offer to do these tasks at home long before you suggest moving out of the dorm.

CHAPTER 13

What Can You Do with a Sociology Degree?

Choosing a Life, Not a Job

E very now and then, you notice someone who is obviously enjoying his work—the gardener at the botanical gardens, the chef at a sushi bar—and you think, *I'd like that job. It looks like fun.*

Students face these temptations every day. Colleges spread out a smorgasbord of academic appetizers and invite students to sample a little of everything. Liberal arts program are set up so that students take courses in a range of subjects, giving them a basic understanding of the physical sciences, humanities, and social sciences. With each class they take, they are making judgments, deciding they want to delve deeper into one subject and vowing they will never take a second course in another.

The developmental processes of young adults are also part of the mix. College students are at an age when they are exploring all their belief systems, and the college curriculum is set up to encourage investigation, not only of new academic subjects, but also of themselves. One of the most exciting outcomes of a good class schedule is the occasional "Eureka!" that happens when everything comes together. The book a student is reading for an English class portrays the same event as a painting in the art history textbook, and it all ties into this week's lecture in the psychology of religion and Grandma's stories about her childhood in Georgia.

Parents send their child to college for an education, and they hope their student will genuinely enjoy the process of learning, but the ultimate proof of a successful college career is not whether their child enjoyed his classes. When their child walks offstage on graduation day, parents want to know that he will be starting a professional job on Monday morning, he will earn a livable wage, and he has a comfortable future. They hope he will have health insurance coverage. They will cut him some slack only if he's going to graduate school to qualify for an even bigger paycheck and a more comfortable life in a couple of years.

THE NEW SCHOOLS OF THOUGHT

Colleges and universities have changed over time, and their role in career preparation continues to evolve. A century ago, the goal of universities was to turn out "educated citizens" who could read Latin and Greek, had studied certain critical works, and could converse intelligently. Some went on to become physicians, lawyers, politicians, or professors, but the overarching goal for university students was to learn a body of knowledge that would provide an educated view of the world.

Even thirty-five or forty years ago, the fact that a student earned a college degree was proof of potential, but it did not necessarily provide entry to a specific career. Technical colleges and business schools were the path for those who wanted to learn a trade or skill, but colleges and universities taught students "how to learn." When they arrived at college as freshmen, the major question students needed to answer was whether they were headed toward a degree in the sciences or one in the arts. A liberal arts graduate could count on getting a job somewhere—anywhere—then work her way up in the profession. A student who majored in psychology might qualify for an entry-level position in social work, marketing, or business and advance from there. An English degree could lead to journalism, library work, grant writing, or public relations.

During the 1980s and 1990s, though, increasing numbers of students began to look to universities for preparation in a specific job, not for a general education. They questioned the need for courses outside their field of study and challenged the notion that they needed a broad educational background. A student might take every computer course the school offered and then leave without graduating, thinking, *I can get the job I want with what I know right now. Why take a bunch of classes to learn things I'll never need? I'm better off earning a paycheck.*

Today, students, parents, and employers are seeing the value of combining career preparation with a liberal education as a long-term strategy for an ever-changing economy. Every job posting seems to require good communication skills, and students have come to appreciate the importance of what they can learn in speech and writing classes. They can increase their value to an employer and their chances for international work if they know a second or third language and if they can discuss with some competence what they learned in cultural studies. Still, they want a sure entry into the job market with a degree that vouches for career qualifications—like journalism, speech therapy, computer programming, or human resource management.

THE CHANGING MIND

Most students start college with a career focus. In order to get through the day, the week, and the semester, students operate under the assumption that they have a plan in mind—a major that will lead to a career that will, in turn, lead to a lifetime of fulfillment, wealth, and happiness. They don't dwell on those long-term goals every day, but knowing they have a destination keeps them on track.

As students explore a range of college subjects, however, career goals can change—sometimes for the most unexpected reasons. A student might take a course because it's required, but he finds it's the only subject they really makes sense to him. "I like the way philosophy majors think. That constant questioning, looking for the logic and the deeper meaning—it's fun to be challenged like that."

An instructor who loves his subject can bring a lecture to life and draw a student into a field of study. Matt, who was "kind of thinking about a psych major and maybe pre-med," signed up for geology because it was the only four-credit lab class that fit his second-semester schedule. Although much of the course textbook centered on rock identification and plate tectonics, Matt was fascinated by the stories the professor told during class. "This guy can make *rocks* exciting! The day he talked about coral reefs—how changes in rock temperature and water currents can affect the reefs—I was actually disappointed when the lecture ended. I could have listened to him for hours. I would love to know a subject as well as he does."

The next year, Matt took another class from the same professor, and the following summer, he applied for a job in the geology lab. Eventually, he decided to go to graduate school to study hydrogeology, a subject he never knew existed before he started college.

Sometimes students come face-to-face with the reality that they picked the wrong major. If they discover they are bored or disillusioned by the classes in their major, they face a tremendous letdown. Worse, they may find they do not qualify for the major they dreamed of, or that they simply can't work in that field. The student who planned to be a veterinarian will be forced to rethink his goals if he can't pass organic chemistry or if she develops an allergy to pet dander.

The most common reason for switching majors, though, is that students change. The careful, conservative sophomore who settled on a "safe" choice when he started college now recognizes that he has great potential and does not need to limit himself. His wild-eyed, unfocused roommate discovers his passion and becomes centered. Education at its best opens students to new possibilities and encourages them to dare to expand their choices.

The student who is reexamining career goals has a lot to think about and is probably agonizing over her decisions. Aside from the philosophical issues, there are some purely practical considerations: A few, or perhaps even all, of the classes she has taken may not count toward a new major. Some students must essentially start over or transfer to another university that offers the degree they want.

And there is the family factor. Every year, advisers and counselors hear students say, "I wish I could change my major, but I can't do that to my family. They had their hearts set on me becoming a doctor [or majoring in law, being an engineer, or taking over the family business]."

Some parents truly are disappointed. You expect your child to refine and refocus her life plans during college. A change from music history to music therapy may seem like a smart, strategic move, but it is much harder to understand where your child is headed when he switches from business administration to gender studies. A father complains that his son wants to switch from the engineering department to education. "He hasn't really thought this through! I think he's just listening to his friends. They're all English and history majors, and they don't have much respect for science and engineering. But I don't think my son realizes how much less he would earn as a teacher. I'm afraid he's throwing away his future."

Often, though, parents are not so much disappointed as surprised. They don't hear about the thought process their child is going through until the decision is made, so they can't follow the path of exploration that their child is pursuing. As a parent, you can hardly help but ask questions: Are you sure? When did you make this decision? Have you talked to anyone about this? *Why?*

If your child decides to change majors, he may face an additional year of college, which can cost $15,000 to $30,000 or more, depending on the school. At some point, you and your child may need to talk about the consequences of changing direction, but part of the discussion should include weighing the financial costs against a few years—or a lifetime—of being stuck in the wrong career.

THE PLANNING PROCESS

When Sandra's son, Seth, began his senior year, she asked if he had thought about starting his job search yet. "No, not yet. I can't apply for jobs now, can I?" he asked. "It will be next summer before I could start working anyway."

"My boss's son had a job offer months before he graduated," she said. "I think there are some steps you should be taking now." She suggested that he check the school's Web site for the placement office, but an online search produced only a list of links to advanced-placement credits from high school or placement into language and math classes. The next day Sandra called the college to ask, "Is there such a thing as a placement office at the university like we had in our day? Or are students on their own to find jobs? Isn't there some process to connect employers with graduating students?"

Colleges and universities offer career assistance, but most

schools do not "place" their students into jobs. Landing a job is a skill that students need for a lifetime of employment, and a critical part of a complete college education comes from learning to develop a good résumé, write a compelling letter of application, and conduct a convincing interview. All these skills can be polished in career exploration classes and with the help of career advisers. But career development is a four-year, four-step process, and it doesn't pay to take shortcuts. In order for students to find a satisfying career match, they need to give careful thought and attention to each of the steps. Think of career planning as a series of MILEstones on the career path:

M—Matching: Fitting personal values and interests to potential professions.

I—Information gathering: Determining the skills and knowledge needed for a field of study and acquiring an education.

L—Limiting the options: Assessing the range of jobs within a professional field and focusing on a specific career.

E—Employment qualification: Gaining practical experience in the field and applying for a professional position.

M—THE MATCHING STEP

This step ties in with the self-exploration that students are naturally engaged in during their first year or two of college. As they are identifying their personal values, interests, skills, and abilities, they are developing the very information they need to know in order to lay the foundation for their career. What kind of a lifestyle do they want? What personal talents and abilities can they draw on? Do they prefer a daily routine, or do they need constant challenge and stimulation? And how do the answers to these questions match with the career options they are considering?

Whether or not students are ready to identify a career, most young adults have some sense of how they want to spend their lives—they just don't yet have much experience in expressing their vision of the future. A college career adviser can help students think about and describe the kind of life they want to lead.

"Let's take a look at yourself five years from now," the adviser might say. "It's a Monday morning, and you're getting up, getting ready for work. Don't think too much about the details of your job, but imagine what your life will be like.

"Are you living in an apartment? A house? If you look out the window by your bed, what do you see? Are you in a city? In the country? Is it *this* country?

"What clothes are you putting on for work? Jeans and T-shirt? Casual dress? A business suit? A uniform? What kind of shoes are you putting on?

"You head out the door to go to work. Do you get into a car and drive? Do you catch a bus? Walk? Ride a bike?

"What does your workplace look like when you get there? Are you in a big city, a small city, or a rural area? Do you work in an office building? A lab? Maybe you'll be outside all day?

"If you have clients or customers, what are they like? What are they wearing?"

As students think about the way they want to live, they will begin to see that some professions will support that lifestyle, and others will not.

Career advisers also can administer a number of standard tests that help students understand their personality traits and consider how those characteristics relate to specific professions. An introvert probably won't be happy in a position that requires him to meet the public all day, every day. Someone who appreciates order and routine will not want to work in a job with constant surprises. Similarly, the career adviser can help students identify how their natural skills and abilities might apply to different careers, further clarifying job options.

As a parent, you can help by encouraging your child to talk to a career adviser on campus at least once during the freshman and sophomore years, and to check in more frequently during the junior and senior years. You can also help your student identify personal qualities and potential careers by having her think about which extracurricular activities she most enjoys, which classes seem most interesting, what kinds of homework she spends the most time on, and which professors seem most engaging.

Students don't necessarily recognize their own talents and abilities—or their weaknesses—in themselves. The student who has an eye for design or who just knows how to write a perfect paragraph probably thinks that anyone can do the same if they just try. You can talk about your perception of the ways she works best, or how others seem to relate to her. You may have noticed that she is the person all her friends come to when they have problems, or you may believe that she seems happiest when she's working alone. Her high school teachers may all have reported that she became frustrated when she was asked to complete an assignment during class on a short deadline, but she turned in excellent work when she had enough time to rewrite or check her answers.

Discussing these observations with your son or daughter requires tact. The goal is not to criticize or point out shortcomings, but to identify characteristics as strengths. It is not wrong to work slowly or to prefer solitude; there are careers where those characteristics are an asset.

I—INFORMATION GATHERING STEP

In this step, students are looking at what they must do, what they must learn, and how long it will take to qualify for the professions they are considering. The student who wants to become a lawyer will have to determine if he will be able to handle the demands of the coursework, if he has the finances to pay for law school, and if he is willing to devote the time to more education after completing his undergraduate degree. The potential concert violinist must face the daunting question of whether she has the talent and perseverance to prepare for such a competitive field.

During this phase of the career investigation process, students can find strong support on campus. An academic counselor will help define the departmental major and educational qualifications for the professions students are considering. They can discuss the pros and cons of a graduate degree, and connect students with instructors who teach or work in the field for more information.

Students should also be working with their career advising office. In some cases, a career adviser can identify several different academic programs that will lead to the same career. The student who is interested in a corporate career might believe that the college's business program is the only option. However, depending on the kind of job she ultimately wants, she might be better prepared by studying economics in the liberal arts department, marketing in the communications department, or agricultural business in the agriculture department.

In addition, career advisers can help students set up informational interviews with people working in the field who can talk about the real-world experience of the job. The more students know about the career, the better they will be able to understand and prepare for it.

By the end of their second year of college, students should have some sense of a general career area that most interests them and, if they haven't already declared a major, be ready to commit to a field of study. This is a significant step for students, but it can lead to disappointment for parents who had their own ideas about their child's future profession. When you hear that your son is majoring in sociology, you can't imagine how he will ever get a job. Your daughter announces she has decided on European history, and you cannot fathom a career path.

Parents, like their student, need to keep an open mind about the possibilities and continue to go through the stages one step at a time. Sociology majors find jobs in business, human services, criminal justice, social work, and government. A history degree can lead to museum work, diplomatic service, and tourism careers.

L—LIMITING STEP

During the junior and senior years, students will be increasingly immersed in their area of study. They begin to see a subject in depth, and they learn to apply their knowledge and expand their understanding of their major. In these contexts, career options become increasingly clear.

Any academic major is made up of a variety of specialties. A student who decides to study English in order to become a playwright signs up for a Shakespeare course so that he can study some of the best plays of all time. The student sitting next to him is an English major because she loves to analyze symbolism in literature. In the limiting step, students begin to understand the intricacies of a field of study and narrow their focus to the specialty that most interests them. The choices students make at this phase help them see their future more clearly. An architecture student decides that she prefers renovating historic buildings to designing new ones. The math major discovers that some mathematicians are key members on research projects and others develop applications for sports teams, figuring out mathematically how often to try the trick football play—there are more options than just teaching high school geometry.

Some students might still be trying to identify a career; they have two or more options in mind, and they are not ready to give up either one. "I really like biology, but I think I might want to be a lawyer someday. Since most pre-law students get a degree in political science, I probably should change my major to poli-sci."

Not only might a minor or a second major be the answer to combining multiple interests into a satisfying career, but it also could provide a way to distinguish a student from all the others in her class. The aspiring attorney learns that a biology degree with a political science minor is the best possible preparation for a future in environmental law. Similarly, a journalism student decides to get a second major in religious studies so that she can be a religion reporter.

An adviser in the college career center can help students find a mentor in the fields they're considering. Mentors have insights into what skills are currently needed or are likely to be valuable in the near future. Students need to keep up with emerging changes in their field to see the full range of possibilities, and they can get their best information from a mentor, a personable instructor, or a career services adviser who knows the kinds of jobs recent graduates have taken.

Students can also learn the newest trends in their field by joining a student organization related to their academic major. Student groups frequently invite professionals to come to campus to talk about current issues in the profession or take field trips to nearby businesses to see graduates in action.

Parents can help in this stage by encouraging students to take advantage of the full range of career exploration opportunities available to them, and to take note of the people they're meeting. Regina, a communications major, always wrote down the names of guest lecturers in her courses, speakers who addressed her communication club, and anyone she met when she toured her mentor's workplace. When the time came to look for an internship, she sent messages to everyone on her list, asking for advice. "I'm sure some of them wondered, 'Who is this person and why is she writing to me?'" she said. "But it worked. I actually got two internships—a semester-long internship at a news bureau in Dallas, and a summer position working at the Democratic Party headquarters in Washington, D.C."

E—THE EMPLOYMENT STEP

This stage encompasses the serious work of getting an internship and a job. It starts with developing skills for the job hunt and continues through the process of landing a position. It includes preparing a résumé, writing cover letters, making follow-up phone calls, and interviewing first for internships and then for a professional position.

If students wait until graduation to begin their job search, they will discover they have lost valuable time. A typical entry-level job posting is likely to look something like this:

> Recreation supervisor wanted. Job qualifications: Graduation from an accredited college or university with a bachelor's degree. Two years of experience in recreation work involving the planning, promotion, development, and supervision of a recreation program.

Therein lies the catch-22 of the job market: You can't get a job without experience, and you can't get experience without a job. The answer to the problem is internships, those short-term positions that give students a chance to put their classroom skills to work under the supervision of a practicing professional. Internships have become almost a requirement for upperclassmen, particularly in majors such as journalism, marketing, and business. The "demonstrated knowledge" or "previous experience" that employers demand as preparation for an entry-level position must come from somewhere, and students are putting multiple internships together to meet the requirements.

Students struggle to fit yet another obligation into their schedule, and it's especially challenging when the internship is unpaid and must be squeezed in among class, study, and paid employment hours. "I have to have a car to get to my intern job, but having a car means I need money for insurance and gas. Since the internship doesn't pay anything, I guess I have to keep waiting tables."

As internships have become a necessary step in career preparation, they have become increasingly competitive. Landing an internship—even an unpaid position—with a Fortune 500 company seems like a coup. When it comes time to apply for a professional position, however, students will need to be able to document what they learned in the position. A three-month stint of performing menial tasks—such as filing or running errands—even if it is at a major firm, is less useful in the long run than a position at a less prestigious company where the student was able to build a Web site or be part of the development team that created a five-year marketing plan.

Parents can be helpful in the internship search by encouraging their student to consider in advance what the outcomes are likely to be:

- What tasks will the student be doing?
- What will the student learn?
- Does the internship count toward graduation? Some internships allow students to earn academic credits through a career exploration course.
- Is there a chance that an unpaid internship might lead to a paid internship?
- How will this help toward qualifying for a job in the

future? Is that future job the one that the student really wants?

Internships are usually scheduled during the junior year or early in the senior year, but they can come earlier or later. By the first semester of the senior year, then, students should be starting their search for a postgraduate job or a paid internship. Students can check with their campus career service office for the dates of upcoming workshops and job fairs. Résumé-writing workshops will help them produce a polished résumé, and a career adviser will critique application materials and cover letters. Interview workshops will provide tips and experience in interviewing. Students also can go back to the professionals who served as their mentors or internship supervisors to ask for job-seeking advice.

LOOKING FOR WORK IN ALL THE RIGHT PLACES

When recruiters come to campus, students in business, engineering, or other technical fields might find themselves much in demand, while liberal arts majors become convinced that the job hunt is hopeless. Although students have heard for years that their liberal arts background is the best possible preparation for a well-rounded employee, they grow discouraged as they look at job notices that ask for specialized training or technical skills— qualifications they do not have.

Liberal arts students have a solid background for a number of jobs, but they have to work harder to get a job offer. Campus job fairs might not be the answer, and it will take more time and energy to check multiple job sources, study the position listings, and work to convince employers that they are the right person for the job.

Newspaper want ads list only a small percentage of available positions. Online listings and campus job boards will be more helpful, especially for liberal arts majors. And networking works. The internship supervisor who knows that a student is looking for a job can ask his colleagues about openings and provide a reliable reference at the same time.

THE WIRED APPLICANT

Candidates for professional positions know they must have a résumé, but for college students seeking jobs today, an electronic résumé or "portfolio" is becoming the new standard. A one- or two-sheet list of accomplishments and references is a starting point, but in order to compete for the top jobs, students are realizing that it helps to "show, not tell."

By linking to a personal Web site, students can show prospective employers proof of their accomplishments. A writing sample can be posted onto a Web page; a short video clip will demonstrate both presentation skills and computer mastery; a link to the academic transcript provides grade information; a slide presentation can track a community service project from start to finish.

The problem students face in creating a résumé or an electronic portfolio is that they must create one when they're least likely to have any spare time. If the deadline for graduate school applications is two weeks away, they may not have time to write an essay, gather recommendations from professors, and put together a résumé. When they find out that the campus job fair is this week, they will have to buy a suit, practice interviewing, and quickly put together a portfolio. In the frenzy, they can barely remember what they did last month, let alone recall their service learning experience from the previous semester or come up with an explanation of how their summer job served as a step in their career development.

They also have to remember to take down the edgy video they posted on YouTube and edit out the potentially embarrassing comments and photos on their Facebook, MySpace, and Flickr pages. Like it or not, employers are likely to check social networking sites to find out if the personality a potential employee presents in an interview matches the online version.

SELLING ONESELF

College students accomplish amazing achievements not only through research projects on campus and through work experience, but also through their volunteer and organizational efforts. A volunteer for Habitat for Humanity joins forces with members of the community to rehabilitate a home, and students gain experience not only in carpentry, plumbing, laying carpet, and grouting tile, but also in team building, project management, and conflict resolution. A sorority organizes a food drive and stocks the community food shelf for a month and learns about event planning and customer service. Six students recognize that community-college transfer students need extra support when they arrive at the university, so they draft bylaws and establish a new campus organization. In the process, they learn about organizational structure and *Robert's Rules of Order*.

Unfortunately, students seldom recognize the life and career skills they gain from their club activities and community service. Fund-raising, record keeping, membership recruitment, and problem solving are all skills that future employers are seeking. By the time students are ready to graduate, though, they have forgotten the activities they participated in as freshmen, and they fail to see the progress they've made over their college career. Even as freshmen, it makes sense to set aside a bit of time each semester to document involvement in activities and accomplishments. A résumé for an internship or for a professional position after college should not be just a list of memberships and jobs, but also explanations of how the student contributed to the group or the position and the skills that he or she has developed.

Parents can help by encouraging their student to work on career planning and résumé development throughout college, even if she has not yet selected an academic major. Many of the skills that students acquire, both in and out of the classroom, are likely to apply to many careers. Your child may take a job as a ski instructor because it's a good way to get a little money plus free ski time, but she may not recognize that teaching develops patience, experience with a wide range of ages, and leadership experience.

MY PARENTS SPENT $80,000 ON COLLEGE, AND YOU'RE OFFERING ME A SALARY OF $35,000?

Students start their college career thinking they are on the fast track to a high-paying job, and they will be millionaires by the time they're thirty. The reports of students graduating to a six-figure income are legendary. Mark Zuckerberg started Facebook as a Harvard University student and made millions. Every student has heard of someone who made a fortune on eBay or won big playing online poker. When students catch on that their first job after graduation is not likely to provide the dream lifestyle they were expecting—at least not right away—they wonder, *What's wrong with this system?*

Coming from a generation that is accustomed to instant answers, they don't understand that a job interview today doesn't yield an offer tomorrow. The concept that a job search is likely to take three to six months simply doesn't compute. When they follow up with the employer and hear that the company is still conducting interviews or is seeking hiring approval from the executive office, they think they should jump right into graduate school in order to qualify for a better position in two or three years.

Parents, advisers, and faculty frequently have a better long-term view than the student when it comes to developing career strategies. Students are relieved when parents or advisers suggest that working for a nonprofit organization will be good training for a better-paying corporate opportunity in a year or two. Or it makes sense when a professor recommends a couple of years working in the field as preparation for graduate school.

Nevertheless, the future doesn't always present itself on a prescribed schedule. For a large percentage of students, commencement day brings conflicting emotions—they're done with college, but they have nothing scheduled on their BlackBerry calendar for tomorrow.

Neither the student nor his parents should panic if that first professional job is not secured by graduation. Waiting tables or mowing lawns is not the worst option for students during the summer after graduation. A job applicant needs to have some money coming in, but he also needs flexibility for scheduling interviews. The credentials are in hand, and a job will come with persistence. Positions do open up throughout the summer and on into fall, and students might be better off starting the job search once the degree is in hand.

In the meantime, it feels good to spend at least a few months living in the present rather than focusing on the future. As Mei pointed out shortly after she graduated, "High school was all about preparing for college, and college was preparation for a career. Now my mother thinks I should find a job that will pay enough so I can afford my own car and save for a down payment on a house. After that, she'll want me to start looking for a husband so that I can get married and have babies. She's got me on some fast-track schedule, but I really would like to have time to enjoy this stage of my life—being young, not having major responsibilities yet. What I'd really like to do is go to Ireland, work in a pub for six months, and then come back and look for a job related to my major."

Temporary or part-time positions may not be what you and your child planned for postcollege life, but they can lead to career-path jobs. Teaching an exercise course at the YMCA, doing research for a professor's grant project, or raising funds for an election campaign provide transferable skills. The Peace Corps, AmeriCorps, and Teach for America are exciting transition options, giving students experience as well as opportunities to focus on career directions. As an added bonus, some of these volunteer positions can reduce the amount students must repay on their student loans.

Continuing to live in the college community for anywhere from a few months to a couple of years is typical. For students who are still trying to establish career credentials, lining up a summer internship near campus after graduation might improve the résumé and give them the credentials they need for a professional position. Campus career offices host recruiters and post job listings year-round, and at most colleges, alumni can continue to use the career office after graduation. The chance meeting with a professor or a suggestion from a career adviser can supplement the job hunt and boost the student's ego.

Whether or not there's a job waiting as soon as your student steps off the stage at graduation, you're both headed for yet another transition.

QUICK TIPS FOR STUDENTS

- You will change a lot during the four years you spend in college. Don't feel that you have to stick to the career goal you declared as a first-term freshman. If one of your classes seems especially interesting, or if you meet someone with an intriguing job, allow yourself to think about a career in that area.

- While you're keeping your mind open, have some general time lines in mind for making career decisions. You don't need to have your future job figured out by the end of your sophomore year, but by then, you should be ready to identify a general field of study that you think you will enjoy for the rest of your undergraduate career. After your junior year, you will need to narrow the possibilities within that field, and during your senior year, you should be looking at job advertisements to determine the specific types of job that interest you.

- Don't be afraid to tell your adviser, your friends, and your family if you change your career goals. It's okay to change your mind. They want to know what you're planning, and it helps if they understand why you made that choice.

- Talk to your counselor or adviser at least once each year. Not only do advisers keep students on track for graduation, but they also have good tips for thinking about career preparation.

- Take advantage of mentor programs. A mentor will give you insights into the real world of work. Someone who is in the profession right now can tell you what skills she uses on a daily basis, how she got where she is today, and what skills she will need for the job she wants tomorrow.

- When you apply for internships, look for a position that will allow opportunities for on-the-job observation and hands-on experience.

- Talk to the professors in your major. They know the
  field, they know the kind of jobs their former students
  have taken, and they can predict how the profession is
  likely to change in the near future. They can also write
  letters of recommendation that will support your job
  or graduate school applications.

CHAPTER 14

I'll *Always* Be Here If You Need Me

Mentoring for a Lifetime

The last few months of the senior year create a whole new set of concerns for parents. Your student talks convincingly about goals and deadlines, but you see little progress. The hands-off parenting methods that were just beginning to feel comfortable now feel all wrong. All the self-confidence you saw in your child a year ago is evaporating.

When your child was graduating from high school, you were involved in all the decisions. Now, as your student approaches the transition from college to a job or graduate school, the family role is much less obvious. Students *want* advice, but they no longer feel that they should *need* their parents' advice. They have been making all kinds of decisions during the past few years, but until now, the impact has never seemed quite so significant. Faced with multiple opportunities, all of which seem to have potential both for raging success and dashing failure, they would be happy to turn the decision over to someone else. "What should I do? I can't figure it out. *You* tell me!"

At this stage of your child's life, your responsibility is primarily to maintain a respectful distance, encourage your child to think carefully about all aspects of a decision, and support the choices he or she makes. Unfortunately, when it comes to your child's career decisions, you have three strikes against you:

- You don't know all the details, so you cannot make a fully informed recommendation. If, for example, your child is weighing two job offers, the company offering a better salary might seem to you to be the better choice. However, a highly supportive supervisor or better chances for advancement could make the lower-paying job the better option in the long run.
- You are still too emotionally involved to offer an unbiased opinion. An opportunity that will bring your child closer to home may seem more appealing to you than the position halfway across the country. Or maybe you can imagine visiting your son several times a year if he takes a job in Alexandria, Virginia, but not if the job is in Alexandria, Louisiana.
- If your student heeds your advice and something goes wrong, you will feel responsible.

Students know that their first professional job is not likely to provide lifetime employment. Just as they were advised to build their résumé during the college years, they are counseled to continue developing skills and adding to their credentials as they start their career. It's tempting, and even logical, to pay more attention to professional development opportunities in the job offer than to finances. As one recent graduate explained to her mother, "Mom, you need to understand something about our generation. We don't take just any job after graduation. I only want a job on my résumé that will get me where I want to go."

Nevertheless, graduates need to pay the bills. Parents' role at this point is to ask some thoughtful questions to help their child assess her choices.

- Will the salary pay for housing and other expenses in the community where the job is located?
- If he will be moving a great distance, are any moving expenses covered?
- If he must buy a car, will he be able to afford car payments? Insurance? What does auto insurance cost in the area where the job is located?
- How long does he plan to stay in the position? Is it a stepping-stone to a job in another company, or will he have opportunities to advance in this firm?

Parents cannot, and should not be tempted to, negotiate their child's job offer, but you can play a coaching or mentoring role as your son or daughter weighs the proposal. When a recent graduate has never really thought much about various types of insurance plans, investments, or paid time off, a job offer can present a whole new line of questions.

After Hannah was offered a job in Baltimore, she called her father to tell him the good news. "Dad, I got the job! The salary sounds pretty close to what I was hoping for, and don't worry. I asked, and they said I get health insurance. I'm going to take a couple days to think it over, but I'm pretty sure this is what I want."

A day later, Hannah called back to ask for help. "They have a Web site with their benefits package, and I'm supposed to choose what I want from this cafeteria plan. It's really confusing. There's a basic health insurance plan with coverage for dental and vision care, but the deductible for each visit seems ridiculous. I could pick a plan with a lower deductible, but then I have to pay extra for insurance. And I have to figure out something about retirement or stock options or deferred comp. There's a lot of decisions here—apparently I can even get health insurance for my cat. Can you look at the Web site and talk this through with me?"

Hannah's father worked with her to determine a few different scenarios—one that would keep her monthly paycheck higher by taking the basic health insurance and retirement option; one that would lower her discretionary income now but pay for more of the monthly medical prescriptions she needed; and one that would draw down her funds even more but put her on a good path for retirement someday. Hannah chose the middle route, deciding that she would come out ahead with the prescription costs, but because she didn't plan to live in Baltimore more than a couple of years, she would plan to make up the retirement investments on her next job.

In the meantime, though, her father suggested several more questions for her to consider. "You don't need to talk about this with the person who's offering you the job, Hannah, but call the human resources department and tell them you're considering a job offer. Ask if they can tell you a little more about things like parking, vacation and sick time, maybe tuition reimbursement for graduate school courses. See if they can help you understand the benefits a little better."

While parent input is helpful during these job considerations and negotiations, your son or daughter is the one who must fully understand the benefits package. When it comes to asking specific questions about various costs or benefits, don't make the phone calls for your child, but be a sounding board for her questions and concerns.

POISED BETWEEN COLLEGE AND THE REAL WORLD

Students bring high expectations and lofty goals to college, and as graduating seniors, they will critically reevaluate their plans. Sometimes the view from the senior perspective can be disappointing. Belinda had always said she would go to medical school, but her college grades didn't qualify her for any of the top-ranked schools she had hoped to attend. "Do I want to get a medical degree from some school no one has ever heard of? Maybe I should try something else altogether. My English grades were always good."

Occasionally, a student's carefully constructed plans are thrown off track by circumstances beyond his control. Len was graduating with a teaching certificate just when the state was spiraling into a major economic recession. Teachers were being laid off, and he couldn't even get a job interview. "Check back in August," everyone told him. "We'll know better by then whether we'll have any openings."

And sometimes, heavy competition for the best jobs requires applicants to sacrifice short-term benefits for the promise of long-term potential. Valerie's double major in organizational communications and human relations qualified her for a promising two-year training program at a major firm, but the company would only tell her that she would be assigned to one of three sites—in Phoenix, Minneapolis, or San Francisco. "On the salary they're offering, I could afford to live in Phoenix or Minneapolis," Valerie said, "but if they send me to San Francisco, I would be living off my credit cards. How do I accept the job without knowing for sure where they're sending me?"

Just when students are trying to make career or graduate school choices, they're confronting the emotions that come with leaving the first home they have created on their own. The friendships that develop in college are intense. Students feel extremely close to their roommates and their study partners, not to mention a boyfriend or girlfriend. Campus is comfortable, professors have become treasured mentors, and now they must think about leaving it all behind.

And many simply are not ready to face the responsibilities of adult life; they're still busy enjoying college. The idea of leaving school, beginning a career, and finally becoming a grown-up seems like a script for a TV sitcom. It's a nice image, but what does it have to do with reality?

Questioning Carefully

Everyone's expectations are high for the prospective graduate. Throughout the senior year, all the relatives and family will be asking, "What are you going to do after graduation?" "Do you have a job yet?" If students don't have a job lined up, the questions begin to feel like personal attacks.

Students react more positively when the questions are less direct: "Do you think you'll stay in Boston after you graduate?" "How does the job market look for students in your major?" You will still get the update on your child's plans, but your student won't hear your questions as criticism.

POSTCOLLEGE PARENTING

Some families can afford to support their child beyond graduation, but most are ready for their sons and daughters to be on their own. A few will finance their child's graduate program, while others believe that postgraduate studies are the student's responsibility. There are families that will help their child settle into a first home, but others can barely afford a graduation gift.

Your son or daughter should be well aware by now of the family financial situation. Problems usually occur only when students are unclear about expectations or when they do not know that family circumstances have changed.

Richard never considered finances to be a serious issue. His

family had owned a successful printing company for three generations. Not long before Richard finished college, his parents
decided to sell the company and retire. Technology had changed
the business, and as costs for new equipment kept going up, it
made sense to sell out. In fact, they learned, they probably should
have sold the business a few years earlier. They received much
less for the sale than they had hoped.

Meanwhile, Richard had planned a postgraduation summer
trip to Europe with friends. By August, he was having so much
fun that he decided to turn in his plane ticket and extend his trip
an extra couple of months. In late October, cold, rainy weather
caught up with him in Berlin, and he called home to ask his parents to put enough money on his debit card to buy some warm
clothes and pay for a flight home.

He did not expect his mother's explosive reaction. "You
haven't talked to us about any of your plans for months, and now
you're calling to ask for *money*? I'll give you enough for a ticket
to come home, but that's it. You are not to ask us for anything
again. We're on a retirement income, and we just can't pay for
unexpected expenses. You're twenty-two now, and it's time you
were responsible for yourself."

Graduating seniors probably have a sense of what their own
debts will be after college, but they may not understand how much
their parents are still paying. They are unlikely to know what your
financial obligations are to your other children. They are consumed by the responsibility of their debts and commitments, and
it's hard for them to think beyond their own financial situation.

Sometime during the senior year, or at least soon after, a frank
discussion about debts, payment plans, and when or how you
can help will clarify the issues for everyone concerned:

- When do you expect your student to assume all his or
  her financial responsibilities?

- How will college loans be handled?
- What happens if there's an emergency?
- Under what conditions will you help your child financially in the future?

There will be times when unusual circumstances or your child's own choices put you in the position of deciding whether or not to intervene. A year after she graduated from college, Cassie was working as a reporter at a small daily paper. She signed a lease on a one-bedroom garden apartment in a nice housing complex, and she traded in the nine-year-old hatchback her parents had handed down to her for the red sports coupé she had always wanted. After work, she could swim in the pool just beyond her patio or work out in the building's exercise room.

When her coworkers asked her to go out for lunch, though, she never ordered anything but a glass of ice water and a cup of soup. "And can I get extra crackers, please?" she would ask.

With her monthly rent, car payment, and college loan payment, Cassie's salary left her with almost no extra money. She had been a "poor college student" for four years, so she was used to stretching every dollar, but she was not prepared for this kind of budget constraint. Most frustrating, her credit-card debt was mounting, and there was no end in sight.

Parents can find this time of their child's life more difficult than the college years. "Should we help her out?" Cassie's mother asked her husband. "Maybe we could take over her school loans for a year. I hate to see her struggle like this."

"We can't be there to bail her out for the rest of her life," he answered. "We have two other kids to put through college. Cassie could have found a cheaper apartment, and she certainly didn't need to buy that new car as soon as she graduated. She's got to learn to handle her money."

You might reach a point when you ask the inevitable question: Should your child move back home? You know it's always there as the backup plan. Many students and parents think that moving home is a terrific idea. All the pressure would be off for the student. If there's no rent to pay and no groceries to buy, any job should pay enough to live on. As college loans come due, it's much easier to chip away at the bills when there are no monthly housing payments or utility bills. For most students, though, going back home is viewed as a temporary resort, an intermediate step while they pay off credit-card bills or set aside a little money for the down payment on a condo.

REAL LIFE: YOU'RE NOT IN COLLEGE ANYMORE

The routine of a full-time job brings home the fact that college was not a thorough preparation for life. Sure, students learned the skills and gained the intelligence they need for the work world, but adapting to a daily schedule—one that starts at 8 a.m. five days a week—was not part of the academic curriculum. The group projects in college courses may have taught teamwork, but they didn't provide preparation for having an assistant director with the authority to assign the least desirable tasks and noon-hour coverage of the front desk to the new guy.

College students today are accustomed to frequent incentives and rewards, but their supervisors are probably from a generation that expects employees to do their jobs well without prompting and without praise. The special accommodations that recent graduates might view as "no big deal" turn out to be a very big deal to employers focused on the bottom line.

When Kelly received her first performance review, her director pointed out that her good review qualified her for a 3 percent raise. She did some quick calculations and was disappointed to discover that 3 percent wouldn't amount to much of anything on each paycheck. Still, looking at the extra income for the rest of the year, it came out to just about what she needed to pay her auto insurance, which was due next week—a bill she had forgotten to budget for.

"It would really help if I could have my raise in a lump sum now rather than over the next six months," she explained to her boss. "Can I just keep my paycheck the same for the rest of this year, but get that raise all at once? I have a big bill to pay next week."

She couldn't understand why her boss thought she was joking.

Establishing a social life as a graduate also presents challenges. In college, students are surrounded by hundreds of young men and women who are all in much the same stage of life. In the workforce, the person at the next desk might have children to go home to, be waiting for a call from his pregnant wife telling him it's time to go to the hospital, or be counting the days to retirement. It's hard to establish new relationships at work, and where do you go as an "adult" to meet someone? The bar scene seems shallow, signing up for a church group feels contrived, and online dating feels desperate.

Once again, parents hear the problems, but your son or daughter needs to come up with the solutions. For you, the pangs of parenting will continue, taking both familiar and brand-new forms, no matter how old your child is. If he takes a new job in a city where he doesn't know anyone, you will worry that he is all alone. When she moves into a new apartment or buys a house, you will feel a strong urge to visit, or at least see photos. You will need a visual image of your child in any new setting before you can feel entirely comfortable. When something bad happens to your child—job loss, illness, the breakup of a relationship—you will, indeed, feel the pain. You also will share the joy and pride of all your child's successes—a promising relationship, a new job offer, wedding plans, or the birth of a child.

If you find yourself wondering whether or not you're saying and doing the right things for your adult child, be assured that your doubts are entirely normal, and that all parents make their children crazy on occasion. The mother of a thirty-year-old doctoral candidate noted, "It's still hard to figure out when she is telling me something because she wants my advice, and when she just wants me to listen while she thinks out loud. I will always mess that up!"

You are not the only mentor your child will have during his life—by the time he leaves college, he will know that he can turn to his favorite professor, a former supervisor, and his college friends for advice and support. College alumni chapters or fraternity and sorority national organizations encourage former students to seek out support from other alumni throughout the country.

Nevertheless, your child appreciates you, possibly more than you know. Despite all those years of trying to distance from family ties and become independent, college graduates realize that they still want their parents' love and support.

At a graduation reception for student leaders, two seniors were talking about their postcollege plans. Mike was telling his friend that he had decided to stay in Minneapolis for law school. "I know I'm going to want to live in Minnesota after I get my law degree, so it's only logical to go to school here, do my law internships here, and take the bar in Minnesota."

"Do you really want to live in Minnesota for the rest of your life?" the other young man asked. "Don't you want to get away from this cold weather?"

"Someplace warm would be nice, but my family is here," Mike said. "I'll admit, sometimes I curse my ancestors for settling in such a cold place, but I know I want to live near my family. Can't help it. I love 'em."

"Yeah, I know what you mean," said his friend, looking at the floor and shuffling awkwardly. "I love my parents, too. It took a while to realize it, but they're about the best people I know."

QUICK TIPS FOR STUDENTS

- For the entire last half of your senior year, people will ask repeatedly, "What will you do after graduation?" Don't take it personally. You can use their question as a networking opportunity. "I'm looking for a job. Do you happen to know anyone in my field I can talk to?"

- Do not panic if you don't have a job lined up before graduation. The summer after graduation is a good time to fine-tune the résumé, carefully search job listings, and make sure you have good recommendations from professors or former employers. A lot of jobs open up during the summer. Use the months after graduation for the job hunt, not for berating yourself!

- Do not feel bad about taking a "flexible" job after graduation. You need a job that will allow time off for interviews when they come up.

- Talk with your family about postcollege finances so that you're clear on their expectations.

- Tell your parents you appreciate them. They need to hear things like that sometimes.

Appendix A

The Four-Year College Calendar

Each of the college years presents new issues as students develop academic and life skills. Parents will not always know precisely what problems their child is facing at any given time, but there are some common issues that most students face during the four years of their academic career.

Freshman Issues

The freshman year is all about change and self-discovery. The critical issues for freshmen are time management, setting limits, and learning new study skills.

Time management: First-year students often struggle to balance studying, socializing, and personal time. All are important.

Ultimately, the goal is to master the academic responsibilities, but it is important to make time for friendships. Students do learn more from other people than from classroom lectures, and college provides an amazing opportunity to meet other young adults and to learn about their backgrounds and dreams. Students also need time just for themselves. Some personal time to exercise, listen to music, or read a book just for fun allows students to find the energy to handle everything else in their schedules. The occasional quiet hour also gives them a chance to figure out how everything they're learning fits with their own value system and personality.

Setting limits: When a little of something brings pleasure, it's hard to know when to stop. During the first weeks of college, students are tempted to stay up too late or sleep too much, eat too much or skip meals entirely, party excessively or even study too hard. Balance is critical.

Study skills: The read-and-review or memorization methods that worked in high school are not enough to succeed in college. College classes require that students know how to analyze and think critically about what they read. It's not enough to read and understand the day's assignment from the American history textbook; students must be able to explain how the material relates to this morning's news headlines and what it might mean about the human condition. Study skills workshops are available at most colleges, and they are not just for borderline students. Students who are open to finding new ways to study and learn will reap the rewards.

Sophomore Issues

During the second year, students are more comfortable with college. They question themselves less about daily concerns. Nevertheless, students feel like they should have everything under control, but they know they don't. At the same time, they are starting to internalize their personal values, which often means reassessing relationships; the group of friends from freshmen year is honed to fewer, deeper friendships. All the excitement and challenge of the first year is gone, and the adrenaline rush of transition is gone. The traditional sophomore slump hits mid-year and lingers through the spring.

The critical issues for sophomores involve academic complacency; personal and financial risk; and changing interests and goals.

Academic complacency: During their first year, students learned that they could get by with B's and C's. As sophomores, they are comfortable with average work. Sophomores usually are continuing to fulfill their general academic requirements, and they feel like they are biding time until they get into their major. The grades they earn this year, however, can make all the difference when they declare a major or apply for graduate school. Some selective upper-division (junior- and senior-level) programs require a minimum grade-point average during the first two years. Graduate programs almost always look at overall accomplishments. Some slack may be allowed for freshman-year adjustment, but students who are lax the second year can lose future opportunities.

Personal and financial risk: Sophomores often take risks that they didn't dare to attempt as freshmen and that they won't feel the need to take as juniors. Those who had vowed as freshmen not to drink no longer feel so committed to abstinence. This is a year when financial problems can compound, and when relationships get out of control. They may have signed up for three credit cards as freshmen, but this year they start using them.

Changing interests and goals: All the introductory courses students take during their first two years of college have a purpose. In addition to giving them a strong academic foundation, the courses provide a glimpse of the many different aspects within a single, broad subject. Sophomores are ripe for identifying their passion in life, and they still have the time to change their minds.

Junior Issues

The junior year can be the best, or it can lead to significant doubts—about how the past two years were spent and how the next two years can be better. In ideal circumstances, students are in their major, taking classes that interest them. They know the campus, they have learned the routine, and it feels like life is under control. Juniors are taking leadership positions in campus organizations, and they have friends everywhere they look.

Parents seem to worry least about juniors. They can see that their children are making progress. Their students have formally declared a field of study and seem to have a plan for at least the next two years. Like their students, parents have adjusted to the college processes. They know the financial routines, and they trust their student's ability to handle any problems that crop up. For many students, though, the junior year is when they struggle with the choice they made for a major, trying to determine whether this is really what they want to focus on.

The critical issues for juniors involve disillusionment, regrets, and intimate relationships.

Disillusionment: Students who have been waiting to take classes in their major might be disappointed to find that some of the courses they've been looking forward to are not as exciting as they expected. It can be frustrating for students to acknowledge that they are still learning theory, not applying skills.

Regrets: As juniors, students come to recognize the consequences of their earlier failures. The D in calculus that felt like a victory two years ago—"At least I passed, and I don't ever have to take another math class!"—now looks like an eternal albatross. Students try to figure out how they can possibly raise their grades up to a 3.5, and they realize they don't have enough classes left to improve that much. When they look at the three classes they dropped during their first two years in school, they see that they won't be able to graduate on schedule. There is no way to make up twelve credit hours without committing to another semester on campus. This is the year when students also begin to figure out how much debt they will have when they graduate from college. Until now, it was only a number. Now, as they consider the monthly cost of an apartment and the price of a new car, they see what their college debt will mean to their postgraduate lifestyle.

Intimate relationships: During childhood, children turned to parents for support and guidance. Throughout the teen years, they relied increasingly on their friends. Now, as they consider the future, they begin to realize that they will leave family and college friends behind when they move into a career or go on to graduate school. Intimate relationships feel like a lifeline from the present into the unknown future. Although they know rationally that they have plenty of time to find a life partner, it is still common for students during their junior year to make promises for the future to both friends and lovers or to feel devastated when a relationship ends.

Senior Issues

Seniors know their niche in school, and perhaps they have made their mark by leading an organization or earning honors for the college. Just when things should be comfortable, though, they are sweating the next steps. Deadlines come quickly for graduate school exams and applications, and the weight of finding a job hangs over their heads.

The critical issues for seniors involve balancing priorities, racing against time, and facing the unknown.

Balancing priorities: Students who neglected to take all the required lower-division courses must complete them before they can graduate. They are annoyed to be spending time on sophomore-level classes, but they must fulfill the requirements. Meanwhile, they have senior papers or major research projects due. Every new assignment seems to get in the way of a previous commitment

Race against time: The college career that once seemed to stretch way into the future is now boiled down to eight short months. When fall semester begins, seniors already feel as if they're behind schedule. If they're planning to attend graduate school, they should by now have narrowed down their selections. In short order, they must take the Graduate Record Exam or professional school tests, and it takes time to write a compelling grad school application. Students who will be looking for a job need to be polishing a résumé and researching possible openings. Whether they will go to grad school or into a career, everyone needs to find professors who will write letters of recommendation.

Facing the unknown: With the end of school in sight, students begin to fear the future. If they will be moving to another area, they will be leaving everything that is familiar. They are not just finding a new job or enrolling in a new school, they will also be looking for a new apartment, meeting new people, starting new routines. They will be expected to make payments on educational loans. Even if they are staying in the same town, life will change. Friends will be leaving. They will not be part of the same community. It's time to accept responsibility.

Appendix B

Sample College Budget Sheets

EDUCATIONAL INCOME

What is your college's estimated Cost of Attendance? $_____
Fill in the following to determine how you will fund that cost.

Grants $_____
Scholarships $_____
Parent Contribution $_____
  Which consists of:
  Parent Loan $_____
  Parents' Savings $_____
  Parents' Monthly Contribution from Income $_____

Student Contribution $_____
  Which consists of:
  Student Loan $_____
  Student's Savings $_____
  Student's Monthly Contribution from Income $_____

COLLEGE BUDGET

	Yearly Total	Parents' Contribution	Student's Contribution	Grants/Loans/ Scholarships

Education Expenses

Fixed Costs

Tuition	$_____	$_____	$_____	$_____
Fees	$_____	$_____	$_____	$_____

Discussion point: Is there anything that could affect these costs? Some schools provide "tuition caps" for students who take a certain number of credits, e.g., a per-credit tuition rate for up to twelve credits, and a flat fee for thirteen or more credits.

Estimated Costs

Books	$_____	$_____	$_____	$_____
Supplies	$_____	$_____	$_____	$_____

Discussion point: What factors might either raise or lower these expenses? It is cheaper to buy used books, resell books at the end of the semester, and stock up on supplies during the summer to take advantage of back-to-school sales. Is there special software or supplies that your curriculum will require?

Room/Housing

Fixed Costs

Room contract/rent	$_____	$_____	$_____	$_____
Damage deposit	$_____	$_____	$_____	$_____
Utilities (basic service)	$_____	$_____	$_____	$_____
Phone/Computer/TV (basic service)	$_____	$_____	$_____	$_____

Discussion point: Is there anything that could affect these costs? Will the student be renting a dorm refrigerator or loft for the bed? If there is a cable TV option, is it worth the expense?

	Yearly Total	Parents' Contribution	Student's Contribution	Grants/Loans/ Scholarships

Estimated Costs

	Yearly Total	Parents' Contribution	Student's Contribution	Grants/Loans/ Scholarships
Room/apart-ment decorat-ing	$_____	$_____	$_____	$_____
Utilities (us-age charges)	$_____	$_____	$_____	$_____
Phone	$_____	$_____	$_____	$_____
Computer/ TV (usage charges)	$_____	$_____	$_____	$_____

Discussion point: What factors might either raise or lower these expenses? Is a land-line needed? How does a cell-phone plan affect these expenses?

Food

Fixed Costs

Meal plan/ Groceries	$_____	$_____	$_____	$_____

Discussion point: Is there anything that could affect these costs? Can meal plans be changed midsemester if the student is not using all his meals?

Estimated Costs

Meals (not covered by meal plan)	$_____	$_____	$_____	$_____
Snacks not covered by meal plan	$_____	$_____	$_____	$_____

Discussion point: What factors might either raise or lower these expenses? If the stu-dent misses meals covered by the meal plan, who will pay for dining out?

	Yearly Total	Parents' Contribution	Student's Contribution	Grants/Loans/ Scholarships

Personal Expenses

Estimated Costs

	Yearly Total	Parents' Contribution	Student's Contribution	Grants/Loans/ Scholarships
Clothing	$_____	$_____	$_____	$_____
Laundry	$_____	$_____	$_____	$_____
Toiletries	$_____	$_____	$_____	$_____
Household (cleaning items)	$_____	$_____	$_____	$_____
Haircuts and personal exp.	$_____	$_____	$_____	$_____

Discussion point: What factors might either raise or lower these expenses? Are haircuts cheaper at home than on campus?

Health and Wellness

Fixed Costs

	Yearly Total	Parents' Contribution	Student's Contribution	Grants/Loans/ Scholarships
Health Insurance	$_____	$_____	$_____	$_____
Prescriptions, medications	$_____	$_____	$_____	$_____
Medical appointments (Doctor, dentist, optometrist, etc.)	$_____	$_____	$_____	$_____

Discussion point: Is there anything that could affect these costs?

Estimated Costs

	Yearly Total	Parents' Contribution	Student's Contribution	Grants/Loans/ Scholarships
Medical appointments	$_____	$_____	$_____	$_____
Prescriptions, medications	$_____	$_____	$_____	$_____

	Yearly Total	Parents' Contribution	Student's Contribution	Grants/Loans/ Scholarships

Estimated Costs (continued)

	Yearly Total	Parents' Contribution	Student's Contribution	Grants/Loans/ Scholarships
Unscheduled medical costs	$_____	$_____	$_____	$_____
Recreation/ health club fees	$_____	$_____	$_____	$_____

Discussion point: What factors might either raise or lower these expenses? If there are co-payments, who will pay? If parents receive a bill for services, what are your expectations about explanations?

Transportation

Fixed Costs

	Yearly Total	Parents' Contribution	Student's Contribution	Grants/Loans/ Scholarships
Bus fare/bus pass	$_____	$_____	$_____	$_____
Transportation costs to and from school (air-fare, cab, etc.)	$_____	$_____	$_____	$_____
Car payments, if applicable	$_____	$_____	$_____	$_____
Scheduled car maintenance	$_____	$_____	$_____	$_____
Insurance, if applicable	$_____	$_____	$_____	$_____
Parking, if applicable	$_____	$_____	$_____	$_____

Discussion point: Is there anything that could affect these costs? For example, how would you handle parking tickets? What if the student wants to come home for the weekend, and you have not planned for the transportation costs?

Estimated Costs

	Yearly Total	Parents' Contribution	Student's Contribution	Grants/Loans/ Scholarships
Bus fares	$_____	$_____	$_____	$_____
Gas	$_____	$_____	$_____	$_____

	Yearly Total	Parents' Contribution	Student's Contribution	Grants/Loans/ Scholarships

Estimated Costs (continued)

Parking, non-contract	$_____	$_____	$_____	$_____
Repairs	$_____	$_____	$_____	$_____

Discussion point: What factors might either raise or lower these expenses?

Entertainment

Fixed Costs

Athletic season tickets	$_____	$_____	$_____	$_____
Concert season tickets	$_____	$_____	$_____	$_____
Other	$_____	$_____	$_____	$_____

Discussion point: What factors might either raise or lower these expenses?

Estimated Costs

Movies, videos, concerts	$_____	$_____	$_____	$_____
Books, CDs, magazines	$_____	$_____	$_____	$_____
Dating, socializing	$_____	$_____	$_____	$_____

Discussion point: What factors might either raise or lower these expenses? What if a great concert comes to town, but it's beyond your entertainment budget? What if the team qualifies for a postseason tournament or game?

	Yearly Total	Parents' Contribution	Student's Contribution	Grants/Loans/ Scholarships

Interest Payments

Fixed Costs

Educational loans (some may be due while the student is still in school) $\_\_\_\_\_$	$_____	$_____	$_____	$_____

Discussion point: Is there anything that could affect these costs? What if financial issues require an emergency loan?

Estimated Costs

Credit-card interest $_____	$_____	$_____	$_____

Discussion point: What factors might either raise or lower these expenses? How would a late payment affect the cost and who will pay any penalty charges?

Other

Fixed Costs

Savings $_____	$_____	$_____	$_____

Discussion point: It is important to start setting aside funds each year for future expenses. What factors might either raise or lower these amounts?

Estimated Costs

Other anticipated expenses $_____	$_____	$_____	$_____
Miscellaneous unanticipated expenses, including emergencies $_____	$_____	$_____	$_____

Discussion point: What factors might either raise or lower these expenses? What if electronics need repair? Do you see a difference between computer or cell-phone repair or replacement compared to replacement of a TV or DVD player?

Appendix C

Vocabulary of Higher Education

Every college and university has its own unique terminology. If you don't find the term or phrase you're looking for on this list, contact your student's school to ask for a definition.

PEOPLE

Board of Directors/Board of Trustees: The decision-making group that oversees the college or university. Typically, this group is involved in setting policies and establishing budgets and delegates the day-to-day running of the institution to an administrator, such as a president or chancellor, and to academic officers.

Board of Regents: State colleges and universities may be run by a Board of Regents whose members are approved by the state legislature. This board functions much as a Board of Directors or Trustees.

Bursar: The university official or the office where bills and fees are paid.

Chancellor: The senior administrator of an institution or a higher-education system. At some schools, the senior administrator holds the title of president.

Chief Academic Officer (CAO): The primary administrator who oversees the academic responsibilities of a college or university. In some schools, this position is called Provost, Academic Dean, Dean of Faculty, or Vice President of Academic Affairs.

Dean: Colleges and universities are divided into major administrative units, and a Dean is the head of one of those units. There may be a Dean of Liberal Arts, Mathematics and Sciences, Library and Information Services, and the Graduate School.

Dean of Students: An administrator is assigned to oversee the student life or nonacademic side of the college or university. Sometimes the title is Vice President or Vice Provost for Student Affairs or another similar title.

Full-Time Student: A student who is taking a full load of college credits during the semester or trimester. Typically, a full-time undergraduate student is taking at least twelve credits. Taking fewer credits than full-time status can affect a student's eligibility for financial aid, academic scholarships and honors, and health care or auto insurance coverage under a parent's insurance policy.

Provost: See *Chief Academic Officer*.

Registrar: The official or the office responsible for coordinating class registration and for maintaining educational records at the college or university.

Research Assistant/Teaching Assistant: A graduate student who works part-time as an assistant to a faculty member.

Residential Assistant/Residential Adviser: Usually an upperclassman living in a residence hall and serving as an adviser to students. In some colleges, the title might be Community Adviser, Hall Fellow, or some other name, and titles are usually abbreviated to RA, CA, etc. RAs typically undergo fairly extensive training and have supervisory responsibilities to ensure policies and procedures are followed; they can help residents with roommate conflicts and provide guidance related to the college or university, and they will organize social activities for their residents.

Transfer Student: A student who has attended one college or university and later attends another.

FINANCIAL

Cost of Attendance: The estimated cost for attending school for a year. The cost of attendance includes tuition and fees, books, supplies, room and board, transportation, and an estimate of other personal costs.

Family Contribution: An estimation from the college or university of the amount the family should pay toward a student's Cost of Attendance.

Financial Aid/Financial Aid Package: Grants/loans/scholarships/work-study.

Financial Need: The total amount of money the college or university determines that your student requires in financial assistance. That amount is further broken down to reflect scholarships, grants, loans, and student jobs.

FAFSA or Free Application for Federal Student Aid: A form distributed by the U.S. Department of Education to collect information used to determine a student's need for federal financial aid. See www.fafsa.ed.gov/.

Grant: A grant is financial aid that does not have to be repaid.

Work-Study: Student jobs funded through the U.S. government's Federal Work-Study Program that allow students to work on or near campus in order to help pay their college expenses. Work-study is packaged into a student's financial aid award and usually specifies the number of hours a student may work during the semester or the year in a work-study position.

ACADEMICS

Academic Adviser: A staff member or member of the faculty who provides academic advice to students and guides them through the requirements for graduation.

Adjunct Faculty: Faculty members who are hired to teach a specific class; often these are part-time instructors who have full-time jobs in the field they're teaching.

Advanced Placement (AP) Courses: Academically challenging courses taken during high school that prepare students for challenging examinations in the course subjects. If students achieve a specified score on the tests, a college or university may grant college credits for the courses.

Associate Degree: A college degree that requires less than four years of full-time college study; it usually takes two years to earn an associate degree.

Auditing: Registering for a course in order to attend classes without receiving credit or grades.

Bachelor's Degree: Also called a baccalaureate degree, this degree is awarded for the equivalent of four years of college work.

Commencement: Graduation from college.

Community Service/Service Learning, Co-Curricular Learning: Experiences that take students out of the classroom to apply their education in the community. A service learning experience should include active participation along with critical reflection under the guidance of an instructor or supervisor.

Convocation: A campus-wide gathering. The term often applies to a celebration at the beginning of the academic year.

Credit or Credit Hour: College courses are generally described in terms of the number of hours of instruction per week. Students qualify to graduate by earning a specified number of credits; colleges and universities define the number of overall credits as well as the number of credits in a major or minor and in required areas of study.

Curve Grading: Awarding grades based on the overall performance of students in the class. The student with the most questions answered correctly will receive an A; the student with the fewest right answers will fail. Typically, instructors use a "bell curve," awarding the majority of students a C grade, with a few students receiving the A's and F's on the outer side of the bell-shaped curve.

Dean's List: A list of high-achieving students who have earned a specified overall grade-point average during a term. The list is issued by the dean of the college or department.

Distance Learning: College courses can be offered through distance learning by providing instruction via Internet, video, cable television, correspondence, or at off-campus sites via closed-circuit or satellite broadcast.

Double Major: Students can elect to fulfill the requirements of two majors simultaneously.

Early-Action Admission: An application process that allows students to apply and be notified of an admission decision before the school's regular notification dates. Under early-action plans, a student is not obligated to attend the institution and can defer committing to the school until hearing from other colleges and universities.

Early-Decision Admission: An application process that notifies students of an admission decision much earlier than the regular admission deadline. Students who apply under this plan and are accepted agree to withdraw their application from other schools and commit to attending the early-decision school.

Elective: A course that a student may choose to take, but that is not among the courses required for the student's major.

Family Educational Rights and Privacy Act (FERPA): A federal law that protects the privacy of student educational records. At the college level, this law stipulates that responsibility for student records transfers to students. See www.ed.gov/policy/gen/guid/fpco/ferpa/index.html.

Grade Point Average (GPA): The numerical average of a student's grades for the semester or for the entire college record. The GPA is determined by converting the letter grade for each course to a number (A = 4, B = 3, C = 2, D = 1, and F = 0); multiplying the numerical grade by the number of credits offered for that course; totaling the scores for all courses, then dividing by the overall number of credit hours earned.

Incomplete: A grade registered on the student's transcript indicating the student has not met all the requirements of the course. An incomplete is considered a temporary grade; if the class is not completed within a specified time, the grade will become an F.

Independent Study: A course designed under the direction of a faculty member, usually providing more specific investigation of a topic than is offered in a traditional college course.

Internship: A work opportunity allowing students to practice professional skills in a supervised setting. Internships may be offered with or without pay and with or without college credit.

Learning Center or Learning Commons: A center on campus providing assistance in academic areas or study skills. It may include tutoring, online resources, or workshops. Assistance is offered in such areas as reading, writing, math, and sciences, as well as note taking, studying, time management, and test taking.

Major: An academic area that a student chooses as a primary field of study. A certain number of credits are required to be earned within the major in order to graduate.

Master's Degree: A degree requiring the equivalent of one or two additional years of study after the bachelor's or undergraduate degree. In a master's program, students focus more specifically on a field of study.

Midterm Exam: An examination taken about halfway through the semester or trimester.

Minor: An academic area that a student may choose to take several classes in. It does not require as many credit hours as a major but allows a student to put some emphasis on an area outside the major.

Orientation: An introduction to college life. Orientation programs are common for new students, and many colleges and universities also offer orientation programs for parents, for international students, and for transfer students. The programs generally address academic, social, and emotional aspects of starting college, and students frequently register for their first semester's classes at orientation.

Pass/Fail: A system of grading that does not award letter or numerical grades but indicates whether a student has done passing or failing work.

Portfolio: A collection of student work that presents examples of papers or projects. It allows students both to present examples of their work and to reflect on their knowledge and abilities.

Prerequisite: A course or a requirement that must be completed before a student is allowed to register for a more advanced course or to qualify for a program or major.

Probation: A designation indicating that a student's work is not satisfactory. A set of conditions is imposed for students to improve performance by a designated time. Failure to meet conditions will result in expulsion from the school or the program.

Registration: The process of selecting and enrolling in courses.

Rolling Admission: The process of reviewing and making decisions on admission applications as they arrive rather than enforcing application deadlines after which no further decisions will be made.

Semester/Trimester: The academic calendar is broken into terms of study. Schools are either on a semester system, with two semesters making up a year of study, or a trimester system, where the year is divided into three periods of study.

Seminar: A small class, usually focused on a specialized topic that relies heavily on discussions rather than lectures.

Study Abroad: A program where students earn college credit while studying in another country. Programs may be a few weeks, over the summer, a full semester, or an entire year.

Syllabus: An outline and description of a course, usually handed out on the first day of class. The syllabus provides contact information for the instructor and office hours. It also describes the instructor's expectations for the course and gives an overview of topics that will be covered, required and recommended readings, grading policies, and a schedule of tests and due dates for papers or projects.

Transcript: A list of courses the student has taken, grades for each course, and the number of credits earned. The transcript is the formal record of a student's education and upon graduation, it will reflect the successful completion of a degree from the institution.

Tuition: The amount of money charged for courses. Tuition is only one part of the college bill; students will also be billed for fees (including technology fees, student services fees, and sometimes separate course fees), and those who live on campus will be charged for room and board to cover dormitory and dining costs. Other costs may not show up on the college bill but will still be required, such as books and supplies.

Withdrawal: An official process for dropping out of a class or leaving the institution without completing requirements.

Bibliography

American College Health Association. "Meningitis on Campus." www
.acha.org/projects_programs/meningitis/disease_infocfm#overview
(accessed May 25, 2008).

American College Health Association. *National College Health Assessment: Reference Group Executive Summary Fall 2007.* www.acha-ncha.org/docs/ ACHA-NCHA_Reference_Group_ExecutiveSummary_Fall2007.pdf (accessed May 17, 2008).

American Demographics. "Fast Track." April 2001, p. 24.

Arnett, J. J. and J. L. Tanner. *Emerging Adults in America: Coming of Age in the 21st Century.* Washington, D.C.: American Psychological Association, 2006.

Arria, Amelia M., et al. "High School Drinking Mediates the Relationship Between Parental Monitoring and College Drinking: A Longitudinal Analysis." 2008. www.substanceabusepolicy.com/content/3/1/6 (accessed July 5, 2008).

Aseltine, Robert, Susan Gore, Mary Ellen Colton, and B. Lin. "Life After High School: Development, Stress, and Well-Being," in Gotlib and Wheaton, eds., *Stress and Adversity over the Life Course.* Cambridge: Cambridge University Press, 1997, pp. 197–214.

Astin, Alexander W., and G. Erlandson. *Four Critical Years Revisited.* San Francisco: Jossey-Bass, 1993.

Boynton Health Service. *2007 College Health Survey Report: Sexual Health.* University of Minnesota, October 2007.

Bowlby, J. *A Secure Base: Parent-Child Attachment and Healthy Human Development.* New York: Basic Books, 1988.

Burtley, Cleo. "Benefit Helps Parents with College Process." *Business Insurance* 34 (Sept. 2000): 3.

BusinessWeek. "Working Toward a Major in Debt." Sept. 25, 2000.

Carey, Kevin. *A Matter of Degrees: Improving Graduation Rates in Four-Year Colleges and Universities.* Washington, D.C.: Education Trust, 2004. www2.edtrust.org/NR/rdonlyres/11B4283F-104E-4511-B0CA-1D3023231157/0/highered.pdf (accessed May 21, 2008.)

Carney-Hall, Karla C., ed. *Managing Parent Partnerships: Maximizing Influence, Minimizing Interference, and Focusing on Student Success.* San Francisco: Jossey-Bass, 2008. New Directions for Student Services, No. 122.

Carter, Gertrude, and Jeffrey Winseman. "A Prescription for Healing the Whole Student. *Chronicle of Higher Education* 47:47 (Aug. 3, 2001): B24.

Centers for Disease Control and Prevention. "Youth Risk Behavior Surveillance—United States, 2005." Surveillance Summaries, June 9, 2006. MMWR 2006;55 (No. SS-5).

Chickering, Arthur W., and Linda Reisser. *Education and Identity.* San Francisco: Jossey-Bass, 1993.

Coburn, Karen L. "Organizing a Ground Crew for Today's Helicopter Parents." *About Campus.* Washington, D.C. American College Personnel Association, 2006.

College Board. *Trends in College Pricing.* 2006. www.collegeboard.com/prod_downloads/press/cost06/trends_college_pricing_06.pdf (accessed July 5, 2008).

College Board. "Students Relying More Heavily on Private Lenders." 2006. www.collegeboard.com/prod_downloads/press/cost06/student_debt_06.pdf (accessed July 5, 2008).

Crary, David. "Police Take Cyberstalking More Seriously." *Nando Times.* July 2, 2001.

Credit Sense: Responsible Selling and Use of Personal Debt Project. St. Paul, Minn.: Saint Paul Foundation, 2003.

Daniel, Bonnie, and B. Ross Scott. *Consumers, Adversaries, and Partners: Working with the Families of Undergraduates.* San Francisco: Jossey-Bass, 2001.

Davis, Barbara D. "Encouraging Commuter Student Connectivity." *Business Communication Quarterly.* June 1999, pp. 74–78.

Dobkin, Rachel, and Shana Sippy. *The College Woman's Handbook: Educating Ourselves.* New York: Workman Publishing Co., 1995.

Evans, Nancy J., Deanna S. Forney, and Florence Guido-Dibrito. *Student*

Development in College: Theory, Research, and Practice. San Francisco: Jossey-Bass, 1998.

Fahey, Marge. "Checks and Balances," *Insight on the News*. June 4, 2001, p. 31.

Fisher, Bonnie S., Francis T. Cullen, and Michael G. Turner. *The Sexual Victimization of College Women*. U.S. Department of Justice. Dec. 2000.

Futurist, The. "The Web-Connected Generation." Sept. 2001, p. 9.

Gerdes, Eugenia. "Managing Time in a Liberal Education." *AAC&U's Liberal Education*. Spring 2001, pp. 52–57.

Gordon, Virginia N. *The Undecided College Student: An Academic and Career Advising Challenge*. Springfield, Ill.: Charles C. Thomas, 1984.

Higher Education Research Institute. *The American Freshman: National Norms for Fall 2007*. 2008. www.gseis.ucla.edu/heri/PDFs/pubs/briefs/brief-012408-07FreshmanNorms.pdf (accessed February 6, 2008).

Hirsch, Glenn. *Helping College Students Succeed: A Model for Effective Intervention*. New York: Routledge, 2001.

Hoover, Eric. "The Lure of Easy Credit Leaves More Students Struggling With Debt." *Chronicle of Higher Education*, June 15, 2001, p. A35–36.

Howe, Neil, and William Straus. *Millennials Rising: The Next Great Generation*. New York: Vintage Books, 2000.

———. *Millennials Go to College. Strategies for a New Generation on Campus*. American Association of College Registrars, 2003.

Internal Medicine Alert. "Meningococcal Infection in College Students." Sept. 29, 2001, p. 140.

Jamison, Kay Redfield. *Night Falls Fast: Understanding Suicide*. New York: Vintage Books, 1999.

Keeling, R., ed. *Learning Reconsidered: A Campus-Wide Focus on the Student Experience*. Washington, D.C.: National Association of Student Personnel Administrators and American College Personnel Association, 2004.

Kellogg, Alex P. " 'Safe Sex Fatigue' Grows Among Gay Students." *Chronicle of Higher Education*, Jan. 18, 2002, pp. A37–38.

Keppler, A., R. Mullendore, and A. Carey. *Partnering with the Parents of Today's College Students*. Washington, D.C.: National Association of Student Personnel Administrators, 2005.

Kissee, James E., Stanley D. Murphy, Gloria L Bonner, and Laura C. Murley. "Effects of Family Origin Dynamics on College Freshmen." *College Student Journal* 34:2 (2000): 172.

Kobliner, Beth. *Get a Financial Life: Personal Finance in Your Twenties and Thirties*. New York: Simon and Schuster, 1996.

Kuh, George D. *Student Learning Outside the Classroom: Transcending Artificial Boundaries*. Washington, D.C.: U.S. Department of Education, Office of Educational Research and Improvement, Educational Resources Information Center, 1994.

Leibman-Smith, Joan. "Is It September Yet? Even the Best Kids Can Get Ugly as Senior Year Ends." *Newsweek*, May 14, 2001, p. 61.

Light, Richard. *Making the Most of College: Students Speak Their Minds*. Cambridge, Mass.: Harvard University Press, 2004.

Luzzo, Darrell Anthony. *Career Counseling of College Students: An Empirical Guide to Strategies That Work*. Washington, D.C.: American Psychological Association, 2000.

MacDonald, G. Jeffrey. "Parents Learn to Say Goodbye." *USAToday*, Sept. 12, 2007, p. D5.

Marklein, Mary Beth. "Students Apply but Not to a Dozen Colleges." *USA Today*, April 8, 2007.

Maslow, Abraham. *The Farther Reaches of Human Nature*. New York: Viking, 1971.

McGuire, Kara. "Credit Card Rewards: Upon Further Inspection . . ." *Minneapolis-St. Paul Star Tribune*, June 7, 2008. www.startribune.com/lifestyle/yourmoney/19609349.html?location_refer=$sectionName (accessed June 8, 2008).

———. "What College Graduates Need to Know About Money." *Minneapolis-St. Paul Star Tribune*, May 24, 2008. www.startribune.com/lifestyle/yourmoney/19218044.html?location_refer=$sectionName (accessed May 24, 2008).

Mincer, Jilian. "Post-College Coverage." *Wall Street Journal*, April 20, 2008. http://online.wsj.com/article/SB120865139014228955.html (accessed July 26, 2008).

National Center for Public Policy and Higher Education. *Measuring Up 2000: The State-by-State Report Card for Higher Education*. http://measuringup2000.highereducation.org/completion.cfm (accessed July 5, 2008).

National Institute on Alcohol Abuse and Alcoholism. "A Call to Action: Changing the Culture of Drinking at U.S. Colleges," 2008. www.collegedrinkingprevention.gov.

National Institute on Drug Abuse. "Monitoring the Future: National Results on Adolescent Drug Use." 2007. http://monitoringthefuture.org/pubs/monographs/overview2007.pdf (accessed July 4, 2008),

———. "NIDA Info Facts: High School and Youth Trends." December 2007. www.drugabuse.gov/pdf/infofacts/HSYouthTrends07.pdf (accessed July 4, 2008).

———. Quarterly Report, 2008. *Potency Monitoring Project, Report 100*, Dec. 16, 2007 to March 15, 2008. www.whitehousedrugpolicy.gov/pdf/Full PotencyReports.pdf (accessed June 13, 2008).

National Survey of Student Engagement. *Experiences That Matter: Enhancing Student Learning and Success*. 2007. http://nsse.iub.edu/NSSE%5F2007%5FAnnual%5FReport/docs/withhold/NSSE_2007_Annual_Report.pdf (accessed Feb. 7, 2008).

Nellie Mae. "Undergraduate Students and Credit Cards in 2004: An Analysis of Usage Rates and Trends." United State General Accounting Office, 2005. www.nelliemae.com/pdf/ccstudy_2005.pdf (accessed June 21, 2008).

Nelson, Wendy L., Honore M. Hughes, Barry Katz, and H. Russell Searight. "Anorexic Eating Attitudes and Behaviors of Male and Female College Students." *Adolescence* 34 (Fall 1999): 621.

Newton, Fred B. "The New Student." *About Campus* 5:5 (Nov.–Dec. 2000): 8–15.

Office of National Drug Control Policy, Executive Office of the President. "Teen Marijuana Use Worsens Depression: An Analysis of Recent Data Shows 'Self-Medicating' Could Actually Make Things Worse." May 2008, p. 2. www.whitehousedrugpolicy.gov/news/press08/marij_mental_hlth.pdf (downloaded June 13, 2008).

O'Malley, Patrick M. "Maturing Out of Problematic Alcohol Use." *Alcohol, Research, and Health: Focus on Young Adult Drinking* 28:4 (2004–2005): 202–204. http://pubs.niaaa.nih.gov/publications/arh284/202-204.htm (accessed May 24, 2008).

Pare, Michael. "Making College Achievable for All Is Their Goal." *Providence Business News* 15:29 (Nov. 6, 2000): 4.

Pascarella, Ernest T., and Patrick T. Terenzini. *How College Affects Students: Findings and Insights from Twenty Years of Research*. San Francisco: Jossey-Bass, 1991.

———. *How College Affects Students: A Third Decade of Research*. San Francisco: Jossey-Bass, 2005.

Pew Research Center for the People and the Press. "How Young People View Their Lives, Futures and Politics: A Portrait of 'Generation Next.'" Washington, D.C., Jan. 2007.

Randinelli, Tracey. "Making the Grade: Ace Your College Classes with This Advice on Choosing Courses, Selecting a Major, Writing Papers, and Dealing with Professors." *Careers and Colleges* 22:4 (March 2002): 32–37.

Rendon, L., M. Garcia, and D. Person, eds. *Transforming the First Year of College for Students of Color*. Columbia, S.C., National Resource Center for the First-Year Experience and Students in Transition. Volume 38. 2004.

Rickgarn, Ralph L.V. *Perspectives on College Student Suicide*. Amityville, N.Y.: Baywood Publishing. Co., 1994.

———. "The Issue Is Suicide." The Suicide Awareness Fund, University of Minnesota, 2001.

Rose, Patrick, and Edgardo Pimentel. *Benchmarks for Success: Gauging the Performance of College Prevention Efforts*. Southern Illinois University: Core Institute, 2006.

Sahadi, Jeanne. "College in 4 years? Try 5 or 6." *USA Today*, June 22, 2004. http://money.cnn.com/2004/06/21/pf/college/graduation_rates/ (accessed March 30, 2008).

Sampson, Rana. *Acquaintance Rape of College Students*. U.S. Department of Justice, Office of Community Oriented Policing Services. www.cops.usdoj.gov/pdf/e03021472.pdf (accessed May 24, 2008).

Schemo, Diana Jean. "Study Calculates the Effects of College Drinking in U.S." *New York Times*, April 10, 2002.

Schneider, Barbara, and David Stevenson. *The Ambitious Generation: America's Teenagers, Motivated but Directionless*. New Haven: Yale University Press, 1999.

Schulenberg, J., J. L. Maggs, K. J. Steiman, and R. A. Zucker. "Development Matters: Taking the Long View on Substance Abuse Etiology and Intervention During Adolescence," in P. M. Monti, S. M. Colby, and T. A. O'Leary, eds. *Adolescents, Alcohol, and Substance Abuse: Reaching Teens Through Brief Interventions*. New York: Guilford Press, 2001, pp. 19–57.

Sher, Kenneth J, Bruce D. Bartholow, and Shivani Nanda. "Short- and Long-Term Effects of Fraternity and Sorority Membership: A Social Norms Perspective." *Psychology of Addictive Behaviors* 15:1 (March 2001): 42–51.

Simpson, Rae. *Young Adult Development Project*. Cambridge, Mass.: Massachusetts Institute of Technology, 2008. http://hrweb.mit.edu/worklife/youngadult/index.html (accessed July 2, 2008).

Smith, J. Walker, and Ann Clurman. *Generation Ageless: How Baby Boomers Are Changing the Way We Live Today . . . And They're Just Getting Started*. New York: Collins, 2007.

Smith, Lynn. "Finding Good in 'Normal.' " *Los Angeles Times*, June 12, 2001, p. 1.

Stepp, Laura Sessions. "Perfect Problems." *Washington Post*, May 5, 2002, p. F01.

Stevens, Lise M. "Adolescent Suicide." *Journal of the American Medical Association* 286:24 (Dec. 26, 2001): 3194.

Tederman, James S. *Advice from the Dean: A Personal Perspective on the Philosophy, Roles, and Approaches of a Dean at a Small, Private, Liberal Arts College*. Washington, D.C.: National Association of Student Personnel Administrators, 1997.

Tinto, Vincent. *Leaving College: Rethinking the Causes and Cures of Student Attrition*. Chicago: University of Chicago Press, 1993.

Tobin, Eugene M. "Don't Ban Fraternities, Embrace Them. Embrace Them Closely." *Chronicle of Higher Education* 48:16 (Dec. 14, 2001): B24.

Turner, Aaron P., Mary E. Larimer, and Irwin Sarason. "Family Risk Factors for Alcohol-Related Consequences and Poor Adjustment in Fraternity and Sorority Members: Explore the Role of Parent-Child Conflict." *Journal of Studies on Alcohol* 61 (Nov. 2000): 818.

Turrentine, Cathryn Coree, Stacey L. Schnure, D. David Ostroth, and Jeanine A. Ward-Roof. "The Parent Project: What Parents Want from the College Experience." *NASPA Journal* 38:1 (Fall 2000): 31–43.

Turrisi, Rob, Kimberly A. Wiersma, and Kelli K. Hughes. "Binge-Drinking-Related Consequences in College Students: Role of Drinking Beliefs and Mother-Teen Communications." *Psychology of Addictive Behaviors* 14:4 (Dec. 2000): 342–355.

U.S. Department of Health and Human Services, National Institutes of Health. "What Colleges Need to Know Now: An Update on College Drinking Research." 2007. www.collegedrinkingprevention.gov/1College_Bulletin-508_361C4E.pdf (accessed May 24, 2008).

U.S. Government Accounting Office. *Consumer Finance: College Students and Credit Cards*. June 2001. GAO-01-773.

USA Today Magazine. "Encouraging College Students to Exercise." Sept. 2001, p. 9.

Vander Schee, Brian Al. "Parents as a Target Market in College Admissions." *Recruitment & Retention* 20:12 (Dec. 2006). Madison, Wis., Magna Publications.

Vencat, Emily Flynn. "Narcissists in Neverland." *Newsweek*, Oct. 16, 2007. www.newsweek.com/id/52229 (accessed June 30, 2008).

Wagener, Amy, and Kari Much. "How to Manage Eating Disorders on Campus: A Guide for Resident Assistants." *Student Affairs Leader* 36:10 (May 15, 2008). Madison, Wis., Magna Publications.

Wartman, Katherine Lynk, and Marjorie Savage. *Parental Involvement in Higher Education: Understanding the Relationship Among Students, Parents, and the Institution.* San Francisco: Jossey-Bass, 2008. ASHE Higher Education Report 33:6.

Wechsler, Henry, et al. "College Binge Drinking in the 1990s: A Continuing Problem—Results of the Harvard School of Public Health 1999 College Alcohol Study." *Journal of American College Health* 48:10 (2000): 199–210.

Weiss, Larry J. *Parents Programs: How to Create Lasting Ties.* Washington, D.C.: Council for Advancement and Support of Higher Education, 1989.

Wildavsky, Ben. "Is That the Real Price?" *U.S. News & World Report*, Sept. 6, 1999.

Wood, Phillip K., Kenneth J. Sher, Darin J. Erickson, and Kurt A. DeBord. "Predicting Academic Problems in College from Freshman Alcohol Involvement." *Journal of Studies on Alcohol* 58:2 (March 1997): 200–210.

Resources for More Information

BOOKS

Ahmad, Shaheena. *The Yale Daily News Guide to Succeeding in College*. New York: Simon and Schuster, 1997.

Bragdon, Allen D., and David Gamon. *How Sharp Is Your Pencil?* Bass River, Mass.: Brainwaves Books, 1999.

Carney-Hall, Karla C., ed. *Managing Parent Partnerships: Maximizing Influence, Minimizing Interference, and Focusing on Student Success*. San Francisco: Jossey-Bass, 2008. New Directions for Student Services, No. 122.

Coburn, Karen Levin, and Madge Lawrence Treeter. *Letting Go: A Parents' Guide to Understanding the College Years*. New York: Harper Perennial, 2003.

Combs, Patrick, and Jack Canfield. *Major in Success: Make College Easier, Fire Up Your Dreams, and Get a Very Cool Job*. Berkeley, Calif.: Ten Speed Press, 2000.

Daniel, B. V., and B. R. Scott. *Consumers, Adversaries, and Partners: Working with the Families of Undergraduates*. San Francisco: Jossey-Bass, 2001. New Directions for Student Services, No. 94.

Dobkin, Rachel, and Shana Sippy. *The College Woman's Handbook: Educating Ourselves*. New York: Workman Publishing Co., 1995.

Griffin, Carolyn Welch, Marian J. Wirth, and Arthur G. Wirth. *Beyond Accep-*

tance: Parents of Lesbians and Gays Talk About Their Experience. New York: St. Martins Press, 1997.

Harris, Marcia B., and Sharon Jones. *The Parent's Crash Course in Career Planning.* New York: McGraw-Hill, 1996.

Howe, Neil, and William Straus. *Millennials Rising: The Next Great Generation.* New York: Vintage Books, 2000.

————. *Millennials Go to College. Strategies for a New Generation on Campus.* American Association of College Registrars, 2003.

Jamison, Kay Redfield. *Night Falls Fast: Understanding Suicide.* New York: Vintage Books, 2003.

Kobliner, Beth. *Get a Financial Life: Personal Finance in Your Twenties and Thirties.* New York: Simon and Schuster, 1996.

Light, Richard. *Making the Most of College: Students Speak Their Minds.* Cambridge, Mass.: Harvard University Press, 2004.

Litt, Ann Selkowitz. *The College Student's Guide to Eating Well on Campus.* Bethesda, Md.: Tulip Hill Press, 2000.

McDougall, Bryce. *My Child Is Gay: How Parents React When They Hear the News.* New York: Unwin Hyman, 1998.

Peterson's Study Abroad. Lawrenceville, N.J.: Peterson's Guides, 2002.

Quinn, Patricia O. *ADD and the College Student: A Guide for High School and College Students with Attention Deficit Disorder.* Washington, D.C.: Magination Press, 2001.

Scheele, Adele M. *Jumpstart Your Career in College: Build the Skills to Build Your Future.* New York: Kaplan, 2000.

Schneider, Barbara, and David Stevenson. *The Ambitious Generation: America's Teenagers, Motivated but Directionless.* New Haven: Yale University Press, 1999.

Smith, J. Walker, and Ann Clurman. *Generation Ageless: How Baby Boomers Are Changing the Way We Live Today . . . And They're Just Getting Started.* New York: Collins, 2007.

Wartman, Katherine Lynk, and Marjorie Savage. *Parental Involvement in Higher Education: Understanding the Relationship Among Students, Parents, and the Institution.* San Francisco: Jossey-Bass, 2008. ASHE Higher Education Report 33:6.

WEB SITES

Alcohol issues:
www.collegedrinkingprevention.gov
www.edc.org/hec
www.factsontap.org

Gay, lesbian, bisexual, transgender issues:
www.pflag.org

College parenting issues:
www.collegeparents.org
www.universityparent.com/parents

Study abroad:
www.cdc.gov
www.travel.state.gov

Campus health and safety:
www.jedfoundation.org
www.securityoncampus.org
www.ncvc.org/ncvc/Main.aspx
www.ncvc.org/src/main.aspx?dbID=dash_Home
www.stophazing.org
www.rainn.org
www.nationaleatingdisorders.org

Finances
www.finaid.org
www.projectmoney.org/teaching/worksheets.html
www.startribune.com/blogs/kablog
www.fafsa.ed.gov

Index